NAVIES AND FOREIGN POLICY

NAVIES AND FOREIGN POLICY

K. BOOTH

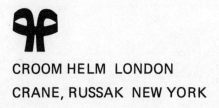

CROOM HELM LONDON

CRANE, RUSSAK NEW YORK

© 1977 K. Booth
Croom Helm Ltd
2-10 St John's Road, London SW11

ISBN 0—85664—323—8

Published in the United States by
Crane, Russak & Company Inc.,
52 Vanderbilt Avenue
New York, N.Y. 10017

ISBN 0—8448—1013—4

Library of Congress Catalog Card No. 76—28612

CONTENTS

For Robert and Thomas

PREFACE

This book is designed as a guide to the specialised study of an instrument of policy, naval power, which historically has played an
important part in the foreign policies of most major states. For
certain countries this relationship has always been closely intertwined.
The relationship between navies and foreign policy is not presently
what it was, but then it never has been in the twentieth century. The
relationship is changing and becoming more complex, but it is not
becoming obsolete. Navies remain an instrument of statecraft. At the
same time, they also consume enormous amounts of money, employ
several million people throughout the world, control terrible
destructive potential, and operate in that watery two-thirds of the
earth's surface which is increasingly a major international issue area.
We live in more complicated times: they demand more complicated
thinking. This book is a preliminary step towards that end. The book is
neither a survey of current naval affairs nor a work advocating the
policies which governments should pursue: rather, it is an introduction
to thinking about the manifold interrelationships between navies and
foreign policy. For all concerned, initially at least, *it's not what you do,
it's the way that you think about it.*

The book has been divided into two parts. Part One examines
the variety of ways in which navies can be instruments of and
influences on foreign policy. Part Two examines the major factors
affecting the character of naval policies. In each part the aim has been
to suggest coherent frameworks for analysis, to indicate relevant literature, and to submit a variety of useful propositions, perspectives,
approaches and rules-of-thumb. The book is made up of large maps and
local guides, sign-posts and check-lists, advice and some equipment
which might help the student of naval affairs to begin to find his way
around the subject, to travel hopefully, and to discover. The message
evident throughout the book is the need to rub together history and
theory, and academics and naval professionals in order to sharpen our
tools for dealing with this complex and significant area of public
policy.

Several explanatory points should be made at the outset. (1) Since
so much knowledge is fragmented and specialised, and since there are
so few integrated individual approaches to this subject, comprehensive-

ness has been chosen rather than depth. This means, for example, that the chapter on naval capabilities is not stuffed with up-to-date information (which in any case would date) but instead attempts to introduce the reader to the range of factors which he might consider when speculating about who can do what. (2) The book has relatively little on war at sea, though there are frequent references to its possibility. This is because the major business of navies in the second half of the 1970s and beyond is not the fighting of nuclear-age Trafalgars, but in using warships to support policy by less drastic methods. (3) Most of the book is about the largest navies rather than small or even medium ones. The latter are not ignored, but it is only the greatest navies which have important foreign policy implications. (4) The focus is on *navies* and *naval* affairs, rather than the wider idea of *maritime* policy. There is, of course, much more to the use of the sea than is encompassed in the idea of naval policy. But the narrower focus provides a definite theme, and, as the reader will discover, no shortage of material. It is stressed throughout the book that the naval focus can only be properly understood in the widest context, which means not only maritime affairs, but also what happens on land.

It is hoped that this comprehensive treatment will help the student of the subject to have a better grasp of the whole, and will encourage him to dig deeper into its specific parts. The study of naval policy has been the Cinderella of strategic studies. It has been badly neglected. The student of strategy has many tools to help him think about the almost *unthinkable* use of the most destructive weapons we have: ironically, he has far fewer tools to help him think about the many *thinkable* uses of modern naval power.

In the writings on naval affairs in the past twenty years or so some ground has been tilled, in one way or another, but it could all be tilled yet more deeply, and produce richer fruit. In the age of Mahan, wars, navies and international relations all appeared relatively more simple than they do today. The demands on those who wrote about navies and foreign policy were correspondingly less. Today, writers about this subject face a world in which war, navies and international relations appear very much more complex, in their human, political, economic and technological dimensions. It is only when our minds are clearer on some of the issues discussed in this book that we can begin to face the growing complexity of the subject with more confidence, and so begin to develop more rigorous and perceptive approaches to the study of navies and foreign policy. Armed with these we will have the basis for better understanding, comparison and forecasting.

*   *   *

This book began as a mind-clearing paper, prepared for the annual conference of the International Studies Association in St Louis, Missouri, March 1974. The panel concerned was organised by Professor George Hudson. It is a pleasure to record my thanks to him for inviting me to participate on his panel, for giving me the general title 'Navies and Foreign Policy' to work under, and for a variety of cheerful support. To make participation possible at that meeting, and subsequently to present the paper to the staff and students of the United States Naval War College and the Center For Foreign Policy Studies, Dalhousie University, I am indebted to the British Association for American Studies, the Maritime Workshop at Dalhousie University, and the University College of Wales. In particular, I am grateful for the support of the Advanced Research Program of the US Naval War College, Newport, R.I., and its President at the time, Vice-Admiral Stansfield Turner: the encouragement and advice (solicited and otherwise) which I have received from him and other officers in the US Navy has been a great help in a subject in which only a few widely scattered academics are involved.

The following read all or parts of the manuscript at various stages, and provided me with useful criticisms and different perspectives. They do not bear any responsibility for the final manuscript – indeed healthy disagreements remain – but their help was invaluable: Captain Richard Hill RN, Professor James E. King, Professor Michael MccGwire, Vice-Admiral Sir Ian McGeoch, Professor Bryan McL. Ranft, Geoffrey Till and Cmdr. Harlan Ullman USN. A special acknowledgement is due to members of the Soviet Navy Study Group at Dalhousie University, before whom various parts of this book were presented in the meetings of 1973 and 1974. In addition, for advice on specific points, I wish to mention John B. Hattendorf, Nicholas Tracy and Peter Vigor. The character of the book has been affected indirectly by many others, not least Inis Claude and John Garnett. For various acts of research assistance I wish to thank Michael Clark and Jane Davis, and I am appreciative of the efforts of the staffs in the Llandinam Library UCW, the National Library of Wales, and the Royal Naval College Greenwich. From the following secretaries I have had all the co-operation I could have wished for: Kay Critchley, Doreen Hamer, Gwalia Watkins and Marian Weston. And lastly, for that essential underway replenishment which keeps everything going, and without which no naval enterprise can for long proceed, I thank my wife Eurwen.

Aberystwyth   Ken Booth

PART ONE: NAVIES AS INSTRUMENTS AND INFLUENCES

1 THE FUNCTIONS OF NAVIES

'Why do we need a navy?' is a recurring question. By indicating the ends for which navies have been and can be used, this chapter provides the beginning of an answer. It can only be a beginning because a full answer will depend upon the national interests and circumstances of whoever asks the question. As he looks at the shop-window of foreign policy instruments, the decision-maker must pay his money (or rather his country's money) and take his pick in the light of policy priorities, national capabilities for action, and beliefs about the utility of different instruments. This chapter is restricted to spot-lighting only the naval corner of that window.

The use of the sea

The functions of navies can be conceived as a trinity, the idea of three-in-one. The unity (the *one-ness*) of the trinity is provided by the idea of *the use of the sea*: this is the underlying consideration in the whole business of navies and foreign policy. The character of the trinity is then defined by the three characteristic modes of action by which navies carry out their purposes: namely the military, the diplomatic, and the policing functions. Within each of these roles navies can serve a large variety of subordinate functions. The trinity can be expressed diagrammatically as shown in Figure 1.

In order to carry out these functions, naval planners have to translate policy objectives into forces of a particular size and composition; they have to decide upon the character and timing of deployment and employment; they have to choose appropriate tactics and so on. The range of operational tasks by which foreign policy objectives are translated into naval happenings is extremely wide.

The theme of navies and foreign policy is *the use of the sea*. Broadly, states are interested in the use of the sea for three purposes: (1) for the passage of goods and people; (2) for the passage of military force for diplomatic purposes, or for use against targets on land or at sea; and (3) for the exploitation of resources in or under the sea. Navies exist as a *means* to further such ends. As it has been understood from earliest times, they exist as part of a state's general maritime policy, whose objective is to attempt to use the sea for one's own purposes, while being in a position to attempt to prevent others from using it in ways

Fig. 1: The functions of navies

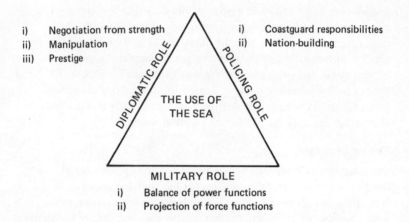

i)   Negotiation from strength   i)   Coastguard responsibilities
ii)   Manipulation   ii)   Nation-building
iii) Prestige

DIPLOMATIC ROLE

POLICING ROLE

THE USE OF
THE SEA

MILITARY ROLE
i)   Balance of power functions
ii)   Projection of force functions

which are to one's disadvantage.

It is appropriate that the *military role* forms the base of the trinity, for the essence of navies is their military character. Actual or latent violence is their currency. It is a navy's ability to threaten and use force which gives meaning to its other modes of action. It derives its diplomatic impact from perceptions of its military character. Obviously it derives its utility in conflicts from its ability to exert brute force successfully. The *diplomatic role* of navies is concerned with the management of foreign policy short of the actual employment of force. Diplomatic applications support state policy in particular bargaining situations or in general international intercourse. The *policing role* is internally as much as externally oriented. These functions are rarely concerned with the armed forces of other states: they are mainly concerned with extending sovereignty over the state's own maritime frontiers.

In considering this trinity several points should be kept in mind. (1) A clear picture of warship functions should afford a basis for comparing and contrasting the naval efforts of different countries, and structure any discussion of the utility of navies. (2) Some of the terms of analysis have various nuances, but for the moment it is well to avoid confusion by semantic exegesis. (3) Like all classifications, a degree of artificiality is unavoidable. This is chronically so in the case of naval operations in peacetime, for the same operation can serve one or more objectives: this mixture of objectives can be separated for analytical purposes, but in practice, in a policy-maker's head, they will probably be present in various degrees of jumble. (4) This presentation of naval functions as a trinity should not be taken to mean that each part is of equal importance. Different states will weigh the importance of each function in the light of their individual maritime problems and interests. (5) The classification is not based upon abstract ideas, but in all cases (except nuclear war) it is based upon an array of empirical evidence.[1]

Policing role

The main aims and subsidiary policy of objectives of this role are as follows:

(1) *Coastguard responsibilities*
  (i) Sovereignty
  (ii) Resource enjoyment
  (iii) Maintenance of good order
(2) *Nation-building*
  (i) Contribute to internal stability
  (ii) Contribute to internal development

Policing takes place mainly in territorial waters, and is concerned with the maintenance of public order in a broad sense. It is a maritime version of the work of the police, border guards, and the idea of 'military aid to the civil authority'. While this role is rarely seen as a part of foreign policy as such, the character and effectiveness with which it is carried out (or not) may have external implications.

Coastguard responsibilities. These tasks are by far the most important within the policing role. They are responsibilities familiar to all coastal states, and may be performed by a separately organised maritime service, a navy, or jointly. These forces attempt to further the basic interests of all coastal states, namely the extension of sovereignty, resource enjoyment in contiguous areas, and the maintenance of good order.[2]

Nation-building. This role involves contributing to internal stability, especially during natural or political turmoil, and contributing to internal development in more settled times. These limited functions are a naval equivalent of the role performed by many armies, going under such names as PUMF (Peaceful Uses of Military Forces) and MACC (Military Assistance to the Civil Community). For obvious geographical reasons, these functions cannot be performed on an extensive scale by navies; however, they can sometimes make a worthwhile contribution, after natural disasters or civil commotions, or in playing a limited modernisation role in some Third World countries.

The coastal policing role is not likely to appeal as an important *mission* to those navies which the jargon describes as 'blue-water'. However, for over one-third of the world's navies, coastguard and nation-building responsibilities represent the extent of their functions (and ambitions). The governments of countries where this is so either do not perceive an external naval threat, or they have no capability to match one. The defence of their maritime frontiers is therefore largely dependent on general international stability. However, even the smallest warships can have external effects which are disproportionate to their military punch. This is particularly the case in the deterrence of small-scale maritime intrusion (especially of the economically motivated type). The willingness to resist can sometimes have political effects bearing no relation to the intrinsic military effort. Iceland's gunboats, one of the most miniscule of forces, have given evidence of this. At the other end of the spectrum of coastguard forces is the US Coast Guard (USCG); this is bigger than the navies of most countries with its destroyer-size 'cutters' and hundreds of aircraft.[3] Essentially the USCG is a para-naval organisation and has been used as such.

Diplomatic role

The main aims and subsidiary policy objectives of this role are as follows:

(1) *Negotiation from strength*
  (i)   Reassure and strengthen allies and associates.
  (ii) Reassure and strengthen friendly governments threatened by serious internal challenge.
  (iii) Reassure and strengthen friendly governments fearing external attack.
  (iv) Change the behaviour of friendly governments when the

latter are facing the threat of external attack.
- (v) Signal 'business as usual' during a crisis.
- (vi) Support or threaten force from the sea to support friendly governments contemplating acquisitive military action.
- (vii) Improve bargaining strength.
- (viii) Threaten force from the sea to support policy.
- (ix) Improve one's ability to affect the course of specific diplomatic negotiations.

(2) *Manipulation*
- (i) Manipulate bargaining positions within an alliance.
- (ii) Demonstrate support to different countries.
- (iii) Gain or increase access to new countries.
- (iv) Build up foreign navies and create proxy threats.
- (v) Create a degree of naval dependency.
- (vi) Provide standing demonstrations of naval power in distant waters to establish the right to be interested.

(3) *Prestige*
- (i) Provide psychological reassurances for the home country.
- (ii) Project a favourable general image of one's country.
- (iii) Project an image of impressive naval force.

The diplomatic role has always been an important one for major navies, and has involved a wide variety of operational tasks. Diplomatic effects are induced by both latent and active means, as will be discussed in the following chapter. The range of functions within this role encompasses actions with a degree of implicit or explicit coercion (negotiation from strength) to actions promising reward (naval aid) to actions seeking to oil the wheels of relationships by improving an image (influence and prestige).

Negotiating from strength. So-called 'political demonstrations of naval force' are a traditional function of navies. It is one which has again risen to prominence because of recent manoeuvrings by super-power warships in different parts of the world. By such actions the superpowers have sought to persuade target states to behave in a favourable manner without the need to use force. In the diplomatic use of warships, the intention is invariably to avoid violence, but this possibility will nevertheless be present in such tasks as assisting associates when they are involved in a conflict. Where there is a possibility of violence, a prudent naval presence must include an ability to be able to fight for control of the air, as well as the sea, and possibly also the ability to project military forces ashore.

Manipulation. The influence tactics of naval diplomacy are designed to have their effects by changing (however incrementally) the political calculations of the relevant observers. Because of this, much thinking has to go into the size, shape and tactics of the force involved if the desired messages are to be effectively communicated. Effects may be induced by negative as well as positive actions. Although the range of influence-building tactics is wide, because their effectiveness depends upon the perceptions of others, this is a rather unpredictable activity.

Prestige. The promotion of a country's prestige and influence is not an operational naval *mission* in the usual meaning of the tern. It is a function of considerable importance nevertheless, and is recognised as such by major navies. This role has relatively few specific operational tasks. With the exception of naval aid, port visits and ceremonial activities, the success of this role is invariably the by-product of overall naval behaviour. Encouraging others to think in desired ways and to listen to one's case with sympathy requires diplomatic as well as naval subtlety.

Military role

The main aims and subsidiary policy objectives within this category can be divided between those pertaining to what we understand as peace, and those pertaining to what we understand as war. The peace-time or *balance of power* functions are as follows:

(1) *Strategic nuclear deterrence*
   (i)   Deter attack on the homeland, and the homelands of the allies.
   (ii) Provide secure situation in which to promote foreign policy interests.
   (iii) Contribute to the nation's ability to negotiate from a position of recognised strength.
   (iv) Counter the deterrent forces of adversaries.
(2) *Conventional deterrence and defence*
   (i)   Prepare for wartime tasks.
   (ii) Deter hostile intrusion into maritime frontiers.
   (iii) Contribute to local maritime stability.
   (iv) Protect national claims in contiguous seas.
   (v)   Extend national claims in contiguous seas.
(3) *Extended deterrence and defence*
   (i)   Protect state activities on the high seas.
   (ii) Protect the lives, interests and property of nationals (and

others) operating in distant waters.
(iii) Protect the lives, interests and property of nationals (and others) threatened by local disturbance or natural disaster.
(iv) Provide the local maritime defence of distant national territories.
(v) Develop operating techniques for the essential wartime tasks in distant waters.
(vi) Build up an infrastructure (including bases and other shore facilities) for the performance of wartime missions.
(vii) Demonstrate commitment to allies.
(4) *International order*
(i) Support an internationally recognised law of the sea.
(ii) Do not support an internationally recognised law of the sea: support and extend national claims.

Strategic deterrence. Four navies presently have the capability of projecting nuclear weapons against their enemies from the sea, and so also of withholding them to affect post-exchange bargaining. China may have such a capability in the near future. A sea-based deterrent force is a very particular and very specialised branch of a navy. The maintenance of 'invulnerability' is a major feature of the operations of a missile-firing submarine (SSBN). Consequently, when they slip under the water and 'get lost' their activities are removed from the daily round of surface and other submarine forces. Nuclear strike-carriers, on the other hand, have always had a more integrated role in naval deployment and planning. Because of improvements in anti-submarine warfare (ASW) techniques, there has been some talk about the problems of protecting seaborne retaliatory forces. If SSBNs become vulnerable to any marked extent, they will require some form of defensive screening (and thus integration with other fleet activities) or further geographical invulnerability.

The sea is used to deploy counters for deterrent forces. This involves the tracking and marking of seaborne nuclear delivery vehicles. In the case of strike-carriers this is a relatively easy task, but this is not so with SSBNs, whose capabilities have continually outrun their challengers'. The counter-deterrent task is now generally agreed to have been the one responsible for the steady geographical expansion of Soviet naval units through the 1960s. Their pattern of forward deployment was basically fixed by the need to try to track and mark US SSBNs and strike-carriers. If war were to break out it would be the Soviet objective to sink as many of these units as possible and so limit the damage inflicted on the Soviet Union.

Conventional deterrence and defence. Most navies do not have a
nuclear weapons capability; their contribution to deterring their
country's enemies is limited to more conventional approaches. To the
traditional so-called 'blue water' navies (the Royal Navy and the US
Navy in particular) there has been a tendency to assume that their role
in peace and war is something which happens *over there*, in distant
waters. For most navies that is not the case: for most of them strategy
begins and ends in the contiguous seas.

Basic maritime defence in the contiguous seas is the mission of just
under two-thirds of the world's navies. Their objective is to extend
metropolitan defence (and possibly offensive potentialities) into
adjoining sea areas, thereby raising the cost of any unwelcome maritime intrusion or interference. 'Contiguous seas' is a more appropriate
phrase than 'coastal defence'. Area defence zones have become so
extended with the growing range of naval weapons that the word
'coastal' now gives a false impression of the potential scope of the
weaponry of the warships of even quite small navies.

Extended deterrence and defence. The sea is also used for
extending deterrence and defence for the protection of one's own
nationals and state activities in distant areas, and for protective
responsibilities for allies and associates. The protection of national
assets and state activities (such as weapons testing) may be carried out
in distant regions by navies which do not regard themselves as oceanic
in a fighting sense. The Dutch Navy has contributed to the maritime
defence of its remaining distant territories. During the process of
colonial withdrawal, the protection of nationals in distant lands was a
regular operational activity, especially for the Royal Navy, and
involved its warships in a variety of limited actions. In previous
centuries, when pirates were very much in evidence, the protection of
nationals on the high seas was a function of primary importance for all
naval powers. Pirates are no longer a large problem (though they still
exist). Harassment by foreign powers is a bigger threat, and naval
building has often been justified by the need to protect a far-flung
national merchant marine. In practice, however, the ratio of naval
units to merchant ships has never been sufficient to defend them in
detail against conceivable threats.

In order to improve their deterrent and defence postures, and to
support policy short of force, fleets and squadrons of the major naval
powers have operated permanently or semi-permanently in distant
waters. Whatever the detailed objectives of such deployments, the

associated requirements are always likely to be exhaustive. Exercises, efforts to improve techniques, readiness and the surveillance of potential enemies involve a great deal of effort. The discharging of tasks relating to major war functions also requires the building up of the necessary infrastructure; this will probably include the acquisition of bases or other facilities in strategically located areas. Forward deployment therefore involves important political implications as well as taxing naval activity.

International order. Underlying the peacetime (balance of power) functions of navies is the objective of international order in general and at sea in particular. The phrase '*maintaining* international order' has been deliberately avoided. Invariably the objective has been to maintain order, but for some naval forces it may be to change the *status quo* by extending national claims, or challenging a naval monopoly. Given the traditional interest of the predominant naval powers (the producers of security at sea) in the freedom of naval movement, and the general interest of states engaged in international trade in safe and dependable transportation, in practice the maintenance of maritime stability has been the norm.

Projection of force functions. If a state is no longer able to secure its objectives by military power, it may feel compelled to resort to military force. It should go without saying that the concept of war is much more confused than in former times, when it had some legal as well as operational discreetness. Wars were declared in former times: now they just happen.

The use of force at sea can be simply divided into four types of war: *(1) general war, (2) conventional war, (3) limited wars and interventions,* and *(4) guerrilla wars.* There is some artificiality in this distinction, but it has a common-sense relevance. Within each category the spectrum of possible violence is wide. The idea of intervention includes everything from the seizure of a town as a hostage, to the support of an international peace-keeping operation, to a large-scale intervention. Limited naval confrontations include everything from harassment to a 'total wet war'.[4]

The operational tasks which navies perform within each type of war will vary enormously in geographical scope and in intensity of violence. However, the objectives are similar, and may be conceived as follows:

Projection of force functions

(i) To meet the level of challenge of whatever level is considered militarily and politically desirable.

(ii)   To challenge and prevent the enemy from using the sea for his own purposes.

(iii)   To command the areas of sea required for allied or national use.

(iv)   To use the seas for the transportation of men and supplies.

(v)   To use the sea for the projection of force against targets on land.

(vi)   To support international peace-keeping operations.

As the intensity and character of a conflict changes, additional tasks may be imposed on the base of each country's minimum defence requirements. Interests and capabilities will be the main determinants. Some countries will be more than satisfied to oppose the enemy's use of the sea: others will wish to use the sea more positively for their own purposes. Different strategies evolve from this dichotomy. A crude but serviceable distinction is usually made between 'sea denial' stagies for those with limited interest and 'command of the sea' (or now more commonly 'sea control') strategies for those with the more positive interests.

However remote war might sometimes seem, it is from their fighting ability that warships have their ultimate significance. By their latent potentiality in peace they can affect the management of politics amongst nations, and by their success or otherwise in discharging their missions in war they can help determine whether their country directs the course of war, or suffers it.

Ends and means

There are several reasons why it is valuable to concentrate on a functional approach.[5] (1) Concentration on policy objectives should encourage the rational selection of the resources to be allocated to naval forces. (2) A mission approach should help the problem of establishing tactical and financial priorities. (3) It should assist the optimum selection of weapons systems. (4) It should ensure that the members of a navy focus on the whole rather than upon one of its parts. (5) Finally, by clarifying why navies might exist for any particular country, one can discuss more sensibly the array of strategies and tactics which they adopt. Before asking 'what is their naval strategy?' one should ask, 'what is their interest in the use of the sea?'

Two warnings are necessary about the functions of navies as presented in this chapter. (1) The list clearly illustrates the comprehensive instrumentality of warships. However, it does not suggest their

utility in any particular role in modern conditions. This difficult
problem is reserved for a later chapter. (2) The trinity should not be
taken as a model in any practical sense. The whole range of functions,
objectives and tasks will not be within the capabilities of the overwhelming majority of countries. Because of volitional or resource
constraints, the majority of navies will be confined to a few of the
functions listed, though these may change with the ebb and flow of
national development, world events and so on. The varying interests
of different countries in using the sea for national purposes will be one
of the themes of this book: from these different interests come
different priorities, levels of capability, strategies and so on.

Having established a preliminary framework for looking at the
functions of navies, the following chapters examine some of the
characteristics of the interrelationships between navies and foreign
policy. In looking at navies as instruments, the emphasis will be upon
the naval support of diplomacy and upon what have been described as
the 'balance of power' functions. From the perspective of the mid-
1970s, these are where the most interesting and important questions lie.

Notes

1.   In drawing up this classification the following sources have been most
     useful: James Cable, *Gunboat Diplomacy. Political Applications of Limited
     Naval Force* (London: Chatto and Windus for the ISS, 1971); Vice-
     Admiral Sir Peter Gretton, *Maritime Strategy: a Study of British Defence
     Problems* (London: Cassell, 1965); L. W. Martin, *The Sea in Modern
     Strategy* (London: Chatto and Windus for the ISS, 1967); Michael
     MccGwire, *Soviet Naval Developments. Capability and Context* (New York:
     Praeger, 1973). Unless stated otherwise, references to MccGwire are to this
     volume; Michael MccGwire, Ken Booth and John McDonnell, *Soviet
     Naval Policy. Objectives and Constraints* (New York: Praeger 1975); Vice-
     Admiral Stansfield Turner USN, 'Missions of the U.S. Navy', *Naval War
     College Review* (hereafter *NWCR*) March-April 1974, pp. 2-17.
2.   See Captain J. R. Hill, 'The Rule of Law at Sea. The Capacity and
     Suitability of Maritime Forces for the Enforcement of International Law
     at Sea' (unpublished thesis, Department of Laws, University of London,
     King's College, 1972), pp. 172-3.
3.   J. R. Hill, 'The United States Coast Guard', *World Survey*, No. 47, Novem-
     ber 1972.
4.   Martin, op. cit., p. 44. Title of speech by Admiral John S. McCain USN,
     May 1966.
5.   These comments are based upon Turner, op. cit., pp. 2-3.

2 NAVAL DIPLOMACY

As the last chapter suggested, warships have always had more than a fighting function. The governments of naval powers have frequently employed their warships in a 'diplomatic' or 'political' mode, hoping to affect the thinking and behaviour of other governments with little or no intention or expectation of using brute force. By *diplomatic* in this context is meant the use of warships in support of a country's general bargaining position, particular negotiating stances and influence-building tactics, and for representational tasks of various kinds. Despite such traditional usage it is both typical and significant that the US Department of Defense, which has invested considerable effort into developing ideas about the use of the military instrument for coercive purposes, appears to have given little 'organised consideration' to the use of the military instrument in support of diplomacy.[1] It is not alone. The question of influence is right at the core of international relationships, but conceptual thinking and case studies remain the exception rather than the rule. It is one of those subjects which seem quite clear as long as they are left alone.

It is the aim of this chapter to discuss some of the elusive and ambiguous problems surrounding naval diplomacy: what do we mean by influence-building? what are the factors which might affect the development of an influence relationship? how can we identify the naval input into an influence relationship? what are the assets and liabilities of warships as diplomatic instruments? what are the characteristic tactics of naval diplomacy? what types of response might such tactics evoke? The difficult question of the present-day utility of warships in this role will be discussed in a later chapter.[2] These are all important problems for the second half of the 1970s, for there is a widespread belief that the navies of the major powers will be periodically and competitively used as diplomatic instruments.

Power and influence

At the outset, the observer of naval diplomacy must accept that the complexity and obscurity of some international relationships will occasionally overwhelm the words which we have to analyse and describe them. The well-established distinction between *power* and *influence* is a case in point. Many difficulties arise. The distinction is

26

usually based on the different tactics used, that is, whether A's effort
to move B in preferred directions involves potentially coercive or
essentially non-coercive tactics: thus power involves 'the ability to
move others by the threat or infliction of deprivations', while influence
is 'the ability to do so through promises or grants of benefits'.[3]

Power and influence both share a number of common characteristics.[4] They are both relational concepts. They are essentially
instrumental, being used primarily for achieving or defending other
goals, rather than being ends in themselves. They are both *processes*,
designed to sustain or change the behaviour of others, and *products*,
resulting in observable outcomes. Neither power nor influence can be
measured other than crudely. The mobilisation of capabilities is not
synonymous with having power or influence: there is no clear
relationship between the capacity to act and the probability of
exercising influence or power. The perceptions of the target decision-
makers are a crucial factor in the development of whichever relationship is intended.

While there is value in preserving a distinction between 'power'
and 'influence' based on the possibility of coercion, it is apparent that
there is hardly ever a clear boundary between them in practice.
A range of possibilities exists in any particular bilateral relationship.
Coercion may exist in the background as an ultimate stimulus or
constraint, although no reference may be made to it. Certainly in any
relationship between a relatively stronger and a relatively weaker state,
the weaker always faces the difficulty of trying to disassociate the
promise of possible benefits, the threat of possible sanctions, or a
danger of a withdrawal of support. This uncertainty is increased by the
very nature of warships: there will always be an inherent ambiguity,
and consequent uncertainty, about the use of essentially coercive
instruments (warships) in ostensibly non-coercive (influence-building)
roles. A clear distinction between the exercise of naval power and the
exercise of naval influence will always be muddied by the relative
subtlety of the stages through which a warship can be transformed
from a platform for a dance-band and cavorting local dignitaries, to a
haven of refuge for nationals in distress, to a gun-platform for shore
bombardment.

If naval acts cannot always be neatly classified in bilateral relationships, the problem is even greater when more than two states are
considered. Thus an act which might be described as an influence-
building attempt between A and B might involve the exercise of power
between A and C. When Soviet warships sailed into Port Said after the

June War this act was designed to build influence with Egypt while exercising coercion (deterrence) against Israel. We must accept that there will rarely be any tidy distinctions in this difficult area of international relationships short of using force. The latter is itself a clear distinction however: while influence and power are concerned with structuring someone's motives, brute force tries to overcome his strength.[5] Naval diplomacy seeks to evoke desired responses without having to apply force.

The emphasis in this chapter is on the potentially less coercive aspects of naval diplomacy. The causal relationships are usually better understood with 'naval power politics', as are its strategy and tactics such as deterrence, crisis management, brinkmanship and so on. 'Naval influence policies', on the other hand, are not so well understood. Before examining specific tactics, it is useful to consider the general factors which affect the influence potential of naval powers, and the influenceability of their targets.

Influencers and influenced

People and governments cannot exercise selection over those who coerce them: they do exercise selection over those they allow to influence them. The most difficult, and for a naval power the most frustrating, point to grasp about naval diplomacy is that whatever the quality and quantity of its warships, and the skill of its seamen, the effectiveness of naval diplomacy is indirect, and depends upon the reactions and understanding of rulers, governments, pressure groups, journalists and mobs whose comprehension of the theology and technology of modern naval strategy probably belongs to a bygone era.[6] Perceptions do not exist in a vacuum, however, and a range of factors affect both influence and influenceability.

The general factors affecting the influence potential of a naval power (very local considerations apart) are the quality, quantity and appropriateness of its capabilities, the skill of its tactical employment, the skill of the diplomatic support behind its naval efforts, the volitional restraints of its government, and the character and effectiveness of the influence-building efforts of its competitors.

To the chagrin of the major naval powers, there is no direct relationship between naval capabilities and diplomatic effectiveness. However, because warships are large and easily countable chunks of hardware, there is often a tendency to see one, with the problem being seen in terms of the beguiling word 'balance': there is often an implicit assumption that just as there is a relationship between

capabilities and the naval balance for war, so there must be a
relationship between capabilities and the peacetime diplomatic 'balance'.
It is tempting, especially for great powers, to assume that twice the
military power should buy twice the political influence. As was stated
earlier, however, the mobilisation of capabilities is not synonymous
with the ability to exercise power and influence. As the leaders of the
superpowers have repeatedly found in the post-war period, the conversion of the base metal of military force into diplomatic gold has
been akin to the alchemist's frustrating search for the Philosopher's
Stone.

The inability to convert military power directly into diplomatic
influence would seem to undermine some of the arguments of the
proponents of 'superiority'. But there is no general answer. Great
capabilities may buy much or little influence, but the same might be
the case with very limited expressions of military power. Those who
are dismissive of the potential political leverage of small amounts of
military power do not always have a strong case. Those commentators
who have minimised the significance of units of the Soviet Navy in
various regions, largely on the grounds that they did not represent a
viable military threat to Western navies, may have made reasonable
military appreciations. Politically such comments may have only
limited relevance. In political terms, in some situations, even a small
presence might have enormous influence potential. The political
influence which even an isolated cruiser might have should not be
assessed in the eyes of Western observers, but in the eyes of the locals,
who, for a mixture of political, historical, economic and military
reasons might be predisposed to seduction. They might see the cruiser
in various guises: as a token of support, as a symbol of a changing
power balance, or as a promise of an alternative source of security.
On a larger scale, President Nasser's attitude to the Soviet naval
presence in the Mediterranean is significant in this respect. He came to
see the strengthening of that presence as being to the advantage of the
whole non-aligned world.[7] The promise it represented in his dreams was
clearly greater than the actual threat which it then posed to the Sixth
Fleet.

Much has to happen before the deploying of a warship becomes a
fact of diplomatic influence. While there is no necessary relationship
between capabilities and the successful wielding of influence, there
may be some relationship. For this to happen, the quality and quantity
of the equipment is important, as is its appropriateness for the task.
Appropriateness is a major consideration, and has become more

troublesome in recent years because of the increasingly specialised ('task-specific') nature of modern warships. So, for example, after a long period when naval officers stressed the importance of sophisticated missiles to fight a nuclear age Trafalgar, latterly there has been increasing talk about the resurrection of guns, because of their visibility and meaning in the low-level activities of naval diplomacy. Clearly, many circumstances are conceivable in which a gun is a more credible threat or promise than a more expensive and more destructive missile. For naval diplomacy the *best* (in terms of a 'bigger bang for a buck') is often the enemy of *good enough*. In this respect there is a requirement for warships to have a general war capability, but also for them to have sufficient flexibility to cope with the less serious but more frequent needs of naval diplomacy. The concept of 'high-low' mix is relevant in this respect: fleets built for worse cases should have the flexibility to operate successfully in lesser contingencies.

The importance of the skill with which naval officers carry out their appointed tasks scarcely needs elaboration. Depending upon the situation, there is a requirement for such qualities as technical competence, decisiveness, patience, diplomatic skill, stubbornness, unflappability, discipline — in fact all the technical and command qualities which naval establishments hope to cultivate in their officers. During the exercise of naval diplomacy, however, the main problem will often be the lack of diplomatic skill on land rather than the lack of professional quality at sea. At least as important as the carrying out of local naval tasks is the provision and orchestration of appropriate diplomatic support. Successful naval diplomacy depends not only on the ships at sea, but also on the skill of the country's diplomats and businessmen ashore. The difficulty of communicating clear messages (unless in this case *uncertainty* was the main signal) is amply illustrated by the various attempts to disentangle the aims of the US administration from its naval behaviour during the Indo-Pakistan war of 1971.[8]

Volitional restraints will also affect influence-building efforts. These restraints will be the result of the importance or lack of importance which a government attaches to the achieving of influence with a particular country, and to its estimate of the likely costs of the influence-building effort. The importance attached will depend upon the government's assessment of its needs and interests, while the costs include both direct costs (economic and human) and potential political costs, such as the possibility of being influenced by the target state (influence is almost always two-way) and any undesirable 'anticipated responses' by the target state or by any other governments which may be competing for influence in it.

The factors just described will affect (but not determine) the influence potential of a naval power. Turning to the factors affecting the influenceability of the target state, it will be seen that the 'psychological environment' of the relevant decision-makers is the main consideration. Influenceability will be mainly affected by the character and quality of the perceptions of its major decision-makers and internal opinion-forming groups, the basic relationship between the countries concerned, the needs of the target country and the type and availability of alternative sources of supply for those needs, and the general responsiveness of the target state.

Ethnocentrism is a particular danger when contemplating an act of naval diplomacy. When assessing the political leverage of units of the Soviet Navy in forward deployment, for example, a Western observer must not project his own beliefs and assumptions about their capabilities and intentions on to rulers, governments or movements which may be socialistically inclined, newly independent, economically backward, desirous of a degree of external military assistance for a regional problem, enthusiastic about the decline of 'imperialism' and so on. While such a country will not want to fall under the control of any white great power, it is obviously likely to be far more responsive to the tactics of Soviet naval influence-building than would be a stable pro-Western Third World country, with no major security problems. But one must not generalise too readily about any country. A clear illustration of the subjectivity which has to be considered in this subject was provided by Soviet naval diplomacy in 1967. However Americans or Israelis perceived the deterrent effects of the rotation of Soviet ships in Egyptian ports vulnerable to attack, the fact is that the Soviet efforts may have been stripped of much of their significance to *Egypt* because important Egyptian opinion did not readily *recognise* the import of the move: in fact, Egyptian 'street opinion', seeing the warships in port, may have been liable to protest about Soviet 'inaction' in the face of the Israeli threat.[9] One man's gesture of support may be another man's idea of passivity.

Interpreting the perceptions of foreign decision-makers is a notoriously difficult task. This is certainly true in assessments of their perceptions of naval matters, whether we are thinking of a particular naval 'balance' in terms of future war, or in terms of influence potential in naval diplomacy. We are all familiar with the problems which Western naval commentators have in assessing the significance of naval balances and the meaning of acts of naval diplomacy, and this is so despite years of expertise and access to relatively extensive and generally reliable information. It is therefore very much more difficult for the foreign policy analyst to assess the political meaning of particular naval 'balances' (or imbalances) in the eyes of alien rulers, governments, parties, mobs and so on. We can only begin to guess at the criteria which different groups adopt. Is their perception based on ideas about relative war-fighting capabilities? If so, on what do they base their judgements — *Jane's*, hearsay, intuition, the propaganda of authoritarian countries or the domestic critics of democratic countries? Do they base their perceptions of the balance in a crisis on estimates of will or capability? Do they know, let alone understand, the naval significance of relevant technical factors? Until such questions can be answered, Western naval observers themselves can only be very impressionistic about the influence potential of their naval forces. At present we know far too little about third-party perceptions of navies and foreign policies to make even reasonably educated guesses about the utility of naval diplomacy.

One factor which will affect the credibility of particular naval forces, however, will be the traditional character of relations between the naval power and its target. The extent of interdependence between them will also affect the disposition of the latter to be impressed by the former's words and actions. Before one state will allow itself to be influenced by another in a politically important way, that state must see the other as being relevant to the furtherance of its own interests. The greater the significance of A for the achievement of B's objectives, the greater is the likelihood that B will be open to A's influence-building tactics. Necessity is the mother of influenceability.

In particular, states with maritime needs are likely to be more vulnerable to acts of naval diplomacy than states without such needs; but this obvious generalisation does not go far. It is probably true that very few countries have such immediate naval problems that they will transform a general maritime interest into an actualised naval need, which will make that state readily responsive to the naval influence-building tactics of one or more suitors. *Responsiveness* is a key word in such relationships. It has been defined as the 'disposition to receive another's requests with sympathy . . . the willingness to be influenced'.[10] It is based on a mixture of such factors as traditional relations, trust, the availability of alternative sources for the satisfaction of national interests, recent experiences and needs, as well as the unique circumstances of the situation under consideration (such as the personality characteristics of the leaders concerned). In this as with the whole subject of naval diplomacy, one cannot progress very far without consideration of detailed case-studies.

Having looked at some of the general factors affecting influence-building attempts, it is necessary now to examine the more specifically naval aspects, beginning with the inherent qualities of warships themselves.

The assets and liabilities of warships as diplomatic instruments

Cromwell's comment that a man-of-war was his 'best Ambassador' has become one of the clichés of naval writings. It has become commonplace because it identified a major role of warships, and suggested some of their essential qualities. As diplomatic instruments, warships have seven basic assets:

(1) *Versatility.* This refers to the ability of warships, either singly or in groups, to perform a range of tasks of a social, humanitarian or political character, as well as of a purely military character. Of all the weapons systems in a country's inventory, warships are clearly the most mutable.

(2) *Controllability.* This quality is based upon two assets possessed by warships in most situations, namely their escalatory potential on the one hand and their withdrawability on the other. Various combinations of warships are well suited to climb the rungs between the lowest maritime confrontation and the highest level of use of force. As instruments of escalation, warships possess a number of advantages over other branches of the armed forces: the increasing use of force can be more clearly graduated, and the absence of resident populations on the sea removes many complicating factors. The non-territoriality of the medium on which warships operate gives them some advantages over other weapon systems as signifiers of national resolve. It means that demonstrations and tests of will can take place, but without necessarily entailing the risks which are the inevitable consequence of a loss of control in international games of chicken on land. Like tank warfare in the desert, naval diplomacy has a clarity and an absence of the collateral complications which are usually present with the use of other instruments of the 'diplomacy of violence'. Similarly, the fact that warships operate at sea will often enable them to withdraw from ostensible commitments with more speed, fewer costs and less loss of face than would be entailed by deployed ground forces, or aircraft and their accompanying logistic tail. In another of the great naval clichés, Bacon wrote that, 'He that

Commands the seas is at great liberty, and may take as much and as little of the war as he will.' The same principle operates in the competition of peacetime naval diplomacy, except that 'command' is not necessary.

(3)   *Mobility.* This refers to the ease with which warships can move, relatively quickly and usually independently to meet the unpredictable situations in near or distant parts which are the stuff of international politics. If they can be spared, warships from widely dispersed points can converge to meet at least some of the needs of a situation, when aircraft or ground forces would be irrelevant, inappropriate, or inaccessible. Whatever their inadequacies, warships may be the only instrument which gives a government options in a particular situation.

(4)   *Projection ability.* Warships are not only relatively mobile, they are also efficient bulk carriers of their own firepower, troops, tanks, aircraft, landing craft, and a variety of other military hardware. This ability enables a combat group to threaten or fight other ships, or to threaten or project force against the land by air strike, amphibious assault, or naval bombardment. The relative freedom of movement across the seas, and the payload which warships and their supports can carry, make them the only means by which some countries can become military powers in distant regions.

(5)   *Access potential.* An old Admiralty maxim was: 'The sea is one'. Many of the utilities of warships arise from the character of the medium in or on which they operate. Although there has been a variety of challenges to the traditional 'freedom of the seas' through a proliferation of national claims and fixed installations, it nevertheless remains true that the movement of armed forces across the sea is much easier than over land or in the air. Consequently, in the third great naval cliché, a country with a navy is potentially a neighbour to all countries with coasts. Without warships, a country's relations with its potential neighbours, however distant, will be reduced in scope. Certainly merchant ships can perform most if not all the transportational tasks of warships, but because they do not have defensive and offensive potential, and because violence remains an irreducible possibility in inter-state relations, states which desire an important degree of independence have no alternative but to provide themselves with the costly insurance of those instruments which will give them some hope in the worst conditions (or fairly bad conditions) of having the desired amount of access with their 'neighbours', be they allies or adversaries, near or distant.

(6) *Symbolism.* The character of warships, especially those of the biggest type, makes them particularly useful and visible signifiers and representatives of a country's intentions and commitments. Laurence Martin has discussed this particular quality of warships with much clarity: he has written that

> A wide variety of naval activities is conducted in peacetime for the express purpose of bringing home to others the power and particularly the naval power of the country in question. ... The conception that ships are small mobile pieces of national sovereignty makes them particularly suitable to symbolise the nation from which they come. For the same reason governments have always paid punctilious attention to the manner in which their vessels and flag are treated and to the reception they accord other nations.[11]

(7) *Endurance.* Although warships have a valuable withdrawable quality, they can also have impressive staying power. They can loiter, with appropriate signals for the situation, either within the visibility of those who are to be impressed, or just out of sight, or at some distance but still within range. They can attempt to make themselves appear either committed or uncommitted or posing a 'vague menace'. Whichever posture they adopt, they can retain an important degree of flexibility. As instruments of diplomacy, warships can be adjacent but removable, but they can also be removed but remain committable.

Warships therefore have many basic characteristics which make them highly suitable instruments of diplomacy. On the other hand they also have a number of important weaknesses. Some situations can blow up so quickly that their relative slowness may rule them out. Short of using force, their effects can only be indirect, through the perceptions of the relevant targets; this means that they are rather unpredictable in their results. In forward deployment warships can invite a range of trouble, as well as being vehicles of opportunity. They can incite hostility, provoke counter-availing forces, add unwelcome responsibilities, encourage unwanted expectations and so on. Furthermore, warships can rarely hope to achieve their required effects acting alone, and therefore need orchestrating with other instruments of diplomacy (which may or may not be present or adequate). Their scope is often limited. While they can sometimes have effects far beyond the shoreline, in many cases they cannot. Rarely can they have the quality of looming menace which an army across an adjacent frontier may have, and rarely can they produce the nerve-racking danger of an alerted air force within range. In sum, while warships as diplomatic instruments do have many valuable characteristics, they also have many limitations. While it is possible to draw up long lists of episodes in which naval forces have been applied for political purposes,[12] we should never let our preoccupation with this instrument obscure the fact that very many more episodes have taken place in which warships have apparently had no role whatsoever.

The last point, the uncertainty surrounding the impact of warships in particular situations, leads on naturally to one of the major difficulties in both the practice and analysis of naval diplomacy. How can we identify the actual effects of naval diplomacy? How do we know if influence is being achieved?

Identifying naval influence

Despite its centrality in international politics, the measurement of influence remains a crude activity. Too often, we have to rely on impressions and assertions, prejudices and preconceptions, newspaper cuttings and quick visits.

One way to avoid being merely impressionistic when discussing influence is to articulate a pertinent set of 'operational criteria'. One of the very few relevant efforts in this regard is Alvin Z. Rubenstein's study of the Soviet-Egyptian influence relationship since the June 1967 war. His criteria have a general salience for any study of great power influence-building efforts in the Third World.[13] Firstly, inferences can be made from shifts (their character, degree, frequency and implications) in B's domestic and/or foreign policies congenial to A. Two riders are necessary: 'often what appears to be influence turns out instead to be *joint interests* of the two parties'; and one can see that influence is of reduced significance when B adapts to A's preferences on *issues that are of low salience* to B, with the cost of such adaption by the latter being minimal.[14] Secondly, influence may exist when A's ability to deal with B on favourable terms noticeably improves. Thirdly, a major increase in the security commitment of A to B suggests a change in A's influence, one that may result in a greater ability to restrain (though not compel) the behaviour of the 'client' and consolidate a more stable dependent relationship. But even here automatic influence cannot be assumed, however, unless A is in a position to control the levers of power in B's domestic politics. Finally, (and Rubinstein makes this less clear), influence must be viewed within a strategic context. Successful influence-building will result in A having B opt for policy outcomes that B prefers but are made possible only by A, which believes they will redound to its long-term regional or global advantage.

In the light of these operational criteria Rubinstein provides a penetrating, if inevitably speculative analysis of the Soviet-Egyptian influence relationship. Interestingly there is little or nothing about the influence effect of the Soviet Navy. From his account of the general relationship, however, several inferences can be made. It might be argued, for example, that the visibility of ships in Soviet relations with Egypt was more an effect of the influence relationship rather than a cause, and that to the extent the USSR had influence over Egypt it was bought by anti-Israeli military aid for the Suez front, not maritime support.[15] Soviet warships can only have been of marginal influence in the development of relations because the Egyptians did not perceive them to be pertinent to their central problem, namely the provision of tanks, air defence and so on for the main battle. Egyptian leaders allowed Soviet warships to use their ports and facilities because their visible presence might contribute to deterring Israeli attacks, and because allowing such usage was a relatively cheap way of sweetening the Soviet leaders to give help where it mattered to the Egyptians; in addition, what was seen by the Soviet Union as a naval facility for its warships was seen by the Egyptians as insurance of a Soviet commitment. The fact that the Egyptians granted naval facilities to the Soviet Union does not mean that the Soviet leaders could count upon moving Egyptian leaders in desired directions. Indeed, Rubinstein's study suggests that despite the size and visibility of the overall Soviet military presence, Soviet influence over Egyptian foreign and domestic policies was quite limited, that Egypt had the ability to undertake independent initiatives, and that the Soviet presence gave Egypt the opportunity to influence the Soviet Union.

The Soviet-Egyptian relationship is a crucial case-study of the naval factor in Soviet influence-building efforts in the Third World. It is a warning against any simplistic notions of 'superpower influence' or of military aid diplomacy directly buying political influence. Some of the Soviet difficulties in its dealings with Egypt were always evident to less hasty observers: but it is only recently that the details have been fascinatingly given by the eye-witness account of Mohamed Heikal. The limited Soviet influence on Egypt has already been referred to. What is equally significant was the Soviet vulnerability to Egypt in a number of respects. (1) One might reasonably conclude that the most significant consideration about the naval factor in Soviet-Egyptian relations was the potential leverage which Soviet naval requirements *gave Egypt* over the Soviet Union. The Soviet squadron in the Mediterranean had *needs* for its operations which made Soviet policy vulnerable to some extent to those countries like Egypt which could supply them.[16] Soviet naval needs resulted in greater Soviet vulnerability to Egypt than Soviet naval strength produced Soviet influence over Egypt. (2) The Soviet leaders did not give the Egyptian leaders all the latter wanted in the way of military supplies, but nevertheless the Soviet leaders became prisoners of the relationship to some degree, as Nasser noted (and exploited). Having once committed itself to supplying Egypt, any Soviet move to cut the flow of weaponry would 'immediately undercut its entire, expensively acquired position in Egypt'.[17] As long as the Soviet Union had interests in Egypt, it had to keep supplying arms. This gave the Egyptians scope for leverage. (3) The Egyptian leaders were able to oppose successfully the 'very insistent' requests by Soviet representatives (Admiral Gorshkov in 1970 for example) for naval facilities at Mersa Metruh and Bernis. Egyptian opposition was strong. Although Soviet arguments were couched in terms which promised that the use of the facilities would redound to Egypt's advantage, the Egyptian leaders were determined not to become too committed to Soviet naval strategy. When the Egyptian leaders saw Soviet global policies coming into conflict with its role as helper of Egypt, Egyptian priorities were clear. The Soviet Union did not get the facilities its navy wanted.[18] Earlier, Nasser had dug in his heels when President Podgorny had made a request for extensive naval facilities, including the right to guard such facilities with Soviet marines and the right of Soviet ships to enter Egyptian ports without prior notice. Nasser lost his temper. 'This is just imperialism,' he said. 'It means we shall be giving you a base.' Podgorny backed down, but the Soviet Union had lost important diplomatic capital.[19] On the whole Nasser was very successful in his dealings with Soviet representatives: he kept them involved, but did not let them dominate.[20] The whole experience of Soviet-Egyptian relations in the late 1960s and early 1970s shows the dangers of commentators being too ready with assumptions about Soviet influence-building attempts in the Third World, and especially of the impact of the naval factor. It is a significant reminder that it is not always clear in such cases *who* influences *whom*.

In addition to elaborating operational criteria, two other approaches might be helpful in deciding what caused what. The first is the regularity answer. For one thing to cause another is for things like the first always to be followed in similar circumstances by things like the second. Thus, in particular bilateral relationships, one might investigate whether there is any pattern between the tactics of naval diplomacy practised by the United States or the USSR and the target country's voting pattern at the United Nations, its stand on East-West questions, its assertiveness in local disputes, its changing policy dispositions, and so on. In the second approach a cause of an effect is identifiable where, if the first event had not taken place, then the second one would not have existed. By a detailed country-by-country analysis one might therefore speculate whether Soviet or US relations with particular countries would have been different had their warships stayed nearer home. When using either the regularity or 'if only' question, a major difficulty is the fact that naval tactics are never the only factor in a relationship, and can rarely be disentangled from a gamut of diplomatic, economic and wider military signals, promises and threats.

Identifying the influence-building potential and achievement of naval diplomacy will always remain a difficult problem, because of the indirectness of the influence process, its incremental character, and the difficulty of separating its effects from the effects of other influence tactics. The influence of warships will always be particularly difficult to assess in what Luttwak calls 'latent suasion'.[21] In addition to the earlier discussion, several final comments may help to prevent an influence relationship being seen in too simple a fashion: (1) We must not be hypnotised by ships at sea, but must see them instead in relation to a country's overall influence-building tactics. (2) We must not mistake what a particular government claims or hopes to be its influence and what its influence actually is: nor must we confuse the effort to achieve influence with its actual achievement. The latter danger is always present because we are likely to know far more, for example, about the policy aims and tactics of the Soviet Union towards a country such as the Somali Republic than the effects of those aims and tactics on Somali behaviour. In this respect the weight of Soviet area specialists as opposed to East African specialists is likely to skew the objective picture of the influence relationship. (3) Whether or not naval tactics increase one country's influence with another, for organisational reasons navies are likely to claim influence potential, while decision-makers will be predisposed to make some political use of naval forces in order to try to maximise what is an increasingly costly investment. (4) We must be careful to distinguish the possible influence of A's acts on B with behaviour by B which might be the result of a coincidence of interests. The pertinent question is: 'Would B have behaved in that way in any case?' This is a particularly important warning because the evidence for influence is often only circumstantial. But if mutual interests exist, warships can be supportive of such a relationship, and so make them more concrete. (5) We must keep in mind that influence is *at least* a two-way process, so it is essential that we are interested in more than the influence of A on B. The multi-dimensionality of the influence process means that we must speculate about the effects of A's acts not only on B's rulers, but on all significant groups in B's political life, on third parties (C, D, E, F and so on), and on political groups within A. To the extent that A's naval acts affect the expectations of all these groups, it has influence-building potential, in a multi-faceted way.

Despite the frequent difficulty of identifying the precise relation-ship between naval causes and political effects, naval powers have always been convinced of the political utility of warships. Consequent-ly a range of tactics has been developed and employed in the furtherance of policy short of applying even limited naval force.

The tactics of naval diplomacy

Naval diplomacy is carried out by means of five basic tactics. The first two tactics, *standing demonstrations of naval power* and *specific operational deployments* represent naval power politics: the rest, *naval aid, operational visits* and *specific goodwill visits* are naval influence politics. There is, needless to say, a considerable degree of interrelationship between these two types of tactics. *Standing demonstrations of naval power* facilitate (and make necessary) routine *operational visits*, and also increase the opportunities for *specific operational deployments* when crises or incidents arise, or *specific goodwill visits* when the conditions are opportune. Furthermore, as was stated earlier, the dividing line between naval power politics and naval influence politics is not easily drawn. Most tactics have an element of carrot and stick. A 'goodwill' visit may also be a demon-stration of an ability of 'access' for coercive purposes.[22] Furthermore, to accept the benefit of naval aid is inevitably to put oneself in the position of being threatened with its withdrawal. Obviously, the scale on which each of the above tactics takes place can vary enormously, depending on the country concerned and the circumstances. The deployments might include anything from a number of ships to a single ship, and from the most powerful aircraft carrier to the humblest mine-sweeper: naval aid might include anything from single ships (or their parts) to a 'gift-wrapped navy' including technicians and advisers.

(1)   *Standing demonstrations of naval power*

'Naval presences' or 'political demonstrations of naval power' are a time-honoured usage of major navies. By threatening ultimately to use force at sea, or to project force ashore, such standing demonstrations seek to deter actions inimical to the deploying state, and to encourage actions that are in the interests of itself and its allies.[23] The act of deterring might be attempted by either the gathering together of preponderant power, or by the insertion of sufficient naval force to contest another state's free use of the seas in the event of war.

Standing demonstrations of naval power can achieve their objectives by several methods. In addition to threatening adversary shipping, they can also threaten littoral nations with amphibious assault, air attack, bombardment, blockade, and exposure through reconnaissance. Furthermore, they might also be regarded as tokens of resolve and concern in the particular area, and a signal that the deploying power may be willing to call upon other military forces.[24] In this respect even a single ship or a small group of ships might be used to demonstrate a government's interest in a matter, and possibly the latter's determination to employ greater power if events do not proceed in the desired way.

The actual detailed actions by which a group of ships can attempt to convey the required political messages are many and various, as are the messages. Edward Luttwak has usefully distinguished five tactical inputs by which naval power might be transformed from the latent to the active mode.[25] These are: (i) *force-level changes.* These could be reinforcements (to augment the intensity of coercive or supportive effects, to show concern, or to pre-empt), or they could be reductions (to signal disengagement, to discourage, to close options); (ii) *display manipulations.* These could be fleet movements and manoeuvres in the target's presumed zone of observation (to evoke coercive or supportive effects or to show concern) or they could be port visits and transits in direct proximity to land for similar reasons; they might involve a display of combat capabilities in action to augment the intensity of the other effects, or they could display specific combat capabilities in action where these are appropriate to counter or pose a specific threat (in order to augment the intensity of the effects already mentioned, or to render coercion and/or support in a narrow and limited fashion). (iii) *Fleet configuration changes.* This involves the increase or reduction of battle readiness (to augment or reduce the intensity of general coercive or supportive effects, or to signal concern or disengagement) or it might involve the selection of a task force out of the normally deployed fleet in order to accentuate specific combat capabilities (to augment coercive or supportive effects or to limit the scope of coercion or support to a narrower range of actions). (iv) *Warship configuration changes.* This involves, for similar reasons to the last set of tactics, the increase or reduction of general or specific warship battle readiness. (v) *Use of capabilities.* This might include intensive reconnaissance (to deter adversary moves, to intensify coercive or supportive effects, or to suggest preparation for particular combat action), or it might include interposition of various types (to reinforce deterrence, compellence, or support, and to make such actions specific), or it might include the deployment of 'symbolic' and non-destructive force for similar reasons. While this classification evokes images of fleet action (especially the Sixth Fleet) this is not necessarily the case. Various *display manipulations, warship configuration changes,* and *uses of capability* can be carried out by one or a few warships. In fact, much naval diplomacy at the lowest level is carried out by single warships operating in distant parts.[26] In addition, a standing demonstration of naval power may carry out its mission, attempting to evoke the desired effects, without making explicit any of the inputs which Luttwak classified; this is achieved by 'latent suasion', which Luttwak defines as reactions evoked by routine and/or undirected deployments. Warships can sometimes have influence just because they are known to be there.

Because the ultimate targets of standing demonstrations of naval power are the brains of decision-makers, not their ships, the skilful transmission of signals is a matter of primary importance. But however skilfully this is done, it is no guarantee that the target decision-makers will perceive them 'correctly'. Nevertheless, as a general rule a standing demonstration of naval power, however accurately or inaccurately its messages have been perceived — *as long as some messages have been perceived* — will be taken into account by all the states in the adjacent region. Those who might be targeted by the warships and what they represent, and those whose actions might be supported by the warships and what they represent, have in their planning to include the likely actions of the naval power and the effects of those actions on different countries. Even bystanders have to take the warships into account, because of what they might represent to the other states with which they have to deal. A rational decision-maker will have to take any local naval presence into account, even if only to disregard it. While it is unlikely these days that any substantial naval presence will remain unnoticed by any littoral state, what is much more uncertain is that the detailed signals which that force might try to convey will be 'correctly' read by observers, who in many cases will have little expertise in deciphering the niceties of naval diplomacy.[27] If, for one reason or another, a standing demonstration fails to induce the desired effects, and its controllers decide to resort to force, then this can be seen as a very serious breakdown of that country's naval power.

(2). *Specific operational deployments*

Specific operational deployments are invariably a special case of the standing demonstration. They refer to the use of one or more warships in a deliberate, determined and active sense in a crisis or low-level engagement. The action may be initiatory or reactive, and its intention may be to deter, to forestall, to support, to complicate, or to contest the actions of other states in specific situations. The desired effects may be sought by a similar range of 'tactical inputs' as described in the section above. By well-timed cruises, perhaps backed by appropriate diplomatic action and a wide variety of tactics, perhaps augmented with harassment or calculated discourtesies, a naval power might attempt to affect various local attitudes in confrontations or negotiations, or might be used to initiate confrontations.

On a number of occasions in recent history it has happened that today's specific operational deployment becomes next year's standing demonstration of naval power. Supportive commitments often take on a momentum of their own, because governments find their prestige becomes heavily involved; it is often easier to insert a presence than remove one. This is certainly the case for any substantial standing demonstration of naval power, especially if it has had an existence for a number of years: thus the disbanding of the US Sixth or Seventh Fleets would be political events of the first magnitude. On a smaller scale, the Soviet Navy's West African Patrol would require a mixture of luck and tact if it were to be withdrawn without any loss to Soviet-Guinean relations; equally it will require the same advantages if it is to be preserved for a long period without irritating those relations or inviting calls for expulsion.[28] While withdrawals are sometimes difficult, however, naval forces do have special advantages in this respect over other armed forces, especially if operating on a small scale in specific deployments: the 'refit' of warships can be used as an excuse to slip away in the same way that diplomats use 'headaches'.

As with standing demonstrations of naval power, specific operational deployments depend for their effectiveness on the desired patterns being created in the minds of the target decision-makers. Once again, failure or the need to use naval force would signify a serious breakdown of the deploying country's naval power.

(3)   *Naval aid*

Naval aid includes not only the sale or gift of warships, but also a range of related activities such as the attachment of naval advisers, mine-clearing, or salvage work in the aftermath of hostilities. Naval aid has been a prominent activity by the major naval powers in the post-war period; the 'fleet strengths' of the navies of the world are made up of many ships of foreign origin, either bought off-the-shelf, or transferred and renamed after first seeing service in another navy. The tactic of naval aid is sometimes seen in combination with merchant shipping and fisheries activity, in order to build up access and relationships with a particular country; this is an extension of what has been called 'the kitchen use of power'.[29]

(4)   *Operational calls*

Operational calls refer to port visits whose basic occasion is the satisfaction of the operational naval requirements of foreign warships operating in or transiting through a particular stretch of water. The basic requirements are rest for the crew and the replenishment of supplies. Essentially, operational calls are carried out for the convenience of the visitor rather than for the courting of the visited. However, such visits can then be used in attempts to make a favourable impression on the country concerned (or at least on those citizens who are aware of the visit) by the behaviour and turn-out of the crew, the technological prowess of the country as embodied in the ship, the general 'image' of the ship, and the entertainment and cultivation of selected locals. Together, the organisers of such visits hope that they might contribute incrementally to the prestige and standing of the visiting power, and so augment its influence over the country concerned.

(5)   *Specific goodwill visits*

As is the case with operational calls, specific goodwill visits may be carried out by warships operating in or transiting through a particular area. However, the difference between the two is that whereas the former is an attempt to maximise the political effects of a necessary visit, the specific occasion for the latter is political. The scale and type of goodwill visits can vary considerably, from a cocktail party for local dignitaries to a much more publicised and ceremonial visit, involving government-to-government relations in some form. In a ceremonial visit the naval power uses one or more warships to make an outward and formal linkage between its own policy and some event, policy or circumstance associated with the host state. Such visits have an inherently symbolic nature, because of the particularly expressive nature of warships. Goodwill visits of whatever type involve a specific attempt to cultivate the host country, with the hope of accumulating diplomatic capital.

The effects of naval diplomacy

All observers of naval diplomacy, be they practitioners or academics, are very concerned with the effects or outcomes of naval diplomacy. In many, if not most, cases the outcomes are not easily observed, because 'influence' is invariably an incremental process, and because it is often impossible to separate the effects of the naval instrument from those of the other instruments of diplomacy (and it is probably true that the foreign policies of major powers today are more orchestrated than ever before). However, there are two sets of distinctions which should be kept in mind in considering naval diplomacy. The first distinctions are those classified by Luttwak between 'latent' and 'active' naval suasion:[30] the second are the distinctions between intended and unintended effects.

Luttwak's *The Political Uses of Sea Power* is an important attempt to bring coherence to the study of the 'political' uses of navies. What is relevant to the present discussion is his division of naval suasion into two types: (a) active (that is, 'reactions evoked by any deliberate action of signal') and (b) latent (that is, 'reactions evoked by routine and/or undirected deployments'). Active naval suasion can be either 'supportive' or 'coercive': in the first case the target (an ally/client) is reassured; in the second case the suasion is either positive ('compellence') or negative ('deterrence'). Latent naval suasion is also of two types, namely, the 'deterrent mode' and the 'supportive mode'. The significance of Luttwak's 'theory of suasion' is its emphasis on the *indirectness* of any political application of naval power. Because it is 'manifest only in others' reactions' and because it operates 'through the filter of others' perceptions' it is inherently unpredictable in its results. This leads to the second set of distinctions, between intended and unintended effects.

The intended effects refer to the rational aims for which a tactic of naval diplomacy is employed. Of course, a rational aim may not be the only or even the main reason for which a specific action takes place. The reasons for a particular action may be any mixture of factors resulting from the outputs of 'organisational processes' and/or 'bureaucratic politics'. The unintended effects refer to those consequences of an act of naval diplomacy which the initiating power either did not foresee or did not desire.

Whether a particular act of naval diplomacy results in intended or unintended effects will depend upon many factors. The two most important factors are the skill and suitability with which the deploying power carries out its tactics, and the perceptions of the relevant observers. As has become increasingly stressed, naval diplomacy operates through the perceptions of others. Such perceptions are both uncontrollable and unpredictable: the problems of transmitting the desired signals and having them 'correctly' interpreted are considerable; the political effectiveness of such signals cannot be measured; and at best their effect can only be indirect. The more naval diplomacy becomes an exercise in the use of naval power, however, the more do third party perceptions of the existing naval 'balance' (or imbalance) come to the fore; but even so, the behaviour of others cannot be controlled to any significant degree unless force is employed, and is employed successfully. The effectiveness of naval diplomacy will therefore always be a somewhat uncertain quality.

Despite the unavoidable uncertainties, a government engaging in naval diplomacy can take several precautions to try to minimise the dangers of misperception (unless the image of uncertainty is the object of the diplomacy). Firstly, it can ensure that its diplomats work to underline the signal(s) which are being transmitted by the naval forces; and secondly, it can attempt to ensure that the detailed naval behaviour is the most appropriate for the circumstances, and is carried out skilfully. Obviously, sailors ashore on a goodwill visit should avoid insulting local customs, while for naval aid to be politically effective, it is more important that warships are supplied which are militarily relevant and within the technical competence of the receiving country, rather than imposing the military preferences or furthering the economic interests of the supplying power. While the perceptions of relevant observers can never be controlled, therefore, the likelihood of misperception can be reduced if detailed care and attention is invested into such matters as the size and composition of the ships used, their operating procedures and tactical behaviour, and associated diplomatic support. In addition, third-party perceptions of a naval balance and the utility of naval diplomacy will greatly depend upon attitudes conveyed by the domestic opinion of the deploying country: whether these are characterised by positive belief and support, or by declining self-confidence, will greatly affect the thinking of potential targets.[31]

In practice, the range of effects evoked by the various tactics of naval diplomacy can be as wide as is conceivable from any other instrument of diplomacy. When used effectively, naval diplomacy in its various guises can reassure, strengthen, symbolise a growing relationship or commitment, establish rights and interests in near or distant regions, impress onlookers with the country's technical competence or diplomatic skill, restrain allies or adversaries, bolster the strength and confidence of allies and associates or third parties, encourage the independent-mindedness of third parties, encourage or dissuade states in relation to particular policies, signal intentions or expectations, create uncertainty when necessary, neutralise the naval diplomacy of adversaries, complicate the problems and planning of adversaries and their associates, deter inimical actions, foreclose the options of competing states, reduce the confidence of selected targets, cause losses of faith in the associates of one's adversaries, discourage opponents, create a different politico-military environment and set of expectations, increase the level of profitable interaction with near or distant countries, gain access to new countries, maintain or improve access with existing associates, and create a degree of dependency and so the possibility for manipulation. In short, effectively employed naval diplomacy can be used (usually incrementally) to maintain or increase a country's political influence over allies, associates and third parties. If naval diplomacy is badly managed, or is misperceived by relevant onlookers, or even if it is skilfully managed but none the less perceived in a perverse manner, it can result in the opposite of all these effects.

Notes

1. Roger Fisher, *Basic Negotiating Strategy* (London: Allen Lane, The Penguin Press, 1971), p. 94.
2. See Chapter Nine.
3. Arnold Wolfers, *Discord and Collaboration. Essays on International Politics* (Baltimore: The Johns Hopkins Press, 1962), Chapter Seven.
4. The comments below are based on the useful discussions by Peter Bachrach and Morton S. Baratz, 'Decisions and Non-Decisions: An Analytical Framework', *American Political Science Review (APSR)*, 57 (September 1963), pp. 632-42 and 'Two Faces of Power', ibid., 56 (December 1962), pp. 947-51; David J. Bell, *Power Influence, And Authority. An Essay in Political Linguistics* (New York: Oxford University

Press, 1975); Joseph Frankel, *International Politics. Conflict and Harmony* (Harmondsworth: Pelican Books, 1973), Chapter 6; K. J. Holsti, *International Politics. A Framework for Analysis* (Englewood Cliffs, N.J.: Prentice Hall, 1972), Chapter 6; Charles A. McClelland, *Theory and the International System* (New York: Macmillan, 1968), Chapter 3; Wolfers, op. cit., Chapter 7; J. David Singer, 'Inter-Nation Influence: A Formal Model', *APSR*, 57 (June 1963), pp. 420-30.

5.   Thomas C. Schelling, *Arms and Influence* (New Haven: Yale University Press, 1966), pp. 2-6.

6.   The best discussion of the importance of perception in naval diplomacy is to be found in Edward N. Luttwak, *The Political Uses of Sea Power* (Baltimore: The Johns Hopkins University Press, 1974).

7.   See Mohamed Heikal, *The Road to Ramadan* (London: Collins, 1975), pp. 47-8.

8.   See, for example, the various interpretations of James M. McConnell and Anne M. Kelly, 'Superpower Naval Diplomacy in the Indo-Pakistani Crisis', *CNA Professional Paper*, reprinted as Chapter 31 in Michael MccGwire, *Soviet and Naval Developments. Capability and Context* (New York: Praeger Publishers, 1973); Lt. Cmdr. Kenneth R. McGruther, 'The Role of Perception in Naval Diplomacy', *NWCR*, Vol. XXVII (2), September-October 1974, pp. 3-20; Commander James F. McNulty, 'Naval Presence – The Misunderstoof Mission', ibid., pp. 21-31.

9.   Luttwak, op. cit., p. 66.

10. Holsti, op. cit., p. 164.

11. L. W. Martin, *The Sea in Modern Strategy* (London: Chatto and Windus for the ISS, 1971), pp. 138-9.

12. E.G. James Cable, *Gunboat Diplomacy. Political Applications of Limited Naval Force* (London: Chatto and Windus for the ISS, 1971), pp. 177-229.

13. Alvin Z. Rubinstein, 'The Soviet-Egyptian Influence Relationship since the June 1967 War', Chapter 10 in Michael MccGwire, Ken Booth and John McDonnell, *Soviet Naval Policy. Objectives and Constraints* (New York: Praeger, 1975). In order to emphasise the more general applicability of Rubinstein's criteria, the Soviet Union and Egypt have been designated as A and B in the following discussion.

14. My italics.

15. That this was the Egyptian priority see Heikal, op. cit., p. 46.

16. The importance of Soviet naval *needs* is argued by Michael MccGwire, 'The Mediterranean and Soviet Naval Interests', Chapter 25 in MccGwire, *Soviet Naval Developments*.

17. Rubinstein, op. cit., pp. 176-7.

18. Heikal, op. cit., pp. 167-8.

19. Ibid., pp. 47-8.

20. Ibid., p. 166.

21. Luttwak, op. cit., Chapter 1.

22. Martin, op. cit., p. 140.

23. Turner, op. cit., pp. 14-15.

24. Ibid.

25. Luttwak, op. cit., Chapter 4.

26. For illustrations, see Cable, op. cit., *passim*.

27. Luttwak has written about this with insight: op. cit., Chapters 2 and 3.

28. On the West African Patrol see Robert G. Weinland, 'The Changing Mission Structure of the Soviet Navy', Professional Paper No. 80, Center for Naval Analyses (hereafter CNA), reprinted in *Survival*, 14, No. 3, April-May 1972, pp. 129-33; Michael MccGwire, 'The Evolution of Soviet Naval

Policy, 1960-74', Chapter 28 in MccGwire, Booth and McDonnell, op. cit., esp. pp. 525-30.

29. Alfred Vagts, *Defence and Diplomacy: The Soldier and the Conduct of Foreign Relations* (New York: King's Crown Press, 1956), p. 236.
30. Luttwak, op. cit., Chapter 1.
31. See Michael MccGwire, 'Epilogue: Western Naval Inputs to the Soviet Policy Process', MccGwire, *Soviet Naval Developments*, pp. 539-40.

3 NAVIES AND PRESTIGE

Prestige is the sex appeal of politics among nations. It encourages or permits its possessors to aspire to, to attempt, to get away with, or to achieve many things which would have been out of reach in its absence. It is generally seen as a desirable quality, and consequently is much cultivated. However, like sex appeal, it can be risky and abused: it can create false expectations in others, as well as its possessors, and these can result in difficult and dangerous situations which are neither envisaged nor welcome. Like sex appeal, international prestige opens a door to a world of opportunities and pitfalls.

Prestige and sex appeal are both attributes and attributions; that is they are qualities which others recognise, respond to, and respect, but they are also based on elements which are thought worthy of recognition, response and respect. Both qualities are more easily appreciated and enjoyed than analysed and achieved. In both cases image is at least as important as reality. In both cases attribution is almost universally sought (whether or not the aspiration is admitted) but not all can attain it. In both cases the attributes which cause recognition of the quality shift a little from age to age, and from region to region. To the flavour of real life, but to the frustration of analysis, both qualities are more immediately recognised than defined.

If the analogy with sex appeal is valid, then prestige is clearly an important if elusive concept in the process of international reltions. It has also been an important theme in the naval policies of many countries at various times.

The idea of prestige

Prestige has been variously defined as: 'reputation for power';[1] 'attention, deference and respect accorded to one state by others';[2] 'a high ranking in any or all of the several components of national power';[3] to be 'well thought of' out of a very wide range of possible qualities;[4] 'a rank or reputation attributed to an individual or a group by others';[5] 'high behaviour' from which authority derives so that those with prestige 'have influence over others because both they themselves *and the people whom they influence* believe it is legitimate − that is, correct and proper − for those individuals to wield that power';[6] 'one of the expedients which are employed by nation-states to maintain an authority or influence extending beyond their own borders' based on 'the influence acquired by past achievement or, more precisely . . . by a reputation for successful persistence in the enforcement of demands, in the implementation of threats and in the fulfillment of under-takings';[7] it is 'influence, reputation, derived from past achievements, associations, etc.'[8] It has similar connotations in most languages.[9]

From these definitions, the idea of prestige clearly contains an important functional element, involving influence and power. It can be conceived not only in terms of what it *is*, but in terms of what it *does*. By relating it to the idea of the national interest, it will be evident that the attribution of prestige is not just a matter of 'face', but also of concrete advantage. Prestige can contribute to security in various ways: having prestige means that military credibility is likely to be 'high' in relation to capabilities; it means that its possessor is likely to be regarded as a valuable ally; it means that its possessor should be in a favourable position to attract military assistance if desired; it means that its possessor should be thought honourable (upholding agree-ments) and, most important, likely to win in conflicts. In diplomacy prestige is equally useful: it can oil the efforts of a country's negotiators. A prestigious state is likely to be invited to major inter-national conferences. It is likely to be listened to with more than diplomatic courtesy, for its words will be invested with a special credibility and authority. Other states may be wary of appearing hostile, for fear of attracting third-party criticism. A prestigious state will tend to get its way because other states will tend to defer to its 'natural' authority. It may become a nodal point of diplomatic inter-course. It will claim, and be accorded, the right to be interested, involved and informed on all issues it thinks relevant. Its propaganda will be relatively effective, for those who are responsive will give its words the benefit of the doubt. In terms of the promotion of the national interest, therefore, the advantages of being thought to possess prestige appear overwhelming. Prestige brings respect, authority, deference and responsiveness. It produces efficient power and influence in foreign policy.

Why prestige is sought

From the preceding discussion the reasons why governments seek prestige would seem to be obvious. Its supportive character would seem to make it 'an indispensable element of a rational foreign policy',[10] for 'what others think about us is as important as what we actually are.'[11] However, the motivations concerned may be more complex than is suggested by the rational pursuit of the 'national interest'.

A second group of motivations behind the search for prestige concerns the ego-satisfaction of the individuals or group which formulate national policy. From this viewpoint prestige is sought not merely or mainly to serve the national interest (although actions are justified in these terms), but as a political end in itself. Prestige is sought not so much to promote other ends, but for the glory and satisfaction which come from having a recognised reputation.[12] People invariably want the status and recognition commensurate with what they regard as their power or worthiness. Those who are satisfied with their status tend to underestimate the pressures and complexes felt by those who are aspiring for recognition, and the time and effort they will be willing to invest in its achievement. This goes for countries as well as individuals. Have there been any political or military leaders for whom the drive for recognition and personal prestige was not one of the motivating forces behind their public behaviour? Personal pride, patriotism and prestige are usually inextricably linked. This is not a cynical comment, merely a reflection of the human commitment to self-interest.

The search for status is sometimes manifest in investments in costly national efforts. Major weapons systems, including warships, are sometimes criticised as wasteful, or incapable of furthering national interests. However, it can be argued that such expenditures might be judged not merely in terms of their usefulness for specific tasks, but in terms of their being the 'accepted appurtenances' of powerful status. From this viewpoint the prestige accruing from them 'may be a sufficient justification for the expenditure of the resources involved'.[13] In a government's investment in a policy of prestige, therefore, national interest, ego-satisfaction, and accepted appurtenance may all play a part.

In most international circumstances belief is at least as important as what we call 'reality'. Prestige is important because it helps structure the psychological environment of different observers. A's image of B affects B's ability to move events in desired directions. Such 'images' are all the more important in a world where military force is not as readily usable as formerly. 'The Prestige Race' is one of the major characteristics of the modern period.[14] While the explicitness of the 'race' might be questioned, acquaintance with decision-makers and bureaucrats would confirm the importance which they attach to reputation and status, in military, diplomatic and economic contexts. Experience has taught them that

The more prestige a government enjoys the greater its ability to
influence the actions of others without resort to either coercion
or material reward.[15]

These words of Grant Hugo are a reminder of the rational purpose for
which governments seek prestige. However, they give no indication of
the possible pitfalls of prestige. This is a common oversight.

The problems of prestige

Prestige is almost universally sought, despite its many pitfalls. The
impulse for its attainment remains strong because prestige is a political
manifestation of the old maxim that the sins of commission are
preferable to the sins of omission. To face the pitfalls of prestige is to
face the problems of success rather than the problems of failure.

The list of possible pitfalls is long. Bluff is the most frequently
recognised 'corruption' of a policy of prestige.[16] Governments run a
serious risk of failure if they base their prestige 'upon the appearances
of power rather than upon its substance'. Bluff is not dangerous if the
actual test of performance can be forever postponed: but 'even the
highest quality of statecraft cannot ensure' such an outcome.[17]
Another corruption of prestige results from apathy, when a government becomes satisfied with 'a reputation for power which is inferior
to the actual power possessed'. Such neglect might invite attack from
its enemies, failure for its policies, and mortal danger to its vital
interests. Another manifestation of such complacency is the temptation for governments to enjoy inherited prestige, while neglecting the
actual underlying capabilities. Vigilance slackens.[18] Overcommitment is
a third major pitfall. In the light of US policy in Vietnam, Morgenthau
attributed this corruption to the danger of governments failing to
appreciate the long and the short term in questions of prestige. A state
may be dragged into dangerous situations out of a belief that it has
constantly to keep proving its ability to win. Retreat, or even defeat,
are not necessarily detrimental to prestige: in some circumstances
overcommitment might be more dangerous.[19] Arrogance can be a by-
product of prestige. This can be destructive both to a state's interests
and to world stability.[20] Arrogance can be produced by 'self-satisfac-
tion and self-confidence generated by the attainment of major-power
status', and may be expressed in 'self-righteousness, rigidity of policy,
preaching and refusals to accept counsel from allies or compromise
from enemies'.

Irrational behaviour might also be an outcome of a policy of prestige.[21] The Cuban missile crisis in 1962 and the US commitment to West Berlin have been cited as examples. In neither case would nuclear war have been a rational outcome, but in both cases it could have been brought about essentially for reasons of prestige. Irrationality might also result when foreign policy actions are taken for reasons of domestic political prestige. This danger was raised for US foreign policy while President Nixon was trying to deal with the problems caused by the Watergate scandal.

The pitfalls of prestige are increased by a number of associated problems. (1) Prestige is a 'cant word'.[22] It is at best vague and at worst misleading to both speaker and audience. (2) It concerns sensitive issues. Because a state's reputation is politically important, fluctuations in this respect may cause international tensions or even conflict.[23] (3) The idea of a 'prestige race' complicates the course of world politics. The 'race' may be seen as a two-sided game in which one state may gain only to the extent that its adversary is humbled. Furthermore, the race is likely to be inconclusive, for the real *influence* component of prestige will be unclear.[24] In the attribution of prestige, belief is what matters. It is therefore vulnerable to all the problems and dangers of misperception. For example, a particular prestige investment might have been motivated primarily by ego-satisfaction, but worst-case forecasting by foreign observers would interpret it in terms of the advancement of foreign policy. If an underdeveloped country acquires modern warships its neighbours cannot be absolutely sure that they are the manifestations of the insecure ego of the national leader. If they choose to play safe, by acquiring countervailing power, they will be in a classic arms race situation. (4) Governments must seek to ensure that the 'signals' and 'indices' which they project are accurately perceived by the target audience. This is not easily achieved.[25] (5) Prestige is a ball to be tossed about in the internal political arena. In the mouths of politicians the idea of prestige can be used 'to inspire a warm glow of approval or an instinctive retch of aversion'.[26] A particular investment might be justified as a fitting symbol of national greatness, or derided as a 'mere prestige project'. (6) In the modern world the content of prestige is harder to appreciate than in former times. Some of the old standards, especially military might, are not as easily translated into prestige. Its cultivation is therefore more elusive from a policy-making viewpoint. When fashions are not clear, the difficulties increase for those who wish to project an appealing image to a range of beholders.

Prestige is therefore a double-sided attribute. It can be an instrument which contributes significantly to the fulfilment of a wide range of state objectives, being inextricably linked with authority, credibility and deterrence. Alternatively, it may become corrupted, or may even start, in a policy of bluff which leads to dangerous exposure if tested. It can result in a failure of policy, danger to vital interests, irresponsibility, overcommitment, self-righteousness, rigidity and arrogance. A policy of prestige might spring from internal (or internalised) motives, having effects but not aims in the international arena. Its unexpected and unwelcome effects might include tension, jealousy or conflict. Wisely pursued, and with good fortune, a policy of prestige can contribute to the maintenance or even the increase of a state's international power: used without care, a policy of prestige can contribute to overcommitment, exposure, lack of vigilance, arrogance and ultimately failure.

What gives prestige?

The attributes which have endowed states with prestige have changed through time and over space.[27] In the sixteenth and seventeenth centuries religious factors, the grandeur of courts, military power, and prowess in exploration were important. In the eighteenth and nineteenth centuries the advancement of industrialisation, the size and vitality of empire, military success, diplomatic standing and sometimes ideology were important. Throughout these four centuries maritime power was significant for what it meant in terms of trade, the use of the sea in war and the expansion of empire. At the start of the twentieth century the expansiveness of territory and the vigour of industrialisation remained of importance, but during the 'Armed Peace' leading up to 1914 status came to be seen in relatively quantifiable terms, through numbers of soldiers and major warships. During the inter-war years prestige initially accrued to those supporting peace and international order, but after the 1920s, with international politics polarised, the attribution of prestige went to the leaders of the different camps.

The differentiation of prestige has increased further as international politics have become more complex. In the early post-war years prestige was based on a mixture of ideological and military leadership. As time passed, and world society developed, the 'status-endowing attributes' became more numerous, as did the interests and outlooks of attributing states. In terms of ideology, it was no longer just Communism and anti-Communism, but favourite brands of each, not to mention varieties of the neutralist model. In terms of economic attributes it is never clear whether growth rates, or standard of living, or achievements at the edge of knowledge such as space exploration produce most prestige. In one way or another, however, economic considerations have become a primary prestige-endowing attribute. If, as seems likely, the problem of economic security intensifies, then the producers of economic well-being will have a centrality in international politics traditionally held by the 'producers' of military security.

While formal religion has declined as a status-endowing attribute, the idea of 'righteousness' in one form or another has some international impact. Throughout the 1960s, with the widespread exposure given to the conflicts in Vietnam, the Middle East and Czechoslovakia, many groups came to accord prestige to governments renowned for non-interference and astute statesmanship. It is therefore possible for even relatively small states to be endowed with prestige if they can successfully project images such as enlightened statesmanship, effective mediation or pristine neutrality.[28] In addition, the cracks exposed in US society and the problems of life under the Soviet system caused attention to be directed to those countries characterised by internal tranquillity, democratic practice, understanding of minorities and external concern but tolerance. Some prestige clearly attaches to the ability of a state to do things: some attaches to the way it does them.

As time has passed, the direct role of military power as an attribute of prestige is less clear. In the less complex international world of the nineteenth century the relationship between perceived military power and the international pecking order was quite direct. This is not so in a world in which the inhibitions on employing force have grown.

Time is a dimension in prestige. Usually attention and deference attach 'almost automatically' to a state that embodies a tradition of international political involvement, with a record of 'challenges met and mastered'.[29] Future expectations might also be important. For a state to appear as the 'wave of the future' can endow it with attention and deference. Opinions differ about the resilience of prestige,[30] but the consensus is that it is rarely merely a 'bubble'.

Ultimately, prestige depends upon the perception of the relevant beholder: in matters of human behaviour image is almost everything.[31] It follows that governments spend much time and effort in projecting their images in the best light, by propaganda and other means. As important as skill in projecting an image is the *responsiveness* of the target. This will depend upon many factors.[32] It will depend upon where the countries concerned lie on the pole of amity or enmity. It will depend upon the way the target structures his outlook on international politics as a result of his historical experience and ideology. Whether world politics are structured in an individual's mind in terms of great powers versus small powers, *status quo* versus revisionist powers, class or racial divisions, the rich-poor (or north-south) divide, the East-West-Third World division, or ideological or economic preferences about domestic politics — all these images (and others) will help determine the responsiveness which in turn helps to determine *who* invests *whom* with *what* prestige.

Geographical factors also affect responsiveness, but not in any uniform way. Distance can minimise transactions, but it can also lend enchantment. A Marxist can more comfortably entertain ideal-istic hopes about Soviet society in Peru rather than in Prague, while the American dream is more seductive when expressed by the voice of Radio Liberty rather than the news on a local Detroit radio station.

It is in the interest of states which want to act effectively to make as many countries as possible like-minded about the essential status-endowing attributes. This is why propaganda is so important, though it is an instrument of only limited effectiveness. Some states have been able to create politically exploitable attitudes out of latent pre-dispositions, but its impact has been relatively limited. It is still in an experimental stage.[33]

In a more complex and differentiated world, the structure and significance of the international pecking order are more uncertain than formerly, though consciousness about rank and ranking remain important. The idea of a pecking order still structures thinking, but it does not produce the authoritative international hierarchy of the past. Nevertheless, in an activity such as foreign policy, in which every little helps, prestige remains one of the bases for the successful pursuit of international power and influence.

The naval element in international prestige: traditional

In recent centuries the great naval powers were invariably *the* great powers of the international system. It is therefore a commonplace to note that navies were important and often favourite instruments in the search for international prestige. On some occasions, during the Age of Exploration or at the turn of this century, they were probably the most important single instrument. For much of modern history the most effective international actors, those most able to direct rather than suffer international relations, have been those most able to use the sea successfully.[34]

The factors which made for the status-endowing quality of successful

navies were many. In a period when war was regarded as a *natural* and
not particularly evil means of international conduct, there was always
a close correlation between military power in all its manifestations and
high international status. Great naval strength made some countries
militarily impregnable. Britain and the United States in particular
could act internationally with high confidence of metropolitan
security. Their strategic policy (and thus their foreign policy) was not
dominated by the destabilising urgency that characterised the major
continental powers: geography and command of the sea gave them the
luxury of a strategy based on the 'long haul' rather than one full of
the neuroses of those based on the idea that 'mobilisation means war'.
Naval power, and naval power alone, enabled certain countries to
become world powers, and because the inhibitions on the use of force
were less, authority and deference automatically flowed to those
who were willing and able to use it successfully. In such an international
milieu, warships were critical factors.

Warships had a diplomatic role. They were pieces of floating
national territory, and because of their size, potential, strength and
invariably aggressive appearance they helped to structure the thought
patterns of observers, even if conflict was not an imminent possibility.
When foreign dignitaries were invited to review a British fleet, as often
happened at the turn of the century, the intention was to leave in their
minds a strong impression of Britain's power, and especially its ability
to project force far beyond its homeland. But the effect of reviews was
not always as intended. Germany discovered this in 1904. The British
observers invited to the Kiel Review were certainly impressed by
Germany's naval might, but the result was to increase mistrust rather
than deference.[35] Whether they produced deterrence or provocation,
warships were certainly 'power in evidence',[36] and as it was argued in
Germany at the turn of the century: 'Power that was not made visible
could not be believed in.'[37]

Because of the traditional utilities of naval power, it came to be
accepted during the age of imperialism that major warships were a
primary symbol of international power and status. Whatever maritime
purpose Tirpitz, the Kaiser and their supporters had for the development of the High Seas Fleet, there was also an emotional element, a
desire that their country's status and standing in foreign eyes would
be commensurate with their own image of the German Empire. They
wanted to see respect accorded to their country, and through this to
themselves. Churchill put it too starkly when he said: 'The British
Navy is to us a necessity, whilst the German Navy is more in the nature

of a luxury.' But would Tirpitz have been so sensitive about Churchill's talk of *Luxusflotte* had he had confidence in its reputation?[38] That Tirpitz's pride was hurt proves that pride was involved. For Germany, as for other naval powers, a thriving and effective merchant marine also helped to play a part in the projection of a successful national image.[39] But it was warships which everywhere demanded primary attention. At the start of this century, a *Dreadnought* was to an aspiring power what Rolls Royce cars have been to Hollywood hopefuls. Both machines were advanced and useful vehicles, perhaps the best that money could buy. However they both symbolised something over and above any purely rational function. They were the 'accepted appurtenances' of having reached the top.

International prestige made the exercise of power an efficient activity. This was true of foreign policy in general and naval activities in particular. The classical example was the *pax Britannica*. It was largely through the image of predominant maritime strength that the British were able 'by persistence . . . to establish that inevitability which is the essence of power'.[40] Although Graham has effectively demonstrated that the *pax Britannica* was not a simple consequence of naval superiority, he nevertheless recognised its indispensable supportive function. It was the prestige of the Royal Navy which enabled Britain to succeed on the grand scale, by exercising an authority on the shores of the Atlantic and Indian Oceans, and on the Mediterranean Sea, out of all proportion to its resources and population.[41]

Naval prestige was important in war as well as peace. A reputation for success provided a 'reservoir of credibility' for gunboats in threatening situations, or isolated warships. Of World War One it has often been argued that the German naval command were worthy opponents of the Royal Navy in talent, ability and experience, but that they were handicapped by more than numbers: 'they were reluctant to fight a navy which enjoyed a centuries-old reputation of near invincibility.'[42] A specific example of this deference was the way Spee turned and fled off the Falkland Islands in December 1914.

Such prestige is not easily or quickly achieved, or maintained. Much time and effort is required. Lord Cunningham put it this way: 'It takes a navy three years to build a ship. It would take three hundred to rebuild a tradition.'[43] Though he was (understandably) exaggerating in a dramatic situation, his words had an important germ of truth. The voyages of the *Hood* in the inter-war years show in detail how a naval tradition was built and maintained. The appearance of the ship, the work of its men, extensive press coverage, and immaculate public relations helped to ensure that the ship had very successful cruises to many parts of the Empire and other parts of the world. The mayor of San Francisco was but the most euphoric victim of a goodwill visit by the *Hood*. 'We surrender our city unto you,' he said. 'We capitulate.'[44] The *Hood*'s effect was powerful. To those who saw it, it was impressive power in evidence.

The traditional status-endowing quality of navies scarcely requires labouring. Such prestige was to be expected in an age when the relationship between naval power and national destiny was so close. In accordance with the spirit of the age people believed Mahan, who argued that the foundations of the growth, prosperity and security of nations were sea power, commerce and colonies.[45] In the intervening period the world has changed. It has become more complex and confused. Inevitably, this has resulted in some changes in the international significance of the possession of naval power.

Navies and prestige: recent times

The traditional linkage between naval power and international status has not been as obvious in the last thirty years. Several factors have contributed to this: the changing utility of military force in general, the decline of imperialism, the longer range of weapons systems, the increased differentiation in the attributes of prestige, and periodic doubts about the future of navies in the modern world. Military power is still crucial in international politics, and it still has to be made visible, but it is not as prominent in the orchestration of foreign policies. The tendency has been for other instruments to be brought into play.

Navies are still regarded by some as being among the accepted appurtenances of status. One would expect all admiralties to have such an outlook, but it goes further than that. In considering the fairly large and modern navies of Latin America, Martin has noted that these countries have some security and diplomatic justifications for warships, but that their fortunate experience of peaceful relations leads one to suspect that the naval balance between them 'may be one of prestige rather than power'.[46] While in some circles it is fashionable to criticise such countries as being backward-looking in their appreciation of the 'essential political indicators', three comments are pertinent: firstly, although the utility of military force has changed in some ways, we still live very much in a military world; secondly, if particular governments believe that navies are status-endowing, and if they can persuade others to be like-minded, then they are; and thirdly, after about twenty years of neglect, the sea (and all that goes with it) has revived as an issue-area in international politics; to be 'sea-minded' is to be more forward-looking today than was imaginable ten years ago.

Powerful navies cannot compensate for national weaknesses in other respects. Impressive warships cannot outweigh a reputation for diplomatic perfidy, ideological impurity, domestic instability, economic mismanagement, or even poor delivery dates in foreign trade. In such circumstances, even an impressive merchant marine will not add much. In any case, except for authoritarian countries, merchant marines are not likely to be orchestrated as part of a national plan: indeed, some important states do not give themselves the chance, with so many of their ships sailing under flags of convenience. In the recent past sumptuous ocean liners were non-military equivalents of *Dreadnoughts* in their symbolism. An echo of this is still heard in some countries, and might explain the extent and depth of British sensitivity and nostalgia concerning the less than noble fate of the *Queens* in recent years.

Big ships still demand attention. An observer of a large foreign warship is likely to have many thoughts running through his mind; amongst these, implicitly or explicitly, enthusiastically or fearfully, is likely to be: 'If the country can produce and run ships like *that*, then it must have great technical skill, industrial strength and military potential.' In this respect aircraft carriers have been particularly compelling. Thus the British carrier was described as 'the hub and symbol of British power, East of Suez'.[47]

In view of its 'second-class' but rising status, the Soviet Navy offers some useful material for speculation about the symbolic and representational roles of warships. Some recent Soviet writings illustrate a number of the points which have been made in this chapter, although the tactical nature of Soviet writings always makes them difficult to assess. The author (or authors) of the Khrushchev memoirs (and the consensus is that it was the 'windbag and gossip' himself) provides us with a small square of light on this elusive aspect of recent Soviet naval policy.[48]

Khrushchev personally believed that the future lay in air power rather than naval power: 'Gone were the days when Britannia ruled the waves and therefore the world. Nowadays the country that rules the air could win the war.' Consequently, he disapproved of Stalin's belief in the importance of a large surface navy to match that of the likely adversaries; he added that '*Naturally*, our top naval officers encouraged him [Stalin] in this direction.'[49] It is clear from Khrushchev's comments that he was strongly opposed to the building of surface warships on grounds of military effectiveness and expense. Here and there, however, Khrushchev uses phrases and comments which suggest that he was vulnerable to arguments about the status-endowing qualities of navies and their value for representational purposes:

> It still made a beautiful picture when the crew lined up smartly at attention on the deck of a cruiser to receive an admiral or call on a friendly foreign port.

But he added that such ceremonies 'were now just an elegant luxury'. This suggests that he would not waste much money on such projects, but that he would use what was at hand. This might explain the ceremonial activity of the *Sverdlovs*. In addition, unable to find a satisfactory military use for the cruisers under construction, the Praesidium decided to scrap them, but as there were 'some men' in the navy 'who couldn't get over' being completely deprived of cruisers, the leadership decided to make 'a few concessions'. Some ships were converted; others were sold. Of more direct relevance is Khrushchev's comment that

> As another concession, I suggested that perhaps we should have a few high class modern cruisers for purposes of calling on foreign ports. The ships were good solely as showpieces, and very expensive showpieces at that . . . We exchanged opinions in the leadership and decided to go ahead as a concession to the military, which was in favour of these ships. Our naval commanders thought that they looked beautiful and liked to show them off to foreigners.[50]

While it would not be wise to make too much of Khrushchev's recollections, it does appear that the leadership was conscious of the symbolic and representational value of large surface warships, and that they were somewhat susceptible to pressure on these lines, even if in the end more importance was attached to economic constraints and military opportunity costs.

Khrushchev clearly indicates that the Soviet naval leadership was conscious of the possible status value of warships during his leadership. Admiral Gorshkov, Commander-in-Chief of the Soviet Navy since

1956, has given ample evidence that this attitude has persisted, if not grown. In his by now famous series of articles, Gorshkov stressed the prestige value of warships for projecting both the military and non-military achievements of the country.[51] As a result of friendly visits, he claimed, people in many countries

> see warships embodying the achievements of Soviet science, technology, and industry, and establish friendly contacts with representatives of the most diverse strata of population of our country.[52]

It might be assumed that Soviet leaders would be conscious of the representational aspects of ships of all kinds, but especially of warships, since Soviet governments have always been sensitive about their diplomatic rights and privileges, and proper ceremonial respect. It is of particular interest to discover that even Khrushchev, the arch-critic of naval 'metal-eaters', found himself rather impressed by the ceremonial value of warships. It is not insignificant that *Sverdlov* was sent to the Coronation Review at Spithead in 1953 and that he chose another *Sverdlov*-class cruiser for his visit to Britain (presumably a country responsive to warships) in 1956.[53]

More recently, and less ostentatiously, Soviet warships are still taking part in official visits, with customary formalities and exchanges of protocol. That Gorshkov should have stressed the prestige which warships allegedly confer is hardly surprising: nor is his conclusion that history demonstrated that a country with world-wide interests such as the Soviet Union ought to have a first-class navy.[54] It is more significant, however, that while Khrushchev was conscious of the representational value of warships, he was far more concerned with the economic costs of the kind of surface fleet which some regarded as the accepted naval appurtenance of a superpower.[55] Prestige is not attributed only to capital-ship navies, however. In these more complex times even small forces can contribute to a country's prestige, if those who deal with them are 'responsive'. The extreme example is Iceland. The activities of its handful of coastguard gunboats have contributed enormously to the respect with which that country is held.

Unimpressive navies, whatever their size, are likely at best to be irrelevant and at worst counter-productive as far as a country's reputation is concerned. A poorly turned-out ship for a state visit, and bad behaviour by its crew, will help shape national stereotypes, though one should not exaggerate the repercussions of a visit or the number of people who will be involved in it. Paintwork and public relations are not necessarily indicators of naval performance in battle, but they might be perceived as indicators of other national attributes. This goes even more for visits involving members of a naval high command. Tactlessness on such occasions can contribute to the undermining of a reputation which has previously been cultivated. On one occasion Admiral Gorshkov arrived in Alexandria and proceeded straight to Cairo for consultation without first paying his respects, 'as courtesy demanded that he should', to the Egyptian Naval Commander in Alexandria. As it happens, the Commander concerned was a 'highly punctilious' officer. He was 'extremely mortified' by Gorshkov's behaviour, and refused to go to Cairo to meet him.[56] As Rear-Admiral Mahmoud Abdul Rahman Fahmy subsequently recounted his tale to his friends and fellow officers, it is hardly likely that it increased the reputation of 'the Russians' in Egypt. International naval prestige, like beauty or ugliness, may be based on attributes which are only skin-deep, but that may be enough to affect a perceiver's attitudes, and consequently his behaviour.

Port visits have been one of the chief tactics by which governments have attempted to enhance their naval prestige. It is an activity which is more complex than formerly, as Martin has attested with more insight than most contemporary commentators:[57] For one thing, he points out, the character of warships themselves has changed: perhaps nothing — not aircraft carriers because they are 'menacing', nor submarines because they are 'sinister' — will recapture the 'awe-inspiring presence' of battleships in the 'full flower of their development'. This is a valid observation, but it pertains largely to special visits. Submarine visits on 'business calls' are not unusual. The main change and complication in port visits, however, is not ship development, but political developments which have affected the responsiveness of potential hosts. Martin has pointed to this crucial factor with clarity. His important point was that:

> Any demonstration of naval power is a demonstration of the capacity to enjoy access to the shores of others. There is therefore inevitably an implied menace in it, except in those circumstances where conflict between the nations concerned is generally agreed to be unthinkable. Many of the newer states of the world, then, obsessed with the necessity of establishing the reality of their independence, recall the days of earlier Western dominance associated with naval power and, indeed, able to observe the

continued and effective use of Western navies in intervention abroad, might well view even the most ostensibly amiable visits askance.

It might be added that even if the host government is well-disposed to a particular visit, its internal opposition might not be. Because large areas of the world are under the control of new states with relatively unstable régimes, Martin concluded that 'it is conceivable that the routine port visit will decline as an instrument of diplomacy and will become a special device to be used more rarely and with discrimination.'

The Soviet Navy has disproved this forecast. The frequency and geographical scope of their visits have risen markedly since the mid-1960s.[58] Although it can be validly argued that the impact of port visits is limited, that they can be counter-productive and that they cannot substitute for other instruments, the fact is that they are often used because equally useful instruments are not at hand. As McConnell has argued, they perform a unique function: they 'cannot create ties but they can cement them, compound and solidify influence, [and] dramatize its existence.'[59]

Obviously the context in which a visit takes place will be an important determinant of its effect. Port visits will usually take place in countries where the visitors can be sure of a warm, or at least correct, welcome. It is probably true that friendly calls have the effect of publicising the nation involved, like a trade fair or cultural visit.[60] On the other hand, if the ceremonial visit is on a high level the impact is undoubtedly greater. Through such visits the host country occupies the time and attention of high dignitaries of a great state, shares in the authority and charisma that surround their persons, and is given dramatic evidence of a more or less far-reaching political solidarity which outlasts their stay.[61] Whether port visits produce more than such intangible effects as good publicity, prestige, goodwill and gratitude is another question. Visits probably cannot be expected to have much direct political or strategic effect unless the country concerned deploys substantial naval power in the area, which might be used in time of tension.[62] However, extensive effects are rarely the intention behind a visit. There are other ways of expressing larger commitments, through alliances and extended deployments. Goodwill visits are a useful way of expressing an orientation by sharing, in a limited, temporary and symbolic way, one's own military establishment with that of the host country:

Beyond this, the visit is a matter of 'here today, gone tomorrow', though there is the implication (weak in most cases, a little stronger in others) that if my 'friend' is here today, he could come back tomorrow if I need him.[63]

The problem for the visiting country is to ensure that positive messages are received from its demonstration of naval access.

Several general conclusions can be drawn from these remarks about port visits. Firstly, ship visits are supportive of a general foreign policy posture, rather than being independently effective. Secondly, the context and arrangements (such as type of ship and public relations) require detailed attention for a visit to produce its desired result. Thirdly, visits to allies in times of tension are of a very different nature to routine calls. A non-visit in such circumstances can be as symbolic as a visit. Finally, the 'market' for goodwill visits, like any other market, can become saturated. However friendly the host country, frequent calls can involve swiftly diminishing returns or a negative reaction.[64] For a mixture of reasons – diplomatic, internal politics, or creeping apathy – a host country will have its own level of tolerance for naval visits. Beyond that point any visitor will wear out his welcome.

Efficient power and influence is still the pay-off of successfully projected naval prestige. Prestige facilitates successful expeditions, as was the case in the US landings in Lebanon in 1958. The 'almost incredible lack of coordination' in this operation was surmounted by 'luck, expert improvisation, and prestige'. Lesser assailants could have scarcely afforded the initial mistakes.[65] Prestige provides a reservoir of credibility. This was also the case in the British-Indonesian confrontation in the mid-1960s. Indonesia deferred to the British because of its naval prestige and expectations about its latent power.[66] Prestige also contributes to influence in alliance decision-making. NATO's Commander-in-Chief Channel (CINCHAN) is British, partly as a concession to British naval prestige.[67]

Naval prestige, as one of the elements in a country's overall military posture, can therefore contribute 'to the general reputation for power that gives a nation leverage in international affairs'. Such a reputation will only grow, however, if the naval instrument is used wisely and with proper style in the eyes of those observers whom it is hoped to impress, and if it is supported by high status in other 'essential political indicators'. Because navies have this potentiality, it does not mean that all or many governments will see it as expedient or feasible to exert

themselves to develop in this direction. In many international
situations navies and naval prestige will be negligible factors. But in
some situations they will count, and be productive of efficient
power and influence; they will affect the thinking of third parties and
produce a degree of authority and deference. 'When? where? and to
what extent?' depends upon the responsiveness of the particular
beholder(s) and the detailed circumstances of the episode.

Responsiveness

It is difficult to be other than impressionistic when considering the
responsiveness of different individuals and groups to the status-
endowing attributes of navies. A bundle of considerations will be
relevant, such as world outlook, historical experiences, geographical
factors, vulnerability to naval pressure, dependence on the sea, and
local political, economic, and ideological circumstances. A government which sees foreign aid as neo-colonialism, for instance, will see
naval deployments by a power with which it has no affinity as
'gunboat diplomacy' revived. Other states, however, might be responsive to any manifestation of military potential. A government which
believes in the diplomatic utility of vast military power and sees a
traditionally direct relationship between military power and international status is likely to accord respect to those countries with such
potential: the Soviet Union is arguably such a case. A willingness to be
impressed by the symbolism and functionality of impressive navies
might not be as certain in some countries as in former times, but
responsive attitudes still exist.

Geographical factors affect responsiveness, but not in a predictable
way. It might be assumed that the larger the stake which a particular
country has in maritime affairs, the greater will be its sensitivity to
naval developments. States with coastlines, maritime traditions, and a
large amount of foreign trade might be expected to be relatively more
susceptible to naval influence than peaceful, self-sufficient, 'land-
oriented' powers. Because maritime capabilities make possible large-
scale interaction between distant countries, having a coastal capital
might be a significant factor in developing politically relevant
responsiveness. In the past it has been argued that capitals far inland
have been unimpressed by naval demonstrations.[68]

The susceptibility of the target group is a basic determinant of the
effectiveness of image-promoting efforts. Direct personal contacts are
often a very useful method of image promotion or specific propaganda.[69] Admiral Gorshkov apparently believes this, although some

of his own efforts have been clumsy.[70] No doubt personal conviction was allied with a desire to impress his political masters when he wrote that

> The friendly visits of Soviet navymen make it possible for the peoples of many countries to become convinced with their own eyes of the creativity of the ideas of Communism, and of the genuine equality of all nationalities in the Soviet state, and to gain a concept of the level of development and culture of representatives of the most varied regions of our immense Motherland . . .
>
> Soviet navymen, from admirals down to seamen, are carrying the truth about the first Socialist country in the world, about Communist ideology and culture, and about the Soviet way of life to the masses of peoples of other states. They are profitably and convincingly spreading the ideas of the Leninist peaceloving policy of the Communist Party and the Soviet government through many countries of the world. It is impossible to overestimate the significance of this ideological influence.[71]

Navies and a well-drilled merchant marine can contribute to face-to-face transmissions of an image, especially as there still appears to be a measure of public fascination with ship visits. Whether the desired image is received is another matter.

In one area it is possible to be more positive about responsiveness. The traditional maritime powers have always been notoriously responsive (and usually very sensitive) to the rise of the new naval powers. Britain's adjustment to the US Navy in the 1920s is an example of the acrimony which this can cause even between basically friendly powers.[72] A navy's sensitivity will be greater, but so will its sense of purpose, if the coming naval power is that of a potential adversary. The 'rise' of the Soviet Navy in the last decade provides some interesting material on this subject.

The eagerness with which observers in the traditional maritime powers have focused on the Soviet Navy has resulted in a veritable naval debate for the first time in many years. The reactions have been of two kinds. Some have been genuinely alarmed at the breaking of the traditional Anglo-American monopoly of naval power. Others have been rather suspicious that at least some of the concern has been exaggerated by naval establishments wanting better ships and by merchant-shippers hoping for subsidies. Whatever the reason, the responsiveness of the traditional naval powers has contributed enormously to the inflation of the prestige of the Soviet Navy.[73] This might have several consequences which are undesirable from a Western viewpoint. An inflated image of the Soviet Navy's impact might become an important input into the Soviet policy process, *proving* to the Soviet naval establishment and others that their navy is a cost-effective instrument of policy: this might increase their predisposition to use it. The inflated image might also become an important input into the Western policy process. Western naval establishments and governments might become victims of their own propaganda: this might decrease their confidence about using their own naval instrument when there is a possibility of Soviet involvement. Some believe that this has already occurred.[74] Finally, an inflated image might confirm in the minds of pro-Soviet and 'progressive' forces around the world that the tide was running with the Soviet Union and that the West was on the defensive.[75] Such beliefs might in turn encourage closer association with the Soviet Union and/or more assertive regional policies. It might increase the worries of those countries which are anxious about the rise of Soviet power: they might conclude that they can no longer depend on the West for help, and that it would be prudent to make deferential adjustments in their policies. The responsiveness of the traditional maritime powers to the prestige aspects of the Soviet Navy can therefore contribute materially to the deference and authority which they and others might accord Soviet foreign policy in different regions and situations.

Whether particular Third World countries are responsive to Soviet naval activities will depend upon many circumstantial factors. Sensitivity to naval matters amongst this varied group of countries is by no means uniform. Since about 1970, however, a number of them have been more concerned than formerly with the level of superpower naval competition off their shores. This has partly been related to their enhanced awareness of the general international political importance of the sea, which in turn has been related to their new interest in the development of the law of the sea. The responsiveness of Third World countries to the Soviet Navy will depend upon a range of factors: the general level of hostility or amity with the Soviet Union; relations with China (which makes radical propaganda out of Soviet naval behaviour); distance and accessibility to the Soviet Union or alternative sources of security; their stage of economic development (including the relevance of the Soviet model or the impact of Soviet aid); the effectiveness of Soviet propaganda; and the character of the political system. The type of Third World state likely to be most responsive to Soviet naval

activities might be expected to have the following characteristics:
to be a regionally significant country (because that is where the Soviet
Union tries to concentrate its aid and propaganda efforts); to be
markedly anti-Western; to have a significant degree of tension with
neighbouring countries (and so desirous of military aid and diplomatic
support); to be socialistically inclined (or recognisably 'progressive');
to be desirous of economic aid (preferably not from a 'neo-
colonialist' power); and to conceive the problems of international
politics within a framework of ideological or racial struggle. Add to
such predispositions a long coastline, a capital close to the sea, an
interest in foreign trade and maritime orientation — and an approxim-
ate profile can be drawn of states which might be most impressed
by the rising image of the Soviet Navy. These indicators do not mean
that states possessing them will automatically be influenced by the
Soviet Union, but they do suggest the countries around which
scenarios about Soviet naval influence might be conceived. At three
widely separated points of the African land mass, Guinea, Egypt and the
small Somali Republic are countries which broadly fit this profile, if
not in every detail. At another corner of Africa there is another country,
South Africa, which has been equally concerned with questions of
Soviet naval prestige, but from a rather different perspective.

Admiral Gorshkov has clearly recognised the importance of local
responsiveness in determining the efficacy of official visits and
business calls. After describing the 'warm feelings' displayed to the
Soviet Union in the cities and countries visited by Soviet ships, and
noting the way such visits were 'warmly recall[ed]' by many official
representatives, he alleged that the following statement by the Foreign
Minister of Yemen was characteristic:

> For the first time in history, ships of a friendly country visited
> our country. In the past many warships have arrived in Aden, but
> they did not carry the banner of friendship, but threats, force and
> robbery.[76]

In some conditions a goodwill visit can usefully support policy, but in
others identical arrangements can be counter-productive. The responsiveness of the locals is a critical factor.

As was pointed out earlier, the efficacy of visits will also be determined by the accompanying public relations and propaganda effort.
Soviet efforts in this direction will be aided by the widely held image
of traditional Western imperialism and the absence of a sophisticated

local understanding of naval matters. So far the targets for Soviet
naval influence have generally been chosen carefully. Soviet planners
have been 'exceedingly cautious' in choosing their courses of action,
and 'by being very discreet in discussing such activities in public, they
have manufactured . , . luck'.[77] In addition, Soviet naval propagandists
have been active in rewriting some recent episodes (such as the June
War) in ways which flatter and exaggerate the role of their own navy.[78]
The credibility accorded such claims will be in direct proportion to the
ignorance and susceptibility of the receiver. Given the world's
abundance of gullibility, the scope for manipulating naval developments will be substantial. The possible prestige impact of the Soviet
'carrier', the *Kiev*, will be interesting in this respect. The sense of
expectation which thrilled some Western commentators as they waited
the possible arrival of a Soviet 'carrier' through the early 1970s
suggested a great willingness on their part to be impressed by the eventual result, and thereby further increase the prestige generally
attributed to the Soviet Navy. Whatever the actual naval missions of
the Soviet 'carrier', be it a command ship, an anti-submarine carrier
or whatever, it may also be an important propaganda vehicle. It may be
used to try to impress onlookers that the Soviet Navy is increasingly
'equal' or comparable or in the same league as the US Navy. There will
be plenty who would like to believe this. Despite all the manifold
differences between the USS *Enterprise* and the *Kiev*, in a world of
unsophisticated propaganda targets, a carrier is a carrier is a carrier . . .

Prestige and internal politics

The prestige factor in naval policy operates in various ways. Not least
of its manifestations concern internal or internalised motivations.
Information in this area is bound to be severely limited, but it is well
to recall that policy is made by individuals who will *feel* the prestige,
'face' and status aspects of policy; that the action of no individual
is entirely removed from self-interest; and that 'self-image' is often an
important factor in the 'games people play'. At the minimum, those
responsible for a country's naval policy are likely to be concerned that
it appears successful, efficient and modern in the eyes of relevant
observers — internal as much as external. This is always more likely to
be the case with those who are sensitive about their status, because
they want it to change for the better, or because they fear that it is
changing for the worse.

Ego-satisfaction will play some part in the efforts of those
responsible for running a navy. It is no longer as easy for political

leaders to indulge their whims as far as naval procurement is concerned: navies do not have the same aura, and spending on warships is more accountable to penny-conscious taxpayers. For a developing country a modern steel plant is a more useful 'accepted appurtenance' than a cast-off cruiser. Nevertheless, navies have been used to indulge the pretentions of some rulers, both democratic and otherwise. As one example appeared in the mid-1960s:

> Efficient, well-designed and potentially useful though the modern corvettes and frigates ordered by Ghana under Nkrumah (and partly endorsed by his successors) undoubtedly are, it seems highly probable that the original motive for acquiring them was more a conviction that nations of stature have warships than any precise notions of how they might be used in a military way.[79]

Similar arguments have been used about the navies of some Latin American countries. The primary motivating factor behind their bigger and better ships has been identified as prestige,[80] or 'mere prestige'.[81]

Unfortunately the study of individual motivation is hampered by a lack of evidence; this should not deter speculation, however, unless one is willing to abandon a possible factor in the shaping of naval policy. One knows how much individual pride, ambition, self-image and desire for status affects policy-making elsewhere. The Gorshkov series is an interesting case-study in the naval field. It might be argued that Gorshkov has been seeking to project the prestige of the navy in order to enhance his own self-image. His concern might have been all the more pressing because of his possible anxieties about his standing within the Soviet naval profession, his major reference group. One certainly cannot judge his reputation amongst this group from his ful-some newspaper-cuttings in the West. While he appears to have been successful in a political sense, it might be argued that from the naval professionals' viewpoint there has been much to criticise in Gorshkov's record as Commander-in-Chief. He could be accused of having been unwilling to stand up against the political leadership on the question of operational concepts, and, more recently, on their attempt to try to do too much with too few ships. In addition, after a period of rising status within the Soviet military establishment, the Navy has perhaps been falling of late, and has failed to have its pro-grammes accepted.[82] For these reasons it is conceivable that the literary energy expended by Gorshkov, and its character, may have been motivated at least in part by his desire to project more successfully his own personality and standing amongst his major reference group. This natural anxiety might have been intensified by his impending retirement. Further speculation along such lines demands a full psychological profile of the individual concerned, but even then we will be guessing. It is in the nature of things that even Gorshkov's pillow is unlikely to be privy to these possible truths.

Prestige in the internal setting is concerned not only with questions of motivation, but also with questions of the domestic reputation of the national navy. Prestige in this context can be a fickle thing, especially in democracies. It is a notable if not rather curious fact that in the nineteenth century, when the Royal Navy had an overwhelming superiority which redounded greatly to Britain's benefit, the prestige of the Navy in the country and in political circles remained low. This affected its funding, which in turn circumscribed its development as a fighting service.[83] This pattern has a contemporary ring to it. An effective navy should not only seek to project international prestige: it should also seek to nurture its prestige in the soil in which it has its roots.

The prestige factor in the internal context is also relevant in discussions of 'bureaucratic politics'.[84] The following propositions will indicate its possible significance: (1) All naval establishments have a vested interest in exaggerating the prestige of navies. (2) Naval establishments will not confine their emphasis on the utility of warships to those of their own country. A boost to the prestige of any navy should increase the prestige of navies in general. Paradoxically, naval officers everywhere have a vested interest in inflating the prestige of all their counterparts, even potential opponents. There is a world-wide in-group of naval establishments: it is bound by common competitiveness but also by a universal professional comradeship. It is a mutual admiration and promotion society. (3) Because naval establishments have a vested interest in exaggerating the prestige and influence of navies, this does not mean that they always exaggerate. Although it flies in the face of fashionable belief, the possibility must at least remain open that naval establishments will be both accurate and honest in their public statements. (4) The bureaucratic opponents of navies will often counter them by using arguments alleging vested interest. Money-conscious politicians and suspicious publics are likely to be predisposed to believe the critics of naval spokesmen. Because naval establishments expect such suspicion, they may be tempted to propose safe margins when establishing their bargaining positions for their programmes. (5) Whether or not there is an element of conscious exaggeration in their claims about the value of navies, naval spokesmen will believe what they say. Of all groups, they are the most responsive on naval matters. They have seen goodwill exercised; they have received the thanks of impressed foreign dignitaries; they know the meaning of superior naval force; they have witnessed the manifold functions which warships can perform; and they might have felt the confidence bestowed by supremacy, or the deference determined by weakness. In their perceptions of the status-endowing qualities of navies, naval establishments will be more traditionalist than the rest of interested opinion. (6) Arguments about prestige will be manipulated on the basis of the maxim that 'where you stand depends upon where you sit.' Prestige arguments will play some part in inter-service bargaining. Arguments about the prestige-worthiness of navies *vis-à-vis* other military forces will be manipulated to prove or support positions or preferences already reached. (7) Declarations by naval establishments on the prestigiousness of navies made essentially for internal consumption will have a reinforcing relationship on the behaviour of their opponents. Time-worn habits will tend to be perpetuated. The action-reaction phenomenon will be reinforced. (8) Prestige is cultivated not only for efficient external power, but also for oiling the wheels of intra-governmental bargaining. In a prestigious service, officers and related civil servants and politicians will operate with enhanced *esprit de corps*. Prestige contributes towards bureaucratic success.[85]

Whatever the attitude of Soviet political leaders to their navy, there is no doubt that the naval establishment adheres to a traditional regard for the prestige-worthiness of naval power. Much of the argument in the Gorshkov series is about prestige, either implicitly or explicitly. It might be expected that a navy whose standing was rising, but whose history has included some dismal moments, would be more status-conscious and assertive in its propaganda than the naval establishment of a country with a more secure conception of its status and a warmer recollection of its past.[86] There is little or no mention in US statements about its navy being an instrument of prestige; it is only pointed out that a respect for US naval power helps deter attack on the United States and its allies. On the other hand there is a great emphasis placed by Soviet naval spokesmen on the value of the navy in enhancing the respect of the USSR as a military, political, economic and scientific power.[87] Gorshkov himself has strongly identified naval power with a country's general international prestige. He has written about the close and direct tie-up in former times between naval power and great power status. He has stressed the utility of navies for general foreign policy effectiveness,[88] for the impregnability of some countries,[89] and for the impact of naval power on affairs in both war and peace,[90] including the transformation of some nations into important powers at a great distance from their own homeland.[91] Historically, he argued that Russia needed a grand fleet to join the ranks of the great powers.[92]

The Soviet Navy, in conjunction with other branches of the armed forces, has been heavily engaged in recent years in an important internal debate on such issues as resource and mission allocation, and institutional recognition. The Navy has ceased to be the Cinderella service. However, it could be argued that the Soviet naval establishment does not feel that it has received an appropriate share of either political influence or general recognition commensurate with its increasing usefulness in support of foreign policy. The system is still dominated by the Army, while the Air Force and Strategic Rocket Forces are other aspirants for increased recognition.[93] In this internal debate arguments about prestige will have had an important role. It would obviously be in the Navy's interest if it could persuade key decision-makers that modern and efficient warships could do much to enhance the country's international prestige. This is another of the reasons for Gorshkov's frequent assertions. In support of such an interpretation of his motives, it could be argued that well-publicised exercises, notably *Okean*, have been aimed by the naval establishment primarily at the minds of the Politburo. Improving efficiency and experience, and impressing Western observers were secondary objectives of *Okean*. Against the Soviet Navy's claims, its internal opponents would argue that its efforts have been costly and counter-productive (by provoking the United States); that other instruments can do particular jobs more cheaply and effectively; and that navies do not bring international prestige. In one guise or another, therefore, prestige arguments will be present in internal debates, and will be manipulated to suit vested interests.

One interesting manifestation of the prestige factor involves the 'promotion' of rivals by foreign navalists. From a bureaucratic politics perspective, it is a cause of no surprise that Admiral Gorshkov has been lionised by so many admirers in Western naval circles. Although there are grounds for arguing that his reputation has not been as soundly based as conventional wisdom suggests,[94] it is almost taken for granted among Western navalist opinion that Admiral Gorshkov has been a 'good thing' for his Navy, and is a naval figure of outstanding historical importance. Thus we have Admiral Zumwalt, the ex-Chief of

Naval Operations in the US Navy calling Gorshkov a twentieth-century
'Russian Mahan'.[95] This comparison does not reflect well on Mahan
as a historian, for objective *history* was not Gorshkov's strong point
(or intention); neither does the comparison augur well for Gorshkov
as a naval strategist, for much of what Mahan wrote became obsolete
rather quickly. Mahan was, however, an effective publicist for a great
and coming navy, 'second to none'. Will Gorshkov be attended
with the same success? One waits to see. But there is one striking
difference in their situations. No nation could have outbuilt the United
States and prevented its rise to naval ascendancy. This is not the case
for the great and coming Soviet Navy. Whether or not it becomes
'second to none' is in the gift of the United States.

The pitfalls of naval prestige

Naval illustrations can readily be found for the three most familiar
'corruptions' of a policy of prestige. Navies can be used to support
a policy of bluff, which obviously can have unfortunate results if the
test of performance cannot be avoided. The reverberations for
Britain's political standing in Asia of the sinking of the *Prince of
Wales* and the *Repulse* in 1941 far exceeded the intrinsic loss of these
warships. A generation earlier the Imperial Japanese Navy had pricked
another bubble of European imperial prestige by the sinking of the
Russian fleet at Tsushima. The prestige factor can lead to other distor-
tions of naval policy. Nkrumah's corvettes and Latin America's
carriers might not only be criticised in economic terms, but also in
terms of their strategic inappropriateness. A grander illustration of this
type of pitfall was the German project before 1939 for a force of
heavy battleships to boost the country's prestige at sea and in the world
at large. This project, whose completion was frustrated by the 'pre-
mature' outbreak of war, resulted in the German Navy having the
'wrong ships' for the war it was called upon to fight.[96] The possible
naval consequences of a 'negative policy of prestige', such as that
pursued by the United States in the inter-war years, has as its most
bitter reminder the Japanese attack at Pearl Harbor in 1941. The
greatest navy in the world was not a credible deterrent to its most
likely enemy. The slackening of vigilance which follows from inherited
prestige was exemplified by the regular failure of the British Admiralty
in the nineteenth century to keep abreast of the latest technical
innovations, out of over-confidence in its reputation and numerical
superiority. Overcommitment, the third major pitfall, involves the risk
of states being dragged into dangerous situations for the fear of what

non-involvement would do for prestige. In that navies can close distances, extend power gradients, and make naval powers into quasi-regional powers in distant areas, warships can be catalysts for action and vehicles for overcommitment. Critics of US policy in Indo-China would argue that the projection capability of the US Navy affected US thinking in this direction. Furthermore, if a dispute arises, or if a country's prestige is slighted (especially its naval prestige), then the possession of powerful naval forces might contribute to their being used when they are not necessarily the most appropriate instrument of policy. The *Pueblo* episode in 1968 might be such an example. In other circumstances prestige factors might produce arrogance in the wielders of a powerful navy. Arrogance can be counter-productive with both allies and adversaries. Arrogance will increase the possibility that warships may be the vehicles by which their possessors will be dragged into local disputes, possibly against their interest. If prestigious powers have naval vessels in the vicinity of a local conflict, their policy will be more complicated, for better or worse. They may be put under pressure (against their will) to 'do something'. This has been a source of apprehension for some years about the Soviet Navy. Can huge swimming bears keep their profile below the horizon? Another problem will occur if a rising navy becomes invested with prestige to the detriment of established naval powers. This will affect third-party perceptions of the naval balance. The established navy might be provoked to react, or over-react. International change has to be handled carefully if it is not to be upsetting and productive of international tension. The sense of rivalry provoked by the deployment of small numbers of Soviet vessels to the Indian Ocean is evidence of this.

False expectations are at the root of pitfalls caused by the prestige factor. The false expectations of the allies and associates of a prestigious naval power (whether the attribute is worthily or otherwise acquired) may encourage them to attempt to push that power further than it wishes on a particular issue. If the naval power refuses to act in the way its supporters think it ought, then disappointment will result. One wonders how the North Vietnamese reconciled the prestige image of the Soviet Navy with the latter's passivity in the face of US naval operations off Vietnam. False expectations can also be created within the prestigious state itself. Becoming a 'victim of its own propaganda', it might be led to pursue policies which are out of gear with its capabilities or political interests. The false expectations embodied in the fast and modern warships of Italy under Mussolini were an example of this. In a different way the British projection of the

Hood and to a lesser extent the German projection of the *Bismarck*
illustrate some of the possible consequences of undue pride. The
Hood did a fine job in the inter-war years as a symbol of British
power. However, this meant that its inability to discharge its basic
function, *to fight successfully*, was all the more of a disaster in 1941.
When the ship was sunk within eight minutes of sighting *Bismarck*,
the loss to Britain was more than an old but impressive battleship and
1400 crew. Pride and prestige also were struck. There was a
'trauma' in Britain and elsewhere at the news of the sinking, a mood
which is now difficult to recapture.[97] Fortunately for the British,
the *Bismarck* itself was sunk shortly afterwards, and the feelings about
the loss of the *Hood* were dissipated. The Germans were as depressed
about the loss of the *Bismarck* as the British had been about the *Hood*.
In their determination to sink the *Bismarck* the British themselves were
spurred on by the thought that the ship represented more than metal,
fire-power and men. Admiral Tovey's message to the King was: 'The
sinking of the *Bismarck* may have an effect on the war as a whole out
of all proportion to the loss to the enemy of one battleship.'[98] This
message contained an element of drama, irresistible in battle, but the
substance of Tovey's argument was confirmed by Hitler himself, who
was no seaman. Hitler's intuition told him that the ship symbolised
the nation, and that German prestige would be dimmed by its
failure.[99]

We no longer live in such exciting days. Only thirty years ago battleships had an impact on events and emotions that those with no
imagination now dismiss as merely curious. But some national pride is
still invested in warships, and it can suffer in consequence. In these
unheroic, but by no means unemotional times, even the capture of an
unarmed electronic surveillance vessel like the USS *Pueblo* can cause a
nation hurt.[100] Ships still represent more than metal and men.

A country's neglect of the prestige factor in naval policy might not
only encourage harassment or attack from adversaries, but might
contribute to an important lack of self-confidence. Negative prestige
might inhibit a naval power from effectively using its real capabilities.
At some cost to its interests, this will affect adversary and third-party
expectations. Some commentators have criticised what they see as
a mistaken policy of negative prestige on the part of the United States
in recent years, resulting from a certain defensiveness on military
matters. The effect of this drift has been that third-party perceptions
of the naval 'balance' are too flattering to the Soviet Navy.

One man's goodwill visit . . .

This chapter has attempted a preliminary ground-clearing on the subject of navies and the prestige factor. It is a subject about which it is impossible to be other than impressionistic and subjective. Apart from suggesting areas where research and speculation are desirable, the following general conclusions have emerged:

(1)   In recent centuries the great naval powers were invariably the great powers of the international system. Naval power alone enabled certain countries to become distant regional or world powers. Warships were the means of projecting 'power in evidence'. In times when communications were primitive and the range of weapons short, power that could not be made visible locally could not be believed in. Warships were never merely gun-platforms: they were also symbols of the power and status of their home country, and they performed a diplomatic role. There was an investment of pride and status in their building and use.

(2)   In most circumstances navies are no longer in the first rank of status-endowing attributes. However, because of the wide range of functions which they can perform, they must still be taken seriously into account in some relationships. This applies to both large and small navies. The prestige-worthiness of navies has varied in accordance with attitudes to the use of military power and force, ideas about the importance of the sea in national destiny, and subjective responsiveness.

(3)   Naval prestige has always provided a reservoir of credibility, which at times has been significant in episodes involving the use or latent use of naval force. Prestige, credibility and deterrence are closely interrelated.

(4)   Except for highly centralised states, merchant fleets are perhaps no longer the projectors of national image that they once were. The rise of national airlines, the decline of the liner, and the growth of flags of convenience have undermined the image-creating potential of national merchant marines.

(5)   The responsiveness of different countries and groups to the projection of naval prestige will be affected by many factors, but efficient power and influence is still the pay-off of successfully projected prestige. The attribution of naval prestige can still be important both militarily, in action or threatened action, and politically, by contributing to incremental changes in the attitudes and policies of relevant decision-makers.

(6)   The attributes and attribution of naval prestige can cause a variety of pitfalls, because of the false expectations which might be

engendered by the symbolism invested in warships. Navies with too much or too little prestige in relation to their own capabilities and intentions may be dragged into a variety of unwelcome situations, including overcommitment, exposure, adventurism, provocation, irresponsibility, irrationality, apathy and failure.

(7)   The prestige factor will be important in a variety of ways in internal politics. Impressive warships are still regarded by some as being amongst the accepted appurtenances of high international status. This belief is certainly held and propagated by naval establishments, though to a varied extent. In addition, naval policy may be propelled by the ego-satisfaction of the individuals which make up the decision-making and naval establishments, and by manoeuvres to promote the institutional health of their navy. Individuals and organisations collectively are usually very conscious about status and all it implies. Resource constraints, however, make it difficult for naval establishments to indulge their whims, but the urgency, sense of commitment, involvement and tensions which accompany their promotion of different policies may be very closely related to self-image and the desire for respect. That such motivations are not countable or easily identifiable does not mean that they are not important. Pride did not become a deadly sin by being in short supply. All naval establishments have a vested interest in making others convinced about the significance of navies. Arguments about the status-endowing qualities of different armed forces will always tend to be present in discussions about the roles and missions of a country's military services. In the world of military bureaucratic politics, there will be lies, damn lies, and arguments about prestige.

(8)   The attribution of naval prestige will depend upon often crude pictures of traditional achievement and future potential. It will also depend upon the minutiae of port visits, and the way the latter are organised, projected through propaganda, and handled through public relations. Port visits as a tactic in the enhancement of naval prestige are a more complex activity than formerly. They require handling with greater discrimination because of the great political changes which have taken place in the world in the last twenty years. One man's goodwill visit may well be another man's gunboat diplomacy.

Notes

1. Hans J. Morgenthau, *Politics Among Nations. The Struggle for Power and Peace* (New York: Alfred A. Knopf, 3rd Edition, 1960), p. 78. This is the most widely known definition of prestige in Western literature on international politics. This definition was unchanged in the latest (fifth) edition of this book, despite the imprint of the Vietnam experience.
2. Donald James Puchala, *International Politics Today* (New York: Dodd Mead Co., 1971), p. 84.
3. N. L. Hill, *International Politics* (New York: Harper and Row, 1963), pp. 282-3.
4. C. O. Lerche and A. A. Said, *Concepts of International Politics* (Englewood Cliffs, N.J.: Prentice Hall, 1963), pp. 231-2.
5. John D. Singer and Melvin Small, 'The Composition and Status Ordering of the International System: 1915-1940', *World Politics*, Vol. XVIII, January 1965, p. 238.
6. M. R. Singer, *Weak States in a World of Powers* (New York: Free Press, 1972), pp. 74-5.
7. Grant Hugo, *Appearance and Reality in International Relations* (London: Chatto and Windus, 1970), p. 141.
8. *The Concise Oxford Dictionary*, 4th Edition, 1951.
9. On the interesting metamorphosis of the word see Harold Nicolson, *The Meaning of Prestige*, The Rede Lecture, April 1937, University of Cambridge (Cambridge: Cambridge University Press, 1937). I am grateful for a 'Note on the Russian word *Prestizh*' by Peter Vigor to the author, April 1974.
10. Morgenthau, op. cit., p. 80.
11. Ibid., pp. 72-82.
12. Puchala, op. cit., pp. 84-7.
13. Joseph Frankel, *International Politics. Conflict and Harmony* (Harmondsworth' Pelican Books, 1973), p. 124.
14. E.g. Lerche and Said, op. cit., pp. 231-3.
15. Hugo, op. cit., p. 141. See also Morgenthau, op. cit., p. 81.
16. See Morgenthau, op. cit., pp. 82-5.
17. Ibid., p. 83.
18. Ibid.
19. Morgenthau, op. cit., p. 85. See Brodie's comments on the prestige factor in the Vietnam episode. Bernard Brodie, *War and Politics* (London: Cassell, 1973), pp. 161-3.
20. Puchala, op. cit., pp. 85-7.
21. J. W. Burton, *International Relations. A general theory* (Cambridge: Cambridge University Press, 1965), pp. 254-6.
22. Hugo, op. cit., pp. 64, 109, 141.
23. C. P. Kindleburger, *Power and Money* (London: Macmillan, 1970), p. 57.
24. Lerche and Said, op. cit., pp. 232-3.
25. See R. Jervis, *The Logic of Images in International Relations* (Princeton, N.J.: Princeton University Press, 1970), pp. 18-19. This argues that there might be more stability to evaluations of prestige than might be expected.
26. Hugo, op. cit., p. 141.
27. Most of the comments in the next few paragraphs are based on Puchala, op. cit.
28. See, for example, Nicolson, op. cit., pp. 23-8, and Ivo D. Duchacek, *Nations and Men* (New York: Holt, Rinehart and Winston, 1971, second

edition), pp. 192-4.

29.   Puchala, op. cit., p. 87.

30.   Cf. Nicolson, op. cit., Introduction and p. 25; Frankel, op. cit., p. 125;
       Hugo, op. cit., p. 158; Duchacek, op. cit., pp. 193-4.

31.   See Kenneth E. Boulding, *The Image. Knowledge in Life and Society*
       (Michigan: The University Press, 1961).

32.   Some of the psychological mechanisms involved in 'prestige influence'
       are discussed by Roger Brown, 'The Principle of Consistency in
       Attitude Changes', in *Social Psychology* (New York: Free Press, 1965).

33.   See, for example, the special issue on 'Propaganda in International Affairs',
       The Annals of the American Academy of Political and Social Sciences,
       Vol. 398, November 1971.

34.   For a eulogy on this theme see Clark G. Reynolds, *Command of the Sea.
       The History and Strategy of Maritime Empires* (New York: William
       Morrow and Co., 1974).

35.   Arthur J. Marder, *The Anatomy of British Sea Power. A History of British
       Naval Policy in the Pre-Dreadnought Era, 1880-1905* (London: Frank
       Cass, 1964), pp. 477-8.

36.   G. S. Graham, *The Politics of Naval Supremacy. Studies in British Maritime
       Ascendancy* (Cambridge: Cambridge University Press, 1965), pp. 110-11.

37.   Quoted by Alfred Vagts, *Defence and Diplomacy: The Soldier and the
       Conduct of Foreign Relations* (New York: King's Crown Press, 1956),
       p. 236.

38.   Geoffrey Bennett, *The Battle of Jutland* (London: Batsford, 1964), p. 25.
       See also Marder, *Anatomy of British Sea Power*, p. 13.

39.   Graham, op. cit., pp. 99-100.

40.   Hugo, op. cit., p. 148. See his interesting comments on the way in which
       British prestige in India was 'so demonstrable as to be almost quantifiable',
       p. 141.

41.   Graham, op. cit., esp. pp. 110-11, 118-19.

42.   Bennett, op. cit., p. 53. For further comments on the German Navy's
       'inferiority complex' see A. J. Marder, *From the Dreadnought to Scapa
       Flow* (London: Oxford University Press, 1961-7), Vol. 1, p. 436; Vol. 2,
       pp. 19, 53; Vol. 5, p. 334. Ironically, the Royal Navy did not enhance its
       glory by the victory of 1918: see ibid., Vol. 5, p. 165.

43.   Said to his staff in Alexandria, during the evacuation from Crete, May
       1941. Quoted by S. W. Roskill, *The War At Sea*, Vol. 1 (London: HMSO,
       1954), p. 419.

44.   Ernle Bradford, *The Mighty Hood* (London: Hodder and Stoughton,
       1959), pp. 84-5. See Ludovic Kennedy's comments about the way in which
       by looking at the *Hood* 'one understood what "Rule Britannia" meant',
       in his *Pursuit: the chase and sinking of the Bismarck* (London: Collins,
       1974), pp. 58-60.

45.   Alfred Thayer Mahan, *The Influence of Sea Power upon History 1660-1783*
       (London: Methuen and Co., 1965, first published in Boston by Little,
       Brown and Co., 1890), Chapter 1, especially p. 28.

46.   L. W. Martin, *The Sea in Modern Strategy* (London: Chatto and Windus
       for the ISS, 1967), pp. 123-4.

47.   Phillip Darby, *British defence policy east of Suez, 1947-1968* (Oxford:
       Oxford University Press for RIIA, 1973), p. 298.

48.   Strobe Talbott (translator and editor), *Khrushchev Remembers. The Last
       Testament* (London: Andre Deutsch, 1974), pp. 19-34.

49.   Ibid., p. 19. My italics.

50.   Ibid., pp. 31-3.

51. Admiral Gorshkov, Commander-in-Chief of the Soviet Navy, wrote his series 'Navies in War and Peace' in eleven instalments of the naval journal *Morskoi sbornik (Naval Digest)* in 1972-3. His statement of 54,000 words has been much debated by Western naval observers. For the most thorough analysis see *Admiral Gorshkov on 'Navies In War And Peace'* (Center for Naval Analyses, September 1974). The complete text of the series was published in translation in the January-November 1974 issues of the *US Naval Institute Proceedings* (hereafter *USNIPs*). Reference to the *Gorshkov Series* are to this translation. See also note 95 below.

52. *Gorshkov Series* (cleared for publication in *Morskoi sbornik (Ms)*, 8 December 1972), reprinted in *USNIPs*, October 1974, Vol. 100, No. 9/ 859, p. 63.

53. The Khrushchev memoirs do not mention the ship, but they do show that he was evidently keen to elevate Soviet prestige as a result of the visit. Talbott, op. cit., p. 60.

54. *Gorshkov Series* (cleared for publication in *Ms* 25 February 1972), reprinted in *USNIPs*, February 1974, Vol. 100, No. 2/852, p. 28.

55. Talbott, op. cit., pp. 33-4. The question of navies and superpower status will be discussed below, pp. 113-16.

56. Heikal, op. cit., p. 180.

57. Martin, op. cit., pp. 139-41.

58. See James M. McConnell, 'The Soviet Navy in the Indian Ocean', Chapter 28 in Michael MccGwire, *Soviet Naval Developments. Capability and Context* (New York: Praeger, 1973), esp. pp. 395-7; and Michael MccGwire, 'Foreign Port Visits by Soviet Naval Units', Chapter 31 in Michael MccGwire, Ken Booth and John McDonnell, *Soviet Naval Policy. Objectives and Constraints* (New York: Praeger, 1958).

59. McConnell, op. cit., p. 396.

60. Martin, op. cit., pp. 139-41.

61. McConnell, op. cit., p. 396.

62. Martin, op. cit., p. 140.

63. McConnell, op. cit., p. 396. The comments above are specifically directed at visits to non-aligned countries. Visits to allies are intended to underline a more extensive range of commitments.

64. Ibid.

65. James Cable, *Gunboat Diplomacy. Political Applications of Limited Naval Force* (London: Chatto and Windus for the ISS, 1971), p. 94.

66. J. R. Hill, 'The Rule of Law at Sea' (unpublished thesis, Department of Laws, University of London, King's College, 1972), p. 230.

67. Laurence Martin, *Arms and Strategy. An international survey of modern defence* (London: Weidenfeld and Nicolson, 1973), pp. 169-70. Unless stated otherwise, references to Martin are to *The Sea in Modern Strategy*.

68. Vagts, op. cit., p. 236.

69. F. C. Barghoorn, *Soviet Foreign Propaganda* (Princeton, N.J.: Princeton University Press, 1964), p. 304.

70. Mohamed Heikal, *The Road to Ramadan* (London: Collins, 1975), pp. 163-4, 180.

71. *Gorshkov Series* (cleared for publication in *Ms* 8 December 1972) reprinted in *USNIPS*, October 1974, Vol. 100, No. 9/859, p. 63.

72. See Stephen Roskill, *Naval Policy Between the Wars I: The Period of Anglo-American Antagonism 1919-1929* (London: Collins, 1968).

73. Michael MccGwire, 'Epilogue: Western Naval Inputs to the Soviet Policy Process', MccGwire, *Soviet Naval Developments*, pp. 539-40.

74. See below, Chapter Five.

75.   The Soviet naval build-up in the Mediterranean encouraged Nasser in this attitude. Heikal, op. cit., pp. 46-8.

76.   *Gorshkov Series* (cleared for publication in *Ms* 8 December 1972), reprinted in *USNIPs*, October 1974, Vol. 100, No. 9/859, pp. 63-4.

77.   R. G. Weinland, 'The Changing Mission Structure of the Soviet Navy', *Professional Paper No. 80*, Center for Naval Analyses, Washington, 1971.

78.   MccGwire, *Soviet Naval Developments*, p. 478.

79.   Martin, op. cit., p. 123. The centre piece of Nkrumah's naval ambition was the *Black Star*. It was never delivered, and was put up for sale after Nkrumah's fall. *Jane's 1973-4*, p. 331.

80.   Martin, op. cit., pp. 123-4.

81.   Cable, op. cit., p. 171.

82.   See MccGwire's interpretation, *Admiral Gorshkov on 'Navies in Peace and War'* (CNA, September 1974), pp. 21-70.

83.   Graham, op. cit., pp. 105-6.

84.   This concept is discussed at length in Chapter Six.

85.   See Crowe's comments about the Royal Navy in this regard, *The Policy Roots of the Modern Royal Navy, 1946-1963* (Ann Arbor: University Microfilms, 1970), p. 371.

86.   With regard to the Soviet Navy's attitude to the US Navy, Michael MccGwire has drawn the analogy with the Avis car-hire firm ('We try harder') while others have talked about the Annie Oakley syndrome ('Anything you can do, I can do better . . .').

87.   Donald Charles Daniel, 'Navies as Instruments of Foreign Policy, USA/ USSR', paper presented at the International Studies Association Convention, St Louis, Missouri, 20 March 1974, pp. 32-4.

88.   *Gorshkov Series* (cleared for publication in *Ms* 28 January 1972) reprinted in *USNIPs*, January 1974, Vol. 100, No. 1/851, pp. 21 ff.

89.   Ibid., p. 26.

90.   Ibid. It would be 'difficult to overestimate the role of the navy' for 'solving the problems of ties between peoples'.

91.   Ibid. (cleared for publication in *Ms* 25 February 1972), reprinted in *USNIPs*, February 1974, Vol. 100, No. 2/852, pp. 36-7.

92.   Ibid., pp. 27-28.

93.   John Erickson, 'Soviet Defence Policies and Naval Interests' in MccGwire, Booth and McDonnell, op. cit., Chapter 4.

94.   See above, note 82.

95.   Col. Herbert Preston, USMC (Ret.) (ed.), *The Red Star Rising at Sea* (a translation of the Series Navies in War and in Peace, with introduction and conclusion by Admiral Elmo R. Zumwalt, USN (Ret.), former US Chief of Naval Operations, and commentaries by other leading US naval officers), p. 138.

96.   Cajus Bekker, *Hitler's Naval War* (London, MacDonald and Jane's, 1974), Chapter I.

97.   Kennedy, op. cit., pp. 90-91.

98.   Ibid., p. 182.

99.   Ibid., p. 223.

100.   Trevor Armbrister, *A Matter of Accountability* (London: Barrie and Jenkins, 1970).

4 THE INFLUENCES OF WARSHIPS UPON FOREIGN POLICY

Navies do not simply execute foreign policy. In international politics, as in life in general, the interrelationships are complicated between instruments and policies, means and ends. The simple image of the functional relationship between the foreign policy purpose and the naval 'instrument' is too clinical, too ideal. In addition to providing capabilities for the fulfilment of goals set by a political authority, warships can also be important *influences* on policies or aspects of policies. By the way in which they are used, or by their very existence, warships can affect the foreign policy aims or routines of particular states; they can create or modify situations and expectations, and thus policies. This chapter will examine some of the ways by which the naval instrument might affect the short- or long-term character of a country's foreign policy.

Warships and threat assessment

Warships can be important influences on a country's foreign policy simply 'because they are there'. The perceived naval capabilities and intentions of other states can affect assessments of 'the threat'; this is perhaps the most powerful of all individual policy modifers. Military security remains a primary obligation for governments, and so a continuing preoccupation. The military threat which a country faces is the consideration which basically structures the whole of its foreign policy, determining alliances and postures, strategies and tactics. To the extent that a government perceives itself to be vulnerable in a naval context, or identifies hostile naval intentions and capabilities on the part of adversaries, so warships can be an important factor in defining the threat.

In the past, when navies had a relatively greater impact on the structure and process of international politics, the problem of naval threats was a continuing preoccupation for those responsible for the security of many states. For some countries in particular, changes in the naval policy of other states were regarded as a major signifier of policy, and usually one which might have to be responded to immediately. Nineteenth-century Britain was the classical example of a country which was preoccupied with the warship-building and naval

behaviour of other countries as an indicator of hostile intentions.[1]
The main illustration of this fixation was the British response to
German naval building at the turn of the century. Because some people
in Britain believed, or purported to believe, that German naval building
could have no rational purpose beyond challenging Britain, the naval
factor acted as the catalyst in the crystallisation of the hostility
between the two states. The perceived challenge to British naval power
is the only cause of the Great War about which there is no substantial
disagreement.

Today, with the relative decline in the significance of naval power,
with the end of overt imperialism, and with the declining utility of
force for territorial conquest in many situations, it might be thought
that the naval factor is not as significant as formerly in defining the
threat for most if not all countries. This is probably true, but the
change is one of emphasis rather than kind, in most cases at least.
Most Third World countries, for example, probably fear the alleged
neo-colonialism of the multinational company rather more than they
fear punishment from the sea in the form of bombardment, marines
or air strikes. But as long as navies exist, such eventualities cannot
always be excluded from the calculations of those responsible for the
security of small states. This is especially so for countries in which
great powers have important strategic and/or economic interests, and
especially for those on which any great power is dependent to any
extent. Base facilities and oil are the two most obvious factors causing
the militarily strong to be dependent to some extent on the militarily
weak. This very dependence may in some circumstances impel the
strong to exercise their military superiority. Militarily weak countries
with important possessions appreciate that the source of their power
is also the cause of their vulnerability. Valuable possessions transform
them into potential military targets.[2]

Naval threats are not merely a small versus great power phenomenon.
The world is full of local conflicts, many of which have an active
military component. In some of these confrontations, an ensuing war
would involve one or both countries seeking to use the sea to its own
advantage. A country such as South Africa, for example, with few
international friends and to some extent vulnerable to blockade, will
always define threats partly in naval terms. The naval factor therefore
helps define the character of the threat and the size of the problem,
and this will determine the state's naval strategy, be it one of control
or denial, be it independent or in conjunction with an ally. Even
states with limited naval power may find the naval factor of

considerable interest, because warships might be the only way for
conceivable adversaries to project military force against them, or it
might be the only way great powers might become quasi-regional
powers. Warships will have impact because, as Martin has put it, they
give 'access'.

The arrival of warships dramatises a country's foreign policy.
However, by providing such 'power in evidence', warships can
exacerbate relations, even with countries with whom the possibility
of hostilities seems remote. This appears to have been one of the
effects of the build-up, actual and potential, of US naval power in
the Indian Ocean. On a number of occasions Sri Lanka has put forward
a proposal for turning the Indian Ocean into a so-called 'Zone of
Peace'. With the expansion of US naval interests there, mainly
focusing on the development of Diego Garcia, India then took the
initiative and protested about US naval policy. (Indian spokesmen
claimed to be equally opposed to the Soviet naval presence, but
apparently no protests were made.) The Indian protest was embarrass-
ing for the US Amabassador in New Delhi, since for some time he and
the State Department had been trying to improve relations between
the two countries.[3] What this episode shows is that even if the possibility of hostilities is remote, the presence of warships can still
crystallise suspicions and hostilities between states where relationships
are not basically cordial. Historically, competitive naval building has
also adversely affected relations between ostensible friends.[4]

The superpowers certainly have to worry about the threat to their
security in naval terms. From the Soviet viewpoint, the high proportion
of strategic nuclear strike carried by the US Navy's carriers and
Polaris type submarines impelled the decision to move to forward
deployment. Soviet nuclear potential at sea also helps to define the
threat at the most destructive level for the United States. The com-
plexities involved in the weighing of Soviet SLBM strength in the
Strategic Arms Limitation Talks is but one manifestation of this. The
naval factor can also be a signifier of intentions (possibly threats)
at other levels. By providing a particular country with extra
capability, naval power might be a necessary but not a sufficient
factor to raise doubts about intentions in particular situations.
Although there has been much concern in some quarters in the West
about Soviet policy in the Third World since the mid-1950s, intensified
by Khrushchev's speech about support for national liberation movements in 1961, it has been the expansion of Soviet naval deployments
which has for some (rightly or wrongly) focused new attention on

the possible threats to Western interests in those countries. The image of Soviet marines hitting Third World beaches has not been a widely held one, but it has been potent for some.[5] The development of a world-wide intervention capability by the USSR would have a major effect on the perceptions and policies of those who do not share the same interests as that country. In this respect the development of a US-style aircraft-carrier programme would be taken by a number of commentators to be the clearest signifier of a movement towards an 'offensive' naval strategy.[6]

In some circumstances other changes in naval technology can affect assessments. The utility of intervention from the sea has further decreased because of the increasing capability and hence threat represented by the self-defence naval forces of many Third World countries. However, the clearest illustration of the way that changing naval technology can affect threat assessment has been in the evolution of Soviet naval strategy since the war. It has had to undergo a succession of shifts in order to try to counter the developing challenge of US naval-based strike power: its mission was to try to limit the damage to the Soviet Union in the event of war.[7] For its part US naval strategy has also been affected by changing Western assessments of the threat represented by the Soviet Navy.[8]

Economic factors can play an important part in threat assessment. Countries or groups of countries whose survival in peace or war is heavily dependent upon the continued use of the sea will have a particular interest in developments threatening that continued use. The NATO allies depend upon maritime transport for the oil supplies on which their industrialised economies depend and for major reinforcement in war. It is hardly surprising that the naval authorities ultimately responsible for securing such usage should be very sensitive about the development of naval capabilities by their adversaries.

Naval indicators therefore remain important, be they the result of the mere existence of warships, or changes in their operating behaviour or technology. There is still an important naval input into threat assessment by a range of countries. Defining and meeting threats or potential threats from the sea can still be an important factor in the way some countries allocate resources, choose allies and associates, and deal with adversaries and potential adversaries.

Warships and foreign policy requirements: allies and associates, bases and facilities

The need to use warships can beget new foreign policy requirements in several ways. Warships which operate only in contiguous seas are unlikely to beget new foreign policy requirements unless their country is faced by a naval threat with which it cannot deal with the forces at its disposal. In such a situation there will be a requirement to engage in a naval arms race, seek allies or associates, appease the putative enemy, or otherwise manipulate relations with it. Navies which have operated at a greater distance from their homeland have faced such problems more frequently. The most interesting, varied and prolonged historical illustration of a country having to readjust in face of changing naval realities was the painful British realisation in the twentieth century of the fact that it was no longer a truly independent naval power on a world-wide scale: its commitments continually exceeded its capabilities. A declining naval power which is either unwilling or unable to reduce commitments or raise capabilities must perforce become adept at the Micawber-like politics of overstretch. And be willing sometimes to face the bloody consequences.

All navies which have operated at a considerable distance from their own shores have invariably raised new foreign policy requirements for their governments. Prominent amongst these requirements has been the need for bases and facilities.

In the past, the requirement for advanced bases for states wishing to project force overseas was mandatory. As Disraeli put it when Britain occupied Cyprus: 'a country, and especially a maritime country, must get possession of the strong places of the world if it wishes to contribute to its power.'[9] For a great power such as Britain, with a massive navy and global commitments, the thin red line of bases was the artery of its empire. It is no wonder that naval men nurtured them with care, looked for improvement, and defined their requirements expansively. This requirement for bases, which arose inevitably out of the technology, foreign policy and naval policy of the time, was pressed vigorously by the naval professionals. It provoked Lord Salisbury to protest that: 'if they were allowed full scope they would insist on the importance of the moon to protect us from Mars.'[10]

Since 1945, however, there has been a considerable decrease in the number of naval bases around the world: the eradication of the British bases has been the most notable feature. The rise of nationalism and the decline of colonialism jointly increased the costs and decreased the benefits of sovereign bases. But some navies still continued to operate in distant waters, and their dependence on bases was reduced by the development of techniques of afloat support. One small reflection of this change was the fact that the amount of fuel supplied to the

Royal Navy at sea increased from 10 per cent in 1949 to over 50 per cent by 1963.[11] Despite the changed cost-benefit ratio of sovereign bases, all navies operating in distant waters nevertheless find considerable use for foreign bases or facilities, for a mixture of recreation, replenishment and repair.

The advantages of bases or facilities for navies operating at a considerable distance from their homeland are self-evident: by sustaining forward presences, they shorten the time necessary for intervention in a local conflict, and make forces readily available; they increase the time ships can spend on station, whatever tasks they are performing; they improve the efficiency of performance by easing the exchange of crews, and by facilitating replenishment; they ease maintenance problems, and they provide opportunities for rest and recreation. In addition, especially today, shore facilities are important in providing facilities for naval-related air activities and surveillance systems. Even such free-wheeling warships as nuclear submarines are operationally affected by the availability of bases. This has been a factor in the SALT talks. The relative advantage to US SSBNs in terms of time on station conferred by the use of forward bases at Holy Loch and Rota justified a Soviet proposal for a relative numerical advantage in compensation. In this and other cases the endurance of modern warships is less than might be supposed: crew needs and the maintenance of very advanced equipment put limits on sustained cruises.

While there might be a number of immediate naval advantages in having the use of base facilities in foreign lands, the political repercussions are not usually beneficial. If, for example, naval operations critically depend upon the use of advanced facilities, then this means that the government which wishes to use them will have to base at least its medium-term strategy in that region on the goodwill or sufferance of the target country. This might not be a decisive factor in some circumstances, because of confidence in the policies of that country, or confidence in the 'authority' relationship, or because good alternatives exist or because the character of the operations is not vital and/or might be expected to be short-lived. However, such circumstances are not likely to be present very often. Uncertainty will be common in an era of sensitive nationalism, frequent domestic instability, and what Martin has called 'competitive meddling'.[12] The policies of some countries can change with surprising rapidity in their bilateral relationships. All this is undermining to foreign confidence in the long-term enjoyment of naval facilities. And it goes without saying that all governments prefer to avoid instabilities in their programmes.

As this century has progressed, long-term confidence about bases has decreased. By developing a base or facility in a foreign country, a state becomes dependent to some extent on the good favours of that country, unless it is willing to consider using force, in which case the costs and benefits of such an explosive alternative have to be weighed up. The local power might demand some say in the way the base is used, and might have the power to threaten its free use in crises.[13] For such reasons as these the naval power may not be willing to pay the necessary price to have the use of the base, especially if there is any doubt about certainty of use, a factor of paramount importance. But there are also costs for the small power. In addition to opening the possibility of client status it also might have to face important opportunity costs, such as forgoing relations with other states. Such is the sensitivity of this issue in a recently decolonised world that small powers have to pay a price if the granting of base rights is rumoured, let alone proposed. President Nasser was certainly sensitive about this subject when Soviet leaders pressed for greater use of Egyptian ports after the June War. He clearly wished to free his country of any taint associated with 'bases', and Soviet persistence on this matter only helped to alienate Egyptian opinion.[14] In view of this it is understandable that Egypt felt a mixture of distaste and provocation as a result of the rumours in mid-1975 that Libya had offered base rights to the Soviet Union.[15]

In addition to any political disadvantages, bases may also entail some military disadvantages. In an anti-colonial era they are almost certain to be a provocation to local nationalists. Furthermore, any vulnerabilities or exposures may be used by adversaries as a point of pressure for bargaining purposes. Costs are entailed in both cases. One solution is an extra exertion of effort to defend the existing position. Historically, naval bases have often had a multiplier effect: in the first place bases are required and are therefore acquired for the efficient deployment of warships; subsequently, additional warships, not to mention soldiers, possibly airmen, and administrators are required in order to preserve and protect them.[16]

Despite the varied political and military costs which might accrue with the use of overseas bases and facilities, it nevertheless remains true that a country may still wish to have access to overseas bases and facilities for its distant naval operations, although the idea of the sovereign base has largely disappeared. This reliance is even true for the US Navy, which, despite its impressive afloat support capabilities, still finds it advantageous to make use of a range of foreign base facilities. The development of the base at Diego Garcia is the best recent example. The US Navy and its supporters have pressed for these facilities, despite the political risks involved at home and abroad. In a number of ways the episode underlines the problems concerning the development of naval bases under modern conditions. Diego Garcia had many advantages: it was remote and scantily populated. In order to make the development of the base even easier, the existing population of the island was removed by a piece of unsavoury Anglo-American connivance. But even if the locals were not able to make their voice heard, the episode was grist to the mill of domestic critics, especially in the United States.[17] If the US Navy finds use for forward facilities, this is even more so for the Soviet Navy, despite its long-established propaganda stance against such manifestations of imperialism and foreign domination. In the last decade the difficulties of sustaining forward deployment on a significant scale have resulted in a Soviet decision to base their naval plans on the availability and use of a number of overseas facilities. They have chosen to follow this course despite the risks and problems entailed, some of which they have already suffered in their relations with Egypt.[18] This has been preferred to the alternative course, that of building large numbers of warships and providing the necessary amount of specialised afloat support facilities. In pointing out this trend in Soviet naval policy, MccGwire has shown that it provides an interesting insight into the Soviet Union's internal priorities, and also gives some indication of the economic constraints within which Soviet naval policy is forced to operate.[19] It is a further example of the potential embarrassments faced by Soviet foreign-policy-makers as a result of the need to make the Soviet economy work to a minimally satisfactory level.

Clearly, the requirement for base rights or the use of facilities can modify a country's foreign policy. If a government feels strongly that there are important advantages to be had from a prolonged naval deployment in distant waters, and if its afloat support and/or organic air cover potential is unsatisfactory, then there is no alternative but to seek the use of bases or facilities. Naval writers, especially those with a degree of professional responsibility, past or present, have always been much more highly conscious of the value of such bases than has the armchair naval strategist. Because the efficient discharge of their job depends upon it, they have often stressed the strategic requirement over any other factors. The attitude of navalists towards South Africa is a good example. Roskill wrote in 1962:

The recent withdrawal of South Africa from the Commonwealth
on an issue of political principle, with scarcely a whisper from our
side of the possible strategic consequences, shows how little the
matter of overseas bases is understood by the British public — in
spite of the fact that as recently as 1956, when the Suez Canal was
closed, it was the ability and willingness of the South African bases
to handle the greatly increased traffic that prevented the
interruption of the whole of our eastern and Australasian trade.[20]

The same arguments were used in Britain in 1969-70, when the question
arose of the sale of arms to South Africa. The issue was given
additional point because of the further closure of the Canal, and the
perception (in some minds) of a significant Soviet naval threat in the
Indian Ocean. Although many complicated emotions were involved
in the South African issue, the desire for good relations with a
country which offered a secure base was thought by some (the 'High
Tory school of naval strategists') to far outweigh the possible foreign
policy repercussions of closely associating with a country whose
domestic policies were regarded as outrageous by most of the Commonwealth. The naval requirement for bases or facilities in distant lands
therefore has the potential of modifying foreign policy in a variety of
different ways. In this case arms sales and the Simonstown base
became an issue which seriously threatened to rupture intra-
Commonwealth relations. Whatever course was chosen by the British
government, whether it was action or inaction, somebody would be
upset. As often happens with *issues*, an atmosphere built up which
made the question of Simonstown seem very significant, but a year
later most people could scarcely credit the stir which had been
created.

The discussion so far has referred (without qualifications) to 'bases'
and 'facilities'. However, the use of these words is politically sensitive.
Perhaps we would all recognise a naval base when we saw one, but
what we would call it is a different matter.

Most commentators are relatively clear about the historical concept
of a naval base. It was a piece of territory over which an external
naval power had sovereign control, embodied in a formal agreement,
and which was often the result of annexation or military pressure.
On such bases naval powers developed the infrastructure for the exercise of that power. Since the Second World War the connotation of
the term 'base' has changed a good deal. From having a legal connotation, it has now come to be something essentially in the eye of the

beholder. With its ring of imperialism and client status, the term 'naval base' is a ready weapon in the hands of propagandists. Such is the sensitivity of the issue that any fairly regular visit by the warships of one country to a friendly port of another is likely to tempt adversary propaganda into calling that port a foreign 'base'. For this reason, and to avoid unduly provoking local opponents, US naval spokesmen seem to eschew the use of the term in relation to their own practice. Soviet sensitivity is probably even greater, given the number of anti-imperialist propaganda points which it has squeezed out of the earlier Western possession of naval bases. Third World countries are more sensitive again. As most of them have recently been freed from colonial control, 'naval bases' are a reminder of a hated past. To offer them would be a slur on their newly won sovereignty. Some countries will want to develop an infrastructure for the exercise of naval power, however, and some countries are willing to provide them with the real estate, but none want 'base' facilities, at least by that name. It is only ambitious adversaries which have *bases*.

The attribution of 'base' or 'facility' is a political appraisal. For ordinary usage, however, the following distinctions might be made: (1) *Port-of-call facilities*. These refer to temporary facilities made available to warships of all countries, subject to the usual entry formalities. The facilities would include rest and recreation for the crew ('run ashore' in Royal Navy terminology), temporary berthings, and replenishments of a non-military type. (2) *Regular base facilities*. The scale of such facilities might vary greatly, but the significant criteria are the exclusive and long-term character of the arrangements. One might talk of regular base facilities if a particular country has access to special privileges in a foreign country for an indefinite period: these privileges might include special docking arrangements, one's own stores, a segregated portside area, and opportunity for repair and maintenance. (3) *Full naval base facilities*. This concept includes the privileges as above, but on a more substantial scale and with the possession of some capability of self-defence. This extensive commitment would appropriately but by no means necessarily refer to a sovereign base.

In addition to the specific requirement for bases, there is also the possibility, arising out of naval requirements, of a demand upon a country's foreign policy to seek a degree of control, or at least influence, over certain strategic areas. There is obviously a particular naval interest in narrow exits, straits, or 'invasion coasts'. The importance of Gibralter, the Baltic exits, the Low Countries, the straits through the Indonesian archipelago, the Turkish Straits and so on is evident for particular navies. The naval interest in having free access through such waters, or in trying to obstruct the access of others, can affect foreign policy in a variety of ways. It might result in pressure to secure rights and concessions; or in a search for allies or proxies in the strategic areas; or in a search for nearby bases or facilities; or in an attempt to secure the neutralisation of the area; or in an attempt to modify international law in favourable ways; or it might even, in grave circumstances, result in an effort to occupy the desired territory with armed force. Mere location is one reason why some areas take on strategic naval significance: the presence of important raw materials is another. The latter may be of importance to the whole economy, or they might be directly related to naval effective-ness. In earlier centuries the timber of Scandinavia gave that region a special significance for Britain, while the conversion of the Royal Navy to oil before World War One meant that secure oil resources became a major foreign policy objective for naval, and then more general industrial, purposes.[21]

Distant responsibilities which involve the use of the seas will, in times of conflict, require the potential of controlling relevant sea areas, or at least denying them to the enemy. If an individual state faced by a serious naval challenge lacks sufficient capability or credibility to discharge its responsibilities alone, then it must seek to augment its own naval power by an alliance with a local state, or with a global naval power which has the capability and is willing to undertake the requisite responsibilities. This sort of problem is one which has characterised the policy of a state which has become overstretched, because it has allowed its power to dwindle in relation to its responsibilities, because it has either not been willing to cut its responsibilities, or it has not been willing or able to increase its capabilities. Such a problem is usually the fate of former great powers, where inherited commitments outlive their waning strength. British dependence on Japan in the western Pacific in the first twenty years of this century is a prime example of how naval requirements can affect foreign policy in this way.

In the variety of ways suggested, naval requirements can create or modify the foreign policy aims of particular states. The invariable consequence of such developments is to create a new degree of dependence on the policies of others. Such a dependence on the part of a naval power may have various repercussions. Particular problems have arisen in the past twenty-five years because confidence in the stability of the attitudes of distant states has not been high. Sovereign bases,

for example, increasingly became primary provocations to local
nationalist movements, and so became difficult to maintain.
Furthermore, while annexation was a reasonably acceptable option in
the past in order to have access to vital areas, it is no longer so regarded
today. A further complication is that any degree of dependence
produces a two-way influence process. Britain discovered this in its
alliance with Japan in the first twenty years of the century. Although
on the naval side Japan carried out its obligations in a way which
made British statesmen grateful, the latter found the alliance an
acute political embarrassment towards the end, when Japan took
actions which were disapproved of by some of Britain's major
associates, notably the United States. The British government was
forced to make a choice which it did not want to make. Because of
the usefulness of the alliance, Britain's own freedom of diplomatic
manoeuvre was constrained and complicated.

In a variety of ways, therefore, navies can beget foreign policy
requirements, which in their turn may result in political embarrassment, or worse. The clinical image of the functional relationship
between policy and instrument of policy is clearly misleading. It is
safer to keep in mind the thought that in some circumstances the
naval tail may wag the foreign policy dog.

Navies and foreign policy responsibilities

The preceding section demonstrated that navies can produce new
foreign policy requirements. If governments attempt to meet these
requirements, they must invariably take upon themselves new foreign
policy responsibilities. History is full of examples of how ostensibly
small commitments can insidiously expand into large and debilitating
entanglements.

Naval bases in foreign lands show in an instructive way how
requirements can bring forth large and possibly difficult responsibilities,
including some responsibility to the local government. Because the
country wanting a base or facility desires stable evaluations as a basis
for medium- or long-term planning, it automatically has a stake in the
preservation of a régime which seems favourably disposed towards it.
It would be an unusual host régime which did not recognise the potential leverage which this partial dependence gave it. In some circumstances
the possibility of the local government exploiting this leverage might
have to be faced, especially if it is in a strategically sensitive area.
The manoeuvrings of Mintoff's Malta are instructive in this respect.
In other cases the behaviour of the naval power might be modified by

its having to take sides in local quarrels on behalf of the country in which it has a base; this might result in the unwelcome but unavoidable alienation of other countries. Furthermore, depending on the local internal situation, the naval power might come to depend almost entirely on a particular local leader for the furtherance of the relationship; any alternative government would not be as welcoming. This would give the local leader a further degree of leverage.[22] Furthermore, too overt an identification between an external naval power and a particular leader might provoke intensified internal opposition to both the naval power and the local leader.

Influence is therefore a two-way process. By making naval powers more vulnerable to the influence of others, forward deployment can be an important policy modifier. The responsibilities which come with trying to exercise influence might be insidious, and might incrementally modify a state's foreign policy in unexpected and, on the whole, undesired ways.

This problem is not exclusively one of distant deployment. A recent analysis of British policy in Ireland has reminded us that Britain's decreasing commitment to that country over the years has possibly been explicable to a greater extent than is generally recognised by defensive and especially naval requirements. With the disappearance of the naval imperative as far as Ireland is concerned, it was forecast that a major incentive for the British commitment would have gone, and that this would allow the relationship to move into a new stage.[23] In many cases the responsibilities which have come with the annexation of strategic areas (or the changing strategic importance of areas controlled for other reasons) have been very far-reaching. Many countries have found, to their cost, that taking on new responsibilities is far easier than either successfully discharging them or honourably relinquishing them.[24]

Changing naval capabilities and changing foreign policy intentions

Navies can beget new foreign policy requirements and responsibilities. They can also create new foreign policy intentions. This is most likely to occur as a result of changes in relative power in a particular region.

In international life, as in private life, it seems likely that one's goals and expectations will be very closely related to one's changing circumstances and especially capabilities. The comparison which has often been made between money and military power is relevant in this case. Just as a windfall gives an individual new freedom for manoeuvre, so the decline of a potential enemy's navy, one's emergence as the

primary power at the end of an arms race, the discovery of a surplus
of naval capability over requirements either generally or regionally, or
the surprise discovery that capabilities developed for one set of tasks
have proved to have valuable utilities elsewhere — all these outcomes
may result in changing naval evaluations and expectations. These might
then result in changed foreign policy intentions. In the circumstances
just mentioned, where the naval windfalls were profitable ones, the
outcome might be an encouragement to a more ambitious or oppor-
tunistic foreign policy. At the least, greater confidence might be
shown in the pursuit of policy. A decline in relative naval power, on the
other hand, might produce a comparable reduction in estimates of
what can be achieved in foreign policy (amongst all parties concerned).
The degree of truculence or deference which one country introduces
into its behaviour with another will be affected to some extent by
its perception of the relevant military balances.

In recent years many naval observers have been watching to see if
changed naval capabilities might result in changed policy intentions as
far as the Soviet Union is concerned. Some have speculated, for
example, that the developing Soviet capabilities might beget new
intentions in the various regions of its forward deployment. While most
observers now acknowledge that the forward deployment of Soviet
units was initially an attempt to counter the Western strategic strike
forces in the latter's areas of deployment, many then argue that the
Soviet leadership, having been accidentally introduced to the possible
political pay-offs of forward naval deployment, have since adopted
more positive (some would say 'offensive') uses of their far-flung navy.
Originally it was essentially a navy-to-navy sea denial strategy, the
pattern of deployment being unrelated to the pattern of Soviet foreign
policy. However, new opportunities have been seen, and better capabilities have come along. It is sometimes argued that these are likely to
produce a more ambitious foreign policy in some regions. Even if
fundamental goals do not change, at least Soviet policy might be more
assertive. With a fleet or squadron in the background providing power
in evidence, and a token of local Soviet interest, might not Soviet
diplomats feel more 'chesty', Soviet trade representatives more
assertive, and Soviet military advisers and technicians more confident?
This is always a possibility, but whether it would do them any good in
the long term is another matter. From a Third World perspective, it
may be that the image of the Ugly Russian would replace that of the
Ugly American.

Weinland has collected together the scanty evidence concerning the

use of the Soviet navy in support of diplomacy. He has shown that
Soviet naval forces deployed forward for primarily strategic defensive
purposes have been used since the late 1960s in a new mode, as 'active
instruments' of Soviet foreign policy, protecting and promoting Soviet
overseas interests. Their role in this capacity has been 'consistently
expanded', not only in scope but also in character, and has moved from
protection to promotion, and from 'passive' to 'active' defence.[25] With
warships deployed forward the intention of 'active counteraction to
imperialist aggression' becomes an option, whether or not it actually
transpires. Confidence and prestige might rise as a result of the new
capabilities which make the Soviet Union a quasi-regional power. The
Western monopoly of naval power will be ended and its planning
will be complicated. Opportunities will be created for offering new
alignments, exerting leverage in specific situations, easing the
establishment of proxies and clients, and subtly threatening non-
co-operating states.

The evidence which Weinland presents is important, but the conclusions may be overdrawn; one should be wary about extrapolating
them into the future. With a longer perspective it can be seen that
Soviet naval diplomacy has not consistently expanded in activity,
but has levelled off, and at a rather low level. But neither can one
extrapolate this into the future: the only certain fact is that with
warships deployed forward, new opportunities become available for
the advancement (not to mention the humiliation) of Soviet foreign
policy.

The possibility that changing capabilities will produce new intentions is a real one. After all, the evaluations of some governments
constantly fluctuate. This underlines an important warning: it is
important to interpret aims in a dynamic and not a static sense.
It cannot be assumed that if a government undertakes a particular
action that it meant to do it all along. It might have started out with
other objectives, but in the course of time its perceptions of its capabilities, interests, and expectations may have changed. If Soviet marines
ever do hit Third World beaches, it would not necessarily represent the
culmination of a blueprint naval strategy dating back to the first
operations of Soviet units out of area in the mid-1960s. When they
look back, almost all governments are surprised at the way things
turn out.

Alterations in relative naval power can be the result of changes in
naval technology. At the highest level of importance there has been
much speculation about the significance of a breakthrough in ASW,

which would permit either one of the superpowers, or both, to track SSBNs, and so provide some basis for a first strike capability. At a lower level of destructiveness, the bee-sting (or shark-bite?) capability of some Third World countries, armed with instant off-the-shelf mini-navies by the Soviet Union, and containing missile-firing fast patrol boats, gives these countries a new confidence in dealing with the larger navies of the external powers. By raising the costs of any naval intrusion, they give themselves (and are given by the Soviet Union) a degree more of diplomatic freedom in their dealings with countries possessing larger navies. This includes the Soviet Union as well as the United States and others.

As well as creating new intentions, warships can also contribute to the perpetuation, perhaps beyond their proper time, of old policies. Warships can channel foreign policy thinking into the maintenance of old roles. It is often argued, for example, that the maintenance of Britain's role east of Suez was more important for the Royal Navy than was the role of the Royal Navy for the maintenance of Britain's position east of Suez. Because the Royal Navy was there, and always had been, the British assumed that they necessarily had a military role to play east of Suez. Instruments which are in some way new (in power or deployment) can beget new intentions: but old instruments can also help to perpetuate old habits of thought, and are thus supportive of old tasks.

The influence of the possession of warships on the will to use them

The possible influence of the possession of warships on the will to use them is a narrower variant of the previous problem. This section is concerned with the way in which the very possession of certain instruments may channel thinking about the resolution of particular problems. The idea that instruments shape the will is an old and valid one, and has manifestations in many aspects of life. It is one of the reasons why British policemen are not armed. It is one of the reasons why, if you give a small boy a hammer, 'he will find that everything he encounters needs pounding.'[26] It is the reasoning behind the old military maxim that 'The only thing which you cannot do with a bayonet is sit on it.'[27]

The idea that weapons shape the will to use them has for long been one of the basic themes of the proponents of disarmament. Woodrow Wilson exemplified this viewpoint. He expressed it very clearly in 1913, a year after his election, the success of which had in part been the result of an isolationist response to the big-navy adventurism of the turn of the century. On the basis of his fear that weapons shape the will to use them, Wilson cancelled fleet movements ordered by the Navy in response to Japanese threats, and ordered the Army to stop making contingency plans in case of a war against Germany.[28]

The fear that weapons shape the will to use them was given a strong impetus in the United States as a result of the Vietnam War. It played some part in 1967 in the Senate's refusal to authorise funds for the procurement of Fast Deployment Logistics Ships. By this time US attitudes to 'limited war' had moved on from the more hopeful attitudes of the early 1960s. It was felt that a fast deployment capability would encourage further interventions, a thought which was made intolerable by Vietnam.[29] The underlying attitude of mind has been most succinctly expressed by Senator Richard Russell. He said: 'If Americans have the capability to go anywhere and do anything, we will always be going somewhere and doing something.'[30]

Many Americans have come to fear their ability to control the instruments at their disposal. In recent years those concerned with naval developments have often transferred these fears to the Soviet Union. There has been speculation whether the Soviet 'helicopter carriers' (even if designated as ASW ships) and naval infantry (even if prmarily geared to general war tasks in the fleet areas) might be used sometime to support other than their primary tasks. These instruments, each created separately with an independent rationale, might be fitted together to form the nucleus of a limited intervention force. Certainly, military instruments are rarely used in exactly the manner for which they were first designed, and military professionals have become accustomed to having to improvise with less than perfect equipment. It is at least conceivable that Soviet naval forces in the eastern Mediterranean or elsewhere might be asked, possibly against the advice of the naval staff, to support a limited intervention in order to assist a friendly government against internal troubles. The order might come from a hard-pressed or ambitious Soviet leadership, sensitive of its prestige.

One actual recent example of the possession of naval force shaping the will to use it was the US response to the *Pueblo* affair. Following the seizure of the ship a large US task force, including three carriers, assembled in the Sea of Japan. Ostensibly it was a show of force to increase North Korea's fear of military reprisals should they keep the ship and crew. The size, deployment and character of the task force was unambiguous, and so conformed appropriately with Schelling's

ideas about the 'idiom of reprisal'.[31] It seemed the appropriate US
response to a seizure of a ship at sea. However, the trouble from the
US viewpoint was that the show of force was not credible to the
North Koreans. Equally important is the possibility that the almost
automatic naval 'idiom of reprisal' detracted attention away from a
more subtle approach which might have been better designed to have
made North Korea move in a desired way.[32]

In May 1975 an episode with some similarities to the *Pueblo* affair
occurred in the Gulf of Siam. In the so-called *Mayaguez* affair it was
also possible to argue that the possession of a relatively adjacent naval
instrument shaped the US will in its response to the Cambodian seizure
of an almost certainly innocent freighter. In this case, though, the
'idiom of reprisal' was more purposeful, if in the event irrelevant.
However, the decisive response had the effect of increasing the
confidence of many Americans and their allies. Certainly there was
none of the humiliation of eight years before. While the detailed facts
of the episode remain somewhat obscure, many commentators felt that
the availability of the naval instrument channelled the US government's
reaction: as Fairhall expressed it, for the US Navy (he should have said
its political masters), 'the despatch of an attack carrier and some
helicopter-borne marines is the automatic reflex action in almost any
distant crisis.'[33] While this 'reflex action' might not be as automatic
as suggested,[34] the belief that it is a characteristic feature remains a
widespread one, in both West and East. The *Mayaguez* affair was seen
as confirming this, because diplomacy was given only a perfunctory
chance. In this respect the memory of the prolonged and humiliating
negotiations over the *Pueblo* might have been an important factor in
the administration's calculations. Whatever one's assessment of the
operation in a narrow sense, it could still be argued that it was a
political success, because of its side-effects in terms of US prestige and
credibility in the immediate aftermath of the collapse in Indo-China.
The *Mayaguez* affair might have been political theatre more than
military strategy, but it was no less politically significant for that.
But the important point in relation to the present discussion is
motivation rather than effect. It was apparent from the timing of
events that the US forces attacked at the first moment they were
tactically able to do so.[35] For better or worse, alternative approaches
were not given a real chance.

The idea that weapons shape the will to use them is not the prerogative of great military powers, as some of the more self-righteous of
the military weak would like to suppose. One need only speculate

about the motivation of whatever Cambodian authority decided to seize the *Mayaguez*. Was the action rational, or was it a case of an instrument shaping a will? A more serious episode in this respect occurred in mid-1973. On 15 May 1973, Israel was due to celebrate the twenty-fifth anniversary of its foundation. A group of wealthy Jews from the United States and Europe chartered the *Queen Elizabeth II* to take them from Southampton to Israel, departing on 15 April. On 17 April President Gaddafi of Libya summoned the commander of an Egyptian submarine stationed in Tripoli. Gaddafi gave the commander a direct order to sink the *QE II*, having ascertained its feasibility. Once the submarine had left Tripoli its commander reported his order to the Egyptian authorities. The latter were appalled, and ordered the submarines back to Alexandria.[36] This hair-raising episode underlines several important elements of contemporary naval strategy, namely that the instrument can shape the will, that the role of personalities should never be overlooked, that the scope for irrationality is often greater than analysts give credit, and that reliable command-and-control arrangements are critical.

To some extent, therefore, having powerful warships does shape the will to use them. But one important caveat should be entered, arising from the inherent qualities of the naval instrument. Warships may shape the will to use them, but they have important advantages over aircraft and battalions: they can be initially used in a non-provocative way; they move in an international medium; and they can be withdrawn with no trouble and possibly little loss. Warships are less intrusive. While the only thing which you cannot do with a bayonet is to sit on it, this is not true of ships. They can be sat on, with a crew busily employed, for day after day.

Some dangers and problems of forward naval deployment

Naval professionals inevitably focus their discussion of warships in distant deployment on their usefulness as instruments which can be used in support of foreign policy. But there is another side to the coin. Any forward deployment entails military and political risks as well as opportunities. Several have already been mentioned in relation to the responsibilities which forward deployment sometimes insidiously brings in its wake. There are many more. Naval history is full of cases of demonstrations somehow slipping out of control, resulting in tension, misperception and danger.[37] Many of these risks are also present in modern conditions.

Firstly, problems might arise as a result of the initiative of local commanders. When communications were poor, this was always a considerable risk. In the early 1930s the US Secretary of State complained that even the Navy Department did not know what initiatives had sometimes been taken by the commanders of US warships in Nicaraguan waters.[38] More recently, ship movements of the Sixth and Seventh Fleets in crisis situations have been first ordered on the initiative of local commanders.[39] Some of the dangers of forward deployment were seen in the attack on the US communications ship *Liberty* on 8 June 1967. With a different set of personalities, the escalatory potential would have been awesome, for as the US Secretary of Defense, Mr McNamara, subsequently said: 'I thought the *Liberty* has been attacked by Soviet forces. Thank goodness, our carrier commanders did not launch immediately against the Soviet forces who were operating in the Mediterranean at that time.'[40] Although Cable would seem to be correct when he argues that the use of limited naval force in modern times is controlled in minute detail by 'express government decision',[41] plenty of dangers remain, even if governments make all reasonable efforts to ensure the strictest command and control. Orders might be misinterpreted. The activities of the local state(s) might be misperceived. Action which is unauthorised might be taken in the heat of a crisis. Commanders on the spot may take independent action on the grounds that they are more fully aware of the dynamics of the local situation. This may be justified, but woe betide them if things go wrong, and they are seen to have avoided the directives of their distant leaders, who are allegedly more aware of and more in control of the 'wider issues'. Even the handling of the Cuban missile crisis, that supposedly model example of clinical crisis management, showed some of the tensions which can arise between political leaders primarily concerned with the 'wider issues' and naval commanders directly concerned with their men and ships and operational success.[42] In addition to the risks already mentioned it must be added that, however carefully warships are controlled in distant waters, they are always to some extent at the mercy of the behaviour, rational or otherwise, of local coastal states. In sensitive areas this risk will obviously be increased. The *Pueblo* and *Mayaguez* episodes were different variants of this possibility, and in both cases there has been spculation that the seizures might have been the result of the initiative of relatively junior Korean and Cambodian commanders.[43]

Secondly, a large-scale forward deployment, whatever its strategic aims (be they sea-denial, commitment to allies, or posing a vague menace) might provoke the hostility of local powers. Local powers might perceive the deployment as a vague menace to themselves, whatever its objective tasks. If they see world politics as being basically divided between rich/large/white powers and poor/small/coloured powers, then a naval demonstration, with all the echoes of imperialism, might crystallise their other resentments against the naval power. A naval deployment might result in some local powers looking for new alignments. As was argued earlier, superpower naval activity has focused opposition against them (and particularly against the United States) on the part of some littoral states of the Indian Ocean and Mediterranean.[44] Provocation is not the only result of large-scale deployments. Single ships can also cause trouble, as the *Pueblo* episode showed, although that ship was practically unarmed. Certainly, some activities by naval vessels in forward deployment will be inherently provocative, even though 'non-belligerent' in an actual shooting sense. Much will depend on the background state of relations between the interested parties. Amongst inherently provocative activities are overt and covert intelligence gathering, or 'radar harassment patrols' such as that begun by the destroyer *Maddox* in the Gulf of Tonkin, 1 August 1965.[45] In this case it is often argued that the US leadership was just looking for a *casus belli*.

Thirdly, if a large-scale presence at sea 'challenges' a traditional monopoly power, by attempting to deny it potential control of the sea, then the reaction of the former monopoly power might have several unfortunate consequences for the challenger. In the first place, it might result in a degree of tension in their relations which the challenging power did not really expect; and secondly, the challenge might in fact be counterproductive by provoking the monopoly state into increasing its naval building, increasing its deployment, and also making efforts to improve its diplomacy in the particular region concerned. It would appear that the Soviet 'challenge' in recent years has produced an unwelcome vigour in US naval activities, as symbolised by the development of new base facilities at Diego Garcia. Although the Soviet Navy has greatly complicated the US Navy's operational problems, it has also at the same time solved its biggest political problem: it has given for most Americans the answer to the question, 'Why do we need a navy second to none?'

Fourthly, forward deployment might result in the state concerned being dragged into local conflicts. Before moving to forward deployment it was relatively easier to stay out of local quarrels. However, with naval units just on or over the horizon, the pressures for some intervention in local disputes will be greater, from local associates, and also because 'weapons shape the will to use them'. In certain circumstances these pressures might be irresistible; at least they will be stronger than before, because a degree of military access is now feasible. Can superpowers keep their heads below the horizon if a major dispute is taking place ashore? Obviously they can, and have. However, forward deployment does increase the possibility of involvement, and the risk of escalation.[46]

The example of the *Maine* is perhaps the most famous historical illustration of the possible catalytic effect of a warship in a sensitive situation.[47] In more recent times the Tonkin Gulf incident is certainly the most profound episode in its long-term consequences. Much uncertainty surrounds the incident: what kind of US and South Vietnamese provocation had taken place prior to the incidents? and what was the nature of the attacks on the US warships? (Or were the latter 'For all I know . . . shooting at whales out there', as President Johnson facetiously, or otherwise, told reporters eight months later?)[48] Whatever the truth of the matter, and certainly before the Pentagon was satisfied about the details, aircraft from the carriers *Ticonderoga* and *Constellation* were ordered to attack targets in North Vietnam. 'So in a way it had begun. We had shown ourselves in an act of war. We had perhaps committed ourselves more than we knew.'[49] What an understatement!

It is a curious coincidence that ships of one sort or another, in one way or another, have had a catalytic effect in all but one of the major wars in which the United States has been engaged in the last eighty years. The only exception was Korea. The explosion and sinking of the battleship *Maine* in 1898 heightened Spanish-American tension to a critical level. The sinking of the British liner *Lusitania* in 1915 with a significant loss of American lives provoked American indignation and sharpened animosities against Germany. The attack on the gunboat *Panay* in 1937 was an important episode in the exacerbation of US-Japanese relations which led to the attack on the *Arizona, Oklahoma, California* and the rest at Pearl Harbor in 1941. Finally, in 1965, there was the *Maddox*, as arrogant with power as the Pacific fleet of a generation before had been passive. By accident or design, its behaviour in the Gulf of Tonkin was such that it was likely to create an incident out of which wars are begun. 'Remember the *Maine*!' was the old cry. But remember also the *Lusitania*, the *Panay* and the *Arizona* and her sister-ships. No Americans of this generation are likely to forget the *Maddox*.

Finally, forward deployment might result in the changed

expectations of local states. Either, as already mentioned, they might fear a new quasi-regional and possibly interventionist power, or they might invest it with increased prestige and thereby expect it to play a role which it had not sought. The Soviet Union could indulge its propagandists when it had no local power: if it has raised expectations as a result of its now having local power in evidence, its political problems will be increased rather than the opposite. With more military power on the scene, it will now be expected to act on behalf of 'friends'. After Sputnik, China attributed increased prestige to the USSR and talked of the east wind prevailing. The Soviet Union, for its part, had no wish to live up to Chinese expectations. Soviet activism, puffed up by Chinese support, would have been dangerous for all concerned: Soviet caution, in the face of Chinese exuberance, had deleterious effects on its relations with China.

This pattern of relations could very well be repeated in the naval context. By visiting ports in east and west Africa at sensitive times, warships of the Soviet Union have been used to try to increase Soviet influence with particular governments. It would not be surprising if these governments have rather higher expectations of Soviet sympathy to them than any Soviet leadership would allow.

The possibility therefore arises that forward deployment might be manipulated by local powers for their own political purposes; this might result in a country being committed to another − or rather being seen to be committed − to a greater extent than it would wish. A small but interesting example of this occurred in October 1974, when an allegedly 'routine' visit by a British squadron to South African waters 'intended to be nothing more than a limited operation for gunnery and communications practice' caused a fine rumpus within the British Labour Party, not to mention rumoured splits between the Foreign Office and Ministry of Defence.[50] What was allegedly conceived as a routine exercise on the part of the Foreign Office was inflated into a 'goodwill visit' by the South African press and authorities; the latter proclaimed the visit to be a demonstration of the 'active support' of Britain, the United States and France to a country which for some years had presented itself as a vital base for operations in the defence of Western sea communications against the growing Soviet naval threat.[51] The British Foreign Secretary was reported to have been 'disturbed' at the way the visit had been exploited. He should not have been surprised. Such an incident is perhaps one of the more predictable outcomes of the never completely controllable developments which occur when warships are sent to operate off distant coasts.

For all these reasons, therefore, although forward deployment can
serve some useful purposes, it does bring along with it some inherent
dangers. These should be remembered, as well as the missions
successfully discharged. It is not necessary to perceive the Soviet
Union as a particularly malevolent country, and its navy as an instrument of leverage, intimidation, or intervention to know that its
operations in forward deployment are a risky new feature of international competition. To minimise the dangers of forward deployment
it is necessary for any country, at the least, to have clear foreign policy
aims, good intelligence, effective command-and-control arrangements,
and unruffled rational leadership in times of crisis. The absence of any
one of these expensive technical considerations or elusive human
qualities is sufficient to change a navy in forward deployment from an
instrument of opportunity to a vehicle of risk.

Some costs of naval power

This chapter has shown some ways in which warships can have
deleterious effects on foreign policies. They can shape or undermine a
country's efforts in unpredictable and undesirable ways. This risk is
particularly important for countries such as the United States and the
Soviet Union which are faced by the problems besetting the *possessors*
of power: for most countries *weakness* of various sorts is their main
worry. Particularly in the aftermath of Vietnam, Western thinking is
concerned not just with the benefits that international power brings,
but also with the problems caused by the possession of that power;
it is concerned not just with the advantages bestowed by the attribution
of prestige, but also with the pitfalls of being thought prestigious; it is
concerned not just with the impulse to win friends and influence
people, but is also concerned with the obligations, problems and
entanglements caused by two-way influence processes. In a more
disenchanted and wordly-wise period, it is only natural to regard
warships as sources of political costs, as well as instruments of foreign
policy.

A discussion of the political costs of navies reveals the other side
of the coin to the clear-cut mission approach. It reveals the 'instrument'
becoming an influence, and not always to the good. The effects which
warships can have on foreign policies can never be fully predicted.
The history of strategy is full of cases of men and weapons being used
for one purpose or in one manner when their original rationale was very
different. Warships in forward deployment can be the cause of new
requirements, responsibilities, changing intentions, crises and war — an

all the different costs which result from such outcomes. There is much that is uncontrollable: analysts must recognise that something has to be left to chance.

It is conceivable of course that forward deployment might have no significant foreign policy pulls in particular cases. It is conceivable that the naval instrument will be perfectly controlled and will be kept to some extent apart from local regional politics, except when needed. Such a picture is possible, but perhaps not very likely. The need for the simplest facilities is likely to produce some modification in behaviour. On the other hand, a persistent requirement for shore facilities may cause a government to accept a significant degree of commitment to a particular country; the commitment might not really be desirable from a foreign policy viewpoint, but might be complied with as a lesser strategic evil. However carefully a particular country controls its naval instrument in forward deployment, it cannot control the reactions of local parties. Such views might range from hostile propaganda about 'gunboat diplomacy' to inflated expectations of support from the naval power concerned. Beyond the homeland, it is easier to put warships in purdah than other branches of the armed forces, but however well they are controlled by their political masters, they cannot subdue the expectations, envy and longings of the locals.

The functions of warships are manifold, and can give a government many options. They can also create headaches; they can change intentions and channel thinking in particular directions; they can have many unintended effects, creating dangers as well as opportunities; and they can cause incremental changes over a prolonged period which might result in new roles and responsibilities. A navy, traditionally one of the favoured handmaidens of foreign policy, can become its nagging and volatile mistress.

Notes

1. See the 'bogey' and 'nightmares' faced by the British in this respect at the end of the last century; Arthur J. Marder, *Anatomy of British Sea Power* (London: Frank Cass, 1964), pp. 65-104. On the perception of the German fleet as hostile, see Marder, *From the Dreadnought to Scapa Flow*, Vol. 1 (London: Oxford University Press, 1961), pp. 120-1, 171-7.

2. This possibility, largely dormant through the 1960s, raised its head in the aftermath of the Arab use of the 'oil weapon' following the October 1973

war. US military intervention to secure Middle Eastern oil supplies became an active strategic question. For a sensible analysis of the 'threat' see *Strategic Survey 1974* (London: the IISS, 1975), pp. 30-2.

3.   *Guardian*, 14 March 1974.

4.   The best example was the antagonism engendered by Anglo-American naval rivalry in the 1920s. The 'naval imbroglio', as Marder has called it, tended to obscure the identity of interests between the two countries, though it was based on no conflicting strategic interests — 'only conflicting national egos and pride'. On its origins, 1917-18, see Marder, *From the Dreadnought to Scapa Flow*, Vol. 5, Chapter V; on its further development see Captain S. W. Roskill, *Naval Policy between the Wars*, Vol. 1 (London: Collins, 1968).

5.   E.g. Lt. Cmdr. Jonathan T. Howe, USN, 'Soviet Beachhead in the Third World', *USNIPs*, October 1968, No. 788, Vol. 94, No. 10, pp. 60-7.

6.   R. W. Herrick, *Soviet Naval Strategy: Fifty Years of Theory and Practice* (US Naval Institute, Annapolis, Maryland, 1968), pp. 144, 149-50, 156-7.

7.   M. K. MccGwire, 'The Background to Soviet Naval Deployments', *World Today*, March 1971, pp. 93-103.

8.   Thomas W. Wolfe, 'Soviet Naval Interaction with the United States and its Influence on Soviet Naval Developments', Ch. 20 in Michael MccGwire, *Soviet Naval Developments* (New York: Praeger, 1973), pp. 245-76.

9.   D. C. Gordon, *The Dominions' Partnership in Imperial Defence, 1870-1914* (Baltimore: The Johns Hopkins Press, 1965), p. 37.

10.   None the less, naval strategy did not have a free hand in the face of economic constraints in the second half of the nineteenth century. Neither British politics nor the Treasury encouraged the modernisation of the navy. See G. S. Graham, *The Politics of Naval Supremacy: Studies in British Maritime Ascendency* (Cambridge: Cambridge University Press, 1965).

11.   Phillip Darby, *British Defence Policy East of Suez* (Oxford: Oxford University Press for RIIA, 1973), pp. 194-5.

12.   L. W. Martin, 'The Utility of Military Force', *Adelphi Papers*, No. 102 (London: IISS, 1973), p. 19.

13.   This uncertainty is fully appreciated by the United States as a result of its experiences in the 1970s. The restrictions imposed by its allies during the October 1973 war, and the efforts of Iceland and Turkey to bargain with the United States over the bases they offer, are both salutary warnings about such relationships.

14.   The Soviet desire for increasing the facilities at their disposal in Egypt at the end of the 1960s, and the determined Egyptian opposition, has been described by Mohamed Heikal, *The Road to Ramadan* (London: Collins, 1975), pp. 46-8, 163-4, 166.

15.   See, for example, the *Guardian*, 24 May 1975.

16.   See the expansion of Soviet 'needs' in Egypt, from an Egyptian perspective: Heikal, op. cit., pp. 46-8, 163-4, 166.

17.   See, for example, the *Sunday Times*, 12 September 1975.

18.   Alvin Z. Rubinstein, 'The Soviet-Egyptian Relationship since the June 1967 War', Chapter 10 in Michael MccGwire, Ken Booth and John McDonnell, *Soviet Naval Policy. Objectives and Constraints* (New York: Praeger, 1975); Heikal, op. cit., especially pp. 165-84.

19.   MccGwire, 'The Evolution of Soviet Naval Policy: 1960-1974', Chapter 28 in MccGwire, Booth and McDonnell, op. cit.

20.   S. W. Roskill, *The Strategy of Sea Power* (London: Collins, 1962), p. 257.

21.   See Marder, *From the Dreadnought to Scapa Flow*, Vol. 1, pp. 269-71.

22. We are familiar with US fears about political changes in foreign countries
     which might bring unfriendly governments into power. The same problem
     affects Soviet perceptions. The Soviet Union felt more committed to
     Nasser (and then Sadat) than vice versa. See Heikal, op. cit., *passim.*
23. *Sunday Times*, 13 January 1974.
24. A good example of how a naval-based intervention can expand and take
     on a life of its own – the multiplier effect – was the allied war of inter-
     vention in Russia, 1918-20. See Roskill, *Naval Policy between the Wars*,
     Chapter 3.
25. Robert G. Weinland, *Soviet Naval Operations – Ten Years of Change*
     (Center for Naval Analyses, Professional Paper 125, August 1974), p. 7.
     Reprinted in MccGwire, Booth and McDonnell, op. cit., Chapter 20.
     pp. 375-86.
26. A. Kaplan, *The Conduct of Enquiry; Methodology for Behavioural
     Science* (San Francisco: Chandler, 1964), p. 28. He called it *'the law of the
     instrument'.*
27. The enforced idleness of the British and German fleets in World War One
     provides some naval manifestations of this phenomenon. Churchill
     believed that the fleet should 'do something'. The men of Grand Fleet
     itself were bored, and *yearned* for an offensive strategy. The C-in-C,
     Jellicoe, was worried because the stronger he made Beatty, who led the
     battle cruisers, 'the greater is the temptation for him to get involved in
     independent action'. Meanwhile, inactivity was demoralising the German
     Fleet. Marder, *From the Dreadnought to Scapa Flow*, Vol. 2, pp. 46, 176,
     412-20, 432.
28. Vincent Davis, *The Politics of Innovation: Patterns in Navy Cases*
     (Monograph No. 3, Monograph Series in World Affairs, Denver: University
     of Denver, 1967), p. 20.
29. Gordon J. F. MacDonald, 'An American Strategy for the Oceans', Chapter
     6 in Edmund A. Guillon, *Uses of the Seas* (Englewood Cliffs, N.J.: Prentice
     Hall, 1968), p. 187.
30. Quoted by Graham T. Allison, *Essence of Decision: Explaining the Cuban
     Missile Crisis* (Boston: Little, Brown, 1971), p. 271.
31. Thomas C. Schelling, *Arms and Influence* (New Haven: Yale University
     Press, 1966), Chapter 4.
32. See the critique of Roger Fisher, *Basic Negotiating Strategy: International
     Conflict for Beginners* (London: Allen Lane, 1969), pp. 89-94.
33. *Guardian*, 6 June 1975.
34. Cf. the caution in the use of the US Navy in the June War; see Howe,
     Jonathan Trumbull Howe, *Multicrises. Sea Power and Global Politics in
     the Missile Age* (Cambridge, Mass.: The MIT Press, 1971), p. 143.
35. *Sunday Times*, 18 May 1975.
36. Heikal, op. cit., pp. 192-4.
37. Vagts describes a number of these examples: Alfred Vagts, *Defence and
     Diplomacy: The Soldier and the Conduct of Foreign Relations* (New York:
     King's Crown Press, 1956), pp. 231-59.
38. James Cable, *Gunboat Diplomacy. Political Applications of Limited Naval
     Force* (London: Chatto and Windus for the ISS, 1971), p. 159.
39. Howe, op. cit., p. 331.
40. Ibid., pp. 102-4. The local US commanders might equally well have
     attacked Egyptian targets, on the assumption that the *Liberty* had been
     attacked by Egyptian forces – a more conceivable possibility.
41. Cable, op. cit., p. 159.
42. Graham T. Allison, 'Conceptual Models and the Cuban Missil Crisis',

American Political Science Review (APSR), 63, No. 3, September 1969, pp. 689-718. Not only was the Navy slow in responding to the Presidential order regarding the blockade line, but it also forced Soviet submarines in the Caribbean to surface. The President had given no orders which would permit US vessels to attack Soviet submarines, and he believed that there had been no contact between the two forces. Morton H. Halperin, *Bureaucratic Politics and Foreign Policy* (Washington, D.C.: The Brookings Institution, 1974), pp. 279-80.

43. Cable, op. cit., p. 34. *The Times*, 17 May 1975.

44. E.g., *The Times*, 14 March 1974.

45. David Halberstam, *The Best and the Brightest* (Greenwich, Conn.: Fawcett Publications, 1972), p. 500.

46. Howe, op. cit., p. 147. One fearsome example of escalatory potential has been US policy towards the Chinese 'offshore islands'. This commitment, made manifest by the Seventh Fleet, brought the United States to the brink of war with China; this might have involved the use of nuclear weapons. Years later, few would argue that the islands were intrinsically or even symbolically worth such drastic efforts. See Morton H. Halperin and Tang Tsou, 'United States Policy Toward the Offshore Islands', *Public Policy*, 15 (1966), pp. 119-38, reprinted in Morton H. Halperin and Arnold Kanter (eds.), *Readings in American Foreign Policy: A Bureaucratic Perspective* (Boston: Little, Brown, 1973), pp. 334-50.

47. Vagts, op. cit., pp. 235-6.

48. Halberstam, op. cit., pp. 500-3.

49. Ibid., p. 503.

50. *The Times*, 24 October 1974.

51. See the South African government publication *Digest*, quoted in the *Guardian*, 7 November 1974. Those interested in promoting the relationship symbolised its 'warmth' by providing ample photographs of happy British sailors being welcomed by pretty girls.

5 TYPES OF NAVIES

Bird-brain or not, our minds are full of pigeon-holes. We have to classify. Behaviour is based on generalisation, which is only another word for organised knowledge. Decision-makers want analogies and comparisons of behaviour in order to provide a comprehensible frame of reference for thinking about the behaviour of others and for considering their own.[1] These impulses have been manifest in various attempts at classifying the naval instrument. It is the object of this chapter to examine some of the problems involved in this activity, and in particular to look at the validity of conceiving navies in terms of historical analogies, types of strategy, operating radius, or organic relationship with foreign policy. As anyone who has attempted the task will know, it is one of the more masochistic academic exercises.

Historical analogies

One familiar way of typing navies is by historical analogy. It has been widely practised because naval establishments have always (or nearly always) been anxious to learn the so-called 'lessons' of history, be they strategic, tactical, technical or organisational. However, this story has often been one of the failure of navies to learn and apply what *with hindsight* appear to have been the obvious lessons.[2] For those interested in learning directly from history, argument by analogy has a particular importance.

The pitfalls of arguing by analogy, including historical analogy, are well known. With respect to any problem under investigation, the relevant similarities must in fact be similar, and there must be no decisively different variables. It does not follow that because two situations share the qualities a, b and c, that they will also share x, y and z. When tempted by beguiling historical similarities, however, it is easy to overlook the pitfalls.

Argument by analogy has produced one issue of current relevance. This is the question of navies and 'superpower' status. Based on the US experience, the idea is widely held that global naval power, including an interventionist capability, is something which a state given the attribution of superpower ought to have. It is therefore argued that because the Soviet Union is a superpower, it ought to have the capabilities of a first-class navy. There is some strategic logic in this

113

argument, but whether it makes (Soviet-defined) political sense is another matter. Whatever justification there is for the view that a first-class navy is one which a model superpower ought to have, there is little reason to suppose that Soviet leaders think in a similar vein. One would expect a navy commander-in-chief such as Gorshkov to be prone to such views,[3] but more significant were Krushchev's adverse comments in this regard.[4] He records that there were 'quite a few loud-mouths' who advocated the building of aircraft-carriers. Their argument was based on the possession of such ships by the United States, Britain and France. They claimed: 'We're a great country, aren't we? Therefore we should have aircraft carriers, too.' Krushchev's stern reply was: 'Nonsense. Such competition is meaningless and wasteful. Competing with the US can cost us billions.' Khrushchev's next words are a useful reminder to those who think that the Soviet Union responds in a mechanical way to strategic stimuli. He argued:

> I believe an important part of our military doctrine should be
> that we do *not* try to compete with our adversaries in every
> area where they are ahead of us; as long as we preserve our nuclear
> deterrent, we will be defending our country effectively and
> serving our people well.

As long as the Soviet 'superpower'[5] has different interests in the use of the sea to the US 'superpower', so will the character of its navy be different. Naval convergence will only occur if they both conceive 'superpower' in the same way, come to share identical interests in the use of the sea, and invest the same level of effort in their naval development.

Those interested in understanding the Soviet Navy today are presented with one historical analogy which on first sight seems particularly striking: the analogy with Germany before World War One. The analogy constantly crops up in conversation, and sometimes in the literature.[6] The argument runs as follows. Imperial Germany was a state with a specific world policy and perspective, *Weltpolitik*, for which the possession of greater naval power was seen as vital by key groups in the country. For many Germans the further development of the country's rising great power status meant, amongst other things, the creation of a navy at least sufficiently strong to challenge the state or states standing between it and its place in the sun. Cannot the same be said about Soviet 'globalism'? Some would answer affirmatively, almost on the basis of the analogy alone.

But the analogy can be taken much further: the ostensible similarities
between Imperial Germany and Soviet Russia can be pushed far
further than is ever done by those who think it precise enough as it
stands. Traditionally, both countries had a basically coastal defence
navy. They had what is loosely called a 'continental' outlook: that is,
they were basically large land powers, with limited access to the sea;
they were basically self-sufficient; and they had overseas interests
which were important but not 'vital'. They were both politically
expansionist. In both countries the army dominated the military
system and the inter-service struggle for funds. In both cases their
main adversaries were the predominant naval powers. In both cases
the expansion of their navies was regarded by the traditional naval
powers as a 'threat'. They were seen as 'continental' powers, for
whom extensive naval power was not vital; consequently the
acquisition of naval strength was perceived as a hostile indicator. And
to cap all the other similarities, the Imperial German Navy and the
present Soviet Navy developed under the influence of two
personalities of great fame, Tirpitz and Gorshkov.

This is a compelling list of similarities. As for differences, one must
point chiefly to the changed international context and changed
attitudes to war. Can we compare the foreign policy of Germany in
the age of naked imperialism with that of the Soviet Union in a post-
colonial world of 'prudential pacifism'? Are Soviet interests in using the
sea today exactly the same as those of the Kaiser? In addition, the
German economy at the start of the century was booming, and the
Navy could be indulged, relatively, by a fanciful leader. This is not the
case with the Soviet Union today: its economy is under strain and it is
presided over by leaders well aware of the opportunity costs of military
spending. The most important difference of all is that compared with
seventy years ago the costs and risks of war have been enormously
inflated. Fear of superpower confrontation, and the decreased utility
of intervention and territorial conquest, puts a large question mark
over the significance of the much-quoted analogy. The similarities
between Tirpitz's Germany and Gorshkov's Soviet Union are striking,
but they do not prove anything.

Historical analogies are sometimes used to develop arguments on
more specific subjects. It is easy to be tempted into the pitfalls. In
this respect, the analogy often drawn between the German submarine
threat of World War Two and the contemporary Soviet submarine threat
is instructive. Again, the similarities in the situations make it tempting,
but is it a valid analogy? MccGwire is one of the few writers (if not

the only one) to stress the essential differences between the U-boat campaign and a possible Soviet campaign against Western seaborne commerce (perhaps as a method of applying pressure short of general war).[7] The initial differences between the two situations are those of time and space. The U-boats had bases from the North Cape to Bordeaux. Britain was a beleaguered island off a hostile continent. At first the transit routes of German submarines were very short. In contrast, the nearest Soviet bases are located 'at the far end of the hostile 1,000 mile long Norwegian Sea' (that is, where NATO ASW counter-measures could be concentrated). The trade routes would automatically swing away from the threat, increasing the transit to the focal areas to 2,000-2,700 miles. In addition, while the German U-boat effort was concentrated (and in May 1943 about three-quarters of their 400 boats were less than two years old) the numerically comparable Soviet submarine strength is dispersed between four distant fleet areas, is more diversified in type, and is generally older in its anti-shipping types. Furthermore, if the campaign were a limited submarine war on commerce — an extreme form of Schelling's 'diplomacy of violence' — then Soviet planners would have to take into account the possibility of escalation into general war. In 1943 the U-boat campaign was being carried out against the background of an existing total war. For all these reasons we may conclude that while the scenario of a Soviet submarine war in shipping should be considered as a rung on the ladder of the Soviet capability to hurt the West, Soviet planners are not likely to be impressed by its potential utility on the basis of the German experience: their problems and risks are greater than those Germany faced. And it must not be forgotten that Germany still lost in the end. Soviet analysts are likely to stress the differences between the two situations, though it is hardly surprising, remembering the dangers of the U-boat campaign, if Western analysts stress the similarities.

In general, historical analogy is an unsatisfactory and unfruitful method of proceeding in strategic studies. Analogies might be suggestive, but they are no more than that. Conclusions, recommendations or policies based on analogies have weak foundations. In this respect the 'historical school' often falls into one of the common fallacies of strategic studies, namely the assumption that 'Was' Equals 'Is' Equals 'Will be'.[8] The much-used Appendix in James Cable's study of *Gunboat Diplomacy* illustrates this.[9] Cable chose 1918 as the start of his study, because the period from that date was alleged to contain a 'degree of contemporary — and future — relevance' on the basis of its technical and political characteristics. He noted that the operation of warships in coastal waters was already hampered by mines and sub-marines, while the concept of the nation-state had taken 'firm root'. However, while the 'concept' had taken root, it took 35-45 more years for national independence to flower in most colonial countries, and in fact many of the usages of 'gunboat diplomacy' to which Cable refers arose out of the turmoil attendant upon the rise of nationalism and the decay of colonialism.[10] Cable's Appendix is valuable, but not for the purpose he recommends, namely future relevance. It cannot be regarded as relevant for forecasting the type or character of what he calls 'gunboat diplomacy' because at least one of the major factors determining naval behaviour in his period — colonialism — has almost disappeared. This is not to suggest that limited naval force has no utility. It is merely to make the simple but overlooked point that because conditions have significantly changed, any projections into the future will be misconceived. There are two other problems relating to such approaches. Firstly, historical 'lessons' and analogies seem curiously potent in their effect on the thinking of some individuals, and often suffice for deeper analysis. Secondly, the historical analogies which spring to an individual's mind are likely to be those which conform to a pre-established position, and can doubtless be used to 'prove' a point. Against such impulses it should be remembered that history can and should be used to illustrate: it cannot and should not be used to prove or predict.

Strategies of control and denial

Another much favoured approach to classifying navies is in terms of basic strategy. Historically, this was a relatively straightforward task. Strategic labels could be given to the navies of different countries and it was relatively well understood what was meant. The navies of Britain and the United States had a *command of the sea* strategy; that of France had a *guerre de course* strategy; and those of Germany and Russia had *coastal defence* strategies. In these and other cases it was clear why the states concerned wanted to use the sea, and conse-quently it was clear why they needed a navy, and of what type. Such understanding is by no means as easily obtained today. With political and technological changes, interests in the use of the sea have changed, and the problems of classifying on the basis of naval strategy have grown.

The dominating idea in contemporary Western naval thinking is that of 'sea control'.[11] It is both a development and replacement of the historic ideas of 'command of the sea' and 'control of the sea'. Unfortunately, the concept of sea control contains a number of analytical difficulties, as does any alternative. In a literal sense it means roughly the same as command of the sea,[12] but it is to be preferred mainly because the latter has very strong historical overtones. 'Command of the sea' inevitably connotes the traditional British theory of naval strategy, which was developed through the centuries and encapsulated by Mahan, and which referred to the sweeping and commanding of the seas by a mixture of fleet action and blockade. Command of the sea is rejected as a satisfactory modern concept because of such historical overtones, and because one cannot *command* the sea in the traditional, almost absolutist sense. But can one *control* it? The answer is affirmative, as long as some important qualifications are borne in mind.

The term 'sea control' has been introduced as 'a deliberate attempt to acknowledge the limitations on ocean control brought about by the development of the submarine and airplane.'[13] As Admiral Turner has put it, the new term 'sea control' is intended to connote 'more realistic control in limited areas and for limited periods of time'. Under present circumstances, it is only conceivable to exert temporary control (air, submarine and surface) in an area while moving ships into position to project power ashore or to resupply overseas forces.[14] The idea of majestically sweeping and commanding the seas has passed. The corollary of a sea control strategy is one of 'sea denial'. In the former the objective is to put oneself into a position whereby one can use the sea for one's own purposes while preventing the enemy from using it for his: in the latter the objective is to deny the enemy the opportunity of using the seas for his own purposes. A sea control strategy will be more taxing than one of denial since one has a positive as well as a preventive interest in the use of the sea. However, the strategies are not strictly opposites. Preventing the enemy from using the sea is implicit in the idea of control[15] while they share many similar tactical objectives.[16]

We can hardly expect clear-cut distinctions from any two or three words used to encapsulate the many variables included in a country's naval strategy. For better or worse, sea control and sea denial have entered the language: they have problems, but so do any alternatives. They are reasonably satisfactory terms as long as the following points and qualifications are borne in mind: (1) They are not opposites. (2) Sea-control is not a universal theory, like the traditional idea of command of the sea was taken to be, with a recognisable baggage of ideas and tactics. (3) The application of the terms is specific rather than general. As a working hypothesis, it might be satisfactory to classify US naval strategy as one of sea control and that of the Soviet Union as sea denial: the United States does have more extensive and positive interests in using the sea. However, in practice the picture is more variegated. In some areas the Soviet strategy would be one of control (e.g. in order to carry out amphibious operations in support of its ground forces in northern Europe). In other areas, such as the eastern Mediterranean, the Soviet objective would primarily be one of denial, attempting to prevent the US strike-carriers and SSBNs from discharging their missions. As the war at sea progressed, there would be a patchwork pattern of the strategies and tactics of control and denial.

(4) This leads on to an old qualification, written about by Corbett and others,[17] namely that in war at sea the most common feature is neither a controlled (or commanded) sea but an uncontrolled (or uncommanded) one. Normally control or command is in dispute. As Corbett put it seventy years ago: 'It is this state of dispute with which naval strategy is most nearly concerned, for when the command is lost or won pure naval strategy comes to an end.'[18] (5) Sea control is concerned with securing maritime communications in wartime. In peacetime one is concerned with being in a position to secure or contest such usage. These are strategies of potential control or denial.

(6) Finally, it should be stressed that control is not attainable in an old sense. General control is not feasible because of the diversity and weight of weapons – including ballistic missiles – which can be directed against ships at sea, while for the same reason limited control can be no more than temporary.[19] To use the sea successfully in war will be increasingly difficult: it will require not only the limited control of the air, surface and subsurface of the area within which one's ships are operating, but also the ability to stop the enemy using aircraft or missiles against that target from ranges which might now extend to hundreds or even thousands of miles. In an absolute sense, sea control is not a feasible proposition: but this certainly does not mean that it is a strategically irrelevant aspiration.

Naval power gradients

'Power' is a notoriously difficult concept. One of its complications arises from the fact that it is both an absolute and a relational idea. This means that classifications of naval power will be either very simple, based on absolute numbers, or very complex, including all the important combinations of relationships. Other problems complicating the classification of naval power concern variables such as fleet dispersal, the relationship between numbers and tasks, alliance considerations, degree of modernisation, level of efficiency and so on. It is no wonder that attempts to classify navies err on the side of simplicity. One classification distinguishes between the status symbol navy, the coast defence fleet, the minor naval powers, and the major naval powers.[20] Another distinguishes between the navies of 'maritime or blue water nations', 'continental nations' and 'small nations'.[21] A more sophisticated approach is Cable's attempt to establish 'operational ceilings' for different navies,[22] but this is of very restricted applicability, since it is concerned only with the possibility of the exertion of limited force at sea.

One way of distinguishing between navies is in terms of geographical reach. This can be conceived in terms of a 'loss-of-power gradient',[23] tapering to a point where a navy's capabilities cease to be effective. Obviously the length and steepness of this gradient will depend upon the relative power of the forces against which it is contending. In terms of the loss-of-power gradient one can distinguish between coastal, contiguous sea, ocean-going and global navies.[24] These in turn can be divided in terms of basic strategic orientation, that is control or denial. Strategic orientation, like reach, will depend upon the particular adversaries considered, and whether they are operating within an alliance.

A *global navy* will have actual or potential deployment on a world-wide basis without denuding forces required for maritime defence in the contiguous seas. It will maintain standing demonstrations or regular patrols in distant waters as a matter of course. It should have sufficient forces to discharge the priority missions simultaneously, without unacceptable overstretch. If control is the objective, there will be a requirement for organic air power on an impressive scale, the ability to intervene with amphibious forces against well-equipped opposition, and the ability to support such operations independently in distant regions. If sea denial is the objective, force characteristics will be determined by the character of the potential enemy's forces and their deployment. Only the United States and the Soviet Union have world-wide interests in using the sea, and the economic capability to contemplate (if not always to achieve) the building of the required warships in reasonable numbers.

Obviously a navy with ocean-going warships has some potentiality of using them in some capacity anywhere in the world accessible to ships. But to have such warships is not the same as having a global capacity: the latter depends upon strength in depth and world-wide interests. Most navies with ocean-going warships have neither the will nor the numbers to operate simultaneously in several parts of the world. An *ocean-going* navy is therefore one which, having some interest in distant waters, will have sufficient naval strength to be able to threaten convincingly to fight independently to control or contest the sea in the areas of interest against all but the most highly sophisticated opposition. However, such a navy will lack sufficient forces to attempt more than one serious operation in distant waters at the same time without support. For control purposes, organic air power is desirable and/or dependable land bases in adjacent areas. Against defended shores, an intervention will probably depend upon the support of allies. An ocean-going navy will be able to undertake small standing demonstrations or regular patrols in distant waters in support of national commitments. The navies of Britain and France may be described as ocean-going, since they have both some capabilities for and some interests in using the sea out of their immediately adjacent sea areas.

The posture of a *contiguous sea navy* is to operate as the seaward extension of the home territorial defence zone. There is little or no requirement to operate outside contiguous waters. The extent of the latter will depend upon the size of the state concerned and its regional interest in using the sea. Force characteristics will be determined by a variety of factors, including economic capability, the character of the 'threat', the need to meet and further alliance interests, or the need to project some amphibious capability against neighbouring shores. Most navies of the world (about 60 per cent) fall into this category, and their strategy is conceived either in terms of an alliance or under the umbrella of a protector.

Finally, there is a *coastal navy*. The basic orientation of such a 'navy' is to have sufficient strength to carry out coastguard functions, but with a minimal capability to handle even a modest naval intrusion. However, in extending territorial law enforcement, such forces do pose some challenge to potential intruders. In most cases states with miniscule navies rely for their maritime protection on allies or on general maritime stability. About 35 per cent of the world's navies fall into this category.

More than anything, these simple distinctions of naval power based on geographical reach give an indication of the great difference in potential between the navies of the United States and the Soviet Union and the rest, and are a reminder of the dependence of the great majority on alliances and/or general maritime stability.

Navies as dependent variables

Dean Acheson was once irritated and bemused by the discovery that some modern students of foreign policy regarded him as a *dependent variable*. Such testiness is not likely from naval establishments. Constitutionally and congenitally, by training and tradition, they are suited to recognising that their role is to vary their behaviour in accordance with their country's foreign policy, as determined by legitimate authority. The analytical problems involved in classifying navies as dependent variables are extremely complex, however.

The obstacles preventing a close 'fit' between types of foreign policy and types of naval employment include: the great difficulty of discovering an acceptable method of classifying foreign policies; the unreliability of the assumption of a rational relationship between foreign policy and naval acts; the fact that navies are influences on policy, as well as instruments; and the problem of the inherent ambiguity of many actions in the fields of both foreign policy and naval employment.

Historically, as with mercantilism or imperialism, there did seem to be a relatively clear relationship between overseas policy and naval posture. However, although the labels 'mercantilism' and 'imperialism' had certain naval connotations, they were exceptions, and even then the naval connotations were not very precise. Today, the labels on foreign policies have become more complex. For this important reason few, if any, writers have attempted to relate types of foreign policy and types of naval employment.

If one cannot satisfactorily categorise foreign policies, it is possible to draw up a serviceable set of distinctions based on the *intensity* of particular *sets* of *relationships*. This approach has the advantage of being relatively specific in terms of associated naval usages. On the basis of various (overlapping) attempts at classifying international political relationships,[25] it is possible to conceive several major stages in a scale of intensity in the relations between two states, extending from amity to enmity. For each stage characteristic naval behaviour will be suggested and illustrations given.

(1)   *Relations of consensus.* This relationship is typical between states that have few disagreements over foreign policy objectives, or have a high degree of mutual responsiveness or a very low level of interaction. Influence is exercised by persuasion and rewards. Punishment is almost inconceivable. The naval aspect of such a relationship is mainly social and diplomatic, involving reassurance visits for long associates and exploratory goodwill visits to 'new' associates. An

illustration of this would be visits by British minesweepers to Canadian ports, or of frigates to the Philippines. If interaction is high, and the two states perceive a common danger, the navies might perform some of the wide range of supportive functions of which navies are capable.

(2)   *Relations of authority*.   In this relationship, when State A wishes to move B in a desired direction, B complies because he 'recognises that the command is reasonable in terms of his own values'. The naval aspect of such a relationship would be that which characterises a dominant partnership in an alliance, or between a great and smaller power with a high degree of interaction. Illustrations of this are the deference accorded to the Soviet Union on naval matters within the Warsaw Pact, or the deference accorded to the United States by a variety of countries in Latin America. The naval behaviour by which such deference is induced might be subtle or crude, depending upon the traditions, outlooks and issues involved in the relationship.

(3)   *Relations of manipulation*.   In contrast with the maintenance (or *status quo*) character of a consensus relationship, this type of relationship has a probing character; there may be some disagreement over some aspect of policy; one state may wish to increase the level of interaction in ways which are to its advantage; or one state may wish to move the other in a desired direction through the promising or grant of benefits. A wide variety of naval activities is conceivable in such a relationship, including naval aid, support in times of trouble, symbolic deployments, and goodwill and reassurance visits. There is no targeting of military capabilities against each other. A number of Soviet naval actions in recent years belong to a manipulative relationship. They have attempted to increase their leverage with various countries, or to strengthen their anti-Western predispositions, by such tactics as naval aid, support in times of trouble, symbolic deployments, or reassurance visits.[26]

(4)   *Relations of power*.   This relationship is marked by the occurrence of threats: these may be to withold rewards, or be specific threats of non-violent punishment, or possibly of 'vague menaces' as a disagreement rises in intensity. The naval aspect of such a relationship might include the withholding of aid, the withdrawal of promises of support in times of trouble, the development of relationships with unwelcome third parties, or the possibility of limited harassment at sea. The Beira Patrol as an aspect of Britain's relations with Rhodesia is an illustration of this type of relationship.

(5)   *Relations of coercion.* In this relationship there are fundamental disagreements over foreign policy objectives. 'Almost all actions
that A takes externally are perceived by B to be a threat to its own
interests.' Tactics include warnings, threats, non-violent punishments,
or ultimately the selective use of force. At least one of the countries
will have the other targeted. The naval aspect of such a relationship
will include standing demonstrations, naval aid to the other's
adversaries, close shadowing of the other's naval activities, warnings of
punishment, and possibly the use of limited force at sea. The wide
variety of naval interaction which takes place between the Soviet and
US navies is reflective of a basically coercive relationship.

(6)   *Relations of force.* In this relationship there is an almost
total disagreement on foreign policy objectives, and 'the areas of
consensus are limited to a few necessities such as communications'.
The degree of involvement is extremely high, and violent punishment
is the typical method by which A attempts to move B. Some rewards
(e.g. peace) might be offered. One or other or both countries has the
other one targeted. The naval aspect of such a relationship depends
upon the level of naval power possessed by each adversary. At the
minimum, naval power will be used to contribute to deterrence, and if
necessary to provide some defence against unwelcome intrusion. At the
maximum it will be used to project force against the other country.
The naval aspect of the US war against Vietnam is an illustration of a
relationship of force.

Conclusions

From the foregoing discussion of the problems of classifying the naval
instrument, the following general conclusions emerge: (1) Naval history
may be used to illustrate points, but it cannot be used to prove what
is happening or predict what will happen. (2) It is unlikely that an all-
embracing, water-tight classification of the naval instrument can be
devised, which is sufficiently specific to be of analytic or practical use.
(3) As long as it is hedged with qualifications, the conceiving of navies
in terms of types of strategy, relative power gradients, and dependent
variables provides some working structures for the subject: it fixes
some lines through the general chaos. (4) The chapter made evident
the enormous gulf in capability and extent of military interest in the
sea between the handful of major navies and those of the great mass
of countries in the world. (5) It demonstrated, in addition, that
whatever the intensity or character of a relationship between two
countries, warships can and do contribute to the support of policy

in a variety of ways. They are an inherently multi-purpose instrument of foreign policy.

Notes

1. See Joseph Frankel, *Contemporary International Theory and the Behaviour of States* (Oxford: Oxford University Press, 1973), p. 36.
2. For one of the few detailed case studies of this problem see Arthur J. Marder, 'The Influence of History on Sea Power. The Royal Navy and the Lessons of 1914-1918', in *From the Dardanelles to Oran* (London: Oxford University Press, 1974), pp. 33-63.
3. See Chapter Three, especially pp. 74-5.
4. Strobe Talbott (translator and editor), *Khrushchev Remembers. The Last Testament* (London: Andre Deutsch, 1974), pp. 33-4.
5. This is a word, incidentally, which Soviet spokesmen avoid when describing their own state. See Robin Edmonds, *Soviet Foreign Policy, 1962-1973* (London: Oxford University Press, 1975), pp. 4-5.
6. Typically, it is alleged that, like Germany before World War One, the Soviet Union is 'trying to act in the grand manner of a great naval power'. The analogy is drawn by Professor William E. Griffith, in Jonathan Trumbull Howe, *Multicrises. Sea Power and Global Politics in the Missile Age* (Cambridge, Mass.' MIT Press, 1971), p. 318.
7. M. K. MccGuire, 'Russian Capability for a Submarine War on Commerce', Appendix VII in J. L. Moulton, *British Maritime Strategy in the 1970s* (London: Royal United Service Institution, 1969).
8. Yehezkel Dror, *Crazy States. A Counterconventional Strategic Problem* (Lexington, Mass.: Heath Lexington Books, 1971), pp. 4-5.
9. James Cable, *Gunboat Diplomacy. Political Applications of Limited Naval Force* (London: Chatto and Windus for the ISS, 1971), pp. 175-229.
10. This is not to say that the world is now so stable that there is no requirement for evacuation: far from it. But that is not the point. The evacuation of nationals from troubled independent states in the 1970s and beyond is a rather different activity from protecting nationals in colonial areas in the decades after 1918.
11. I have spent much time discussing this and related concepts with Michael MccGwire. He disapproves of the way the concept of 'sea control' is used and therefore of what follows. Nevertheless, he bears much responsibility for clarifying my mind about what I think sea control means.
12. What is the difference between 'command' and 'control'? Dictionaries are not helpful: 'command' is given as one of the meanings of 'control', and vice versa. This is well exemplified in Corbett's definition: '*Command* of the sea . . . means nothing but the *control* of maritime communications, whether for commercial or military purposes' (my italics). Julian S. Corbett, *Some Principles of Maritime Strategy* (Greenwich: Conway Maritime Press, 1972. First edition 1911), p. 90.
13. Vice-Admiral Stansfield Turner USN, 'Missions of the U.S. Navy', *NWCR*, March-April 1974, p. 6.
14. Ibid., p. 7.
15. 'Restraint' is one of the dictionary meanings of 'control'.
16. See Turner, op. cit., pp. 8-10, for a list of such tactical objectives in the idea of sea-control, objectives which obviously have to be contested in a sea denial strategy.

17.   Corbett, op. cit., pp. 87-9.
18.   Ibid., p. 87.
19.   Corbett states that this was usually the case with the traditional idea of 'command', whether general or local, op. cit., p. 102.
20.   E.g. *Jane's Fighting Ships, 1973-74*, pp. 73-8.
21.   Clark G. Reynolds, *Command of the Sea. The History and Strategy of Maritime Empires* (New York: William Morrow and Co., 1974), pp. 12-16.
22.   Cable, op. cit., Chapter 4.
23.   See K. E. Boulding, *Conflict and defence: a general theory* (New York: Harper, 1962), pp. 79, 230, 245-7, 260-2, 268-9, 272.
24.   On the basis of information in *Jane's* and the IISS *Military Balance*, the world's main 98 national 'navies' may be divided as follows: 2 are global, 2 are ocean-going, 59 are contiguous sea navies, and 35 are coastal patrol navies.
25.   The classification below is based on: Peter Bachrach and Morton S. Baratz, 'Decisions and Non-Decisions. An Analytical Framework', *APSR*, 57 (September 1963); K. J. Holsti, *International Politics. A Framework for Analysis* (Englewood Cliffs, N.J.: Prentice Hall, 1972), pp. 169-70; Charles A. McClelland, *Theory and the International System* (New York: Macmillan, 1968).
26.   For specific examples, see pp. 257-8.

6 NAVAL HAPPENINGS: THE IMPACT OF PLAYERS AND PROCESSES

It is of some interest that probably the best song of political satire in the English language was written about the running of the Royal Navy. The ditty concerned is the First Lord's Song from *HMS Pinafore*:[1] it relates how the First Lord reached the highest office without any technical expertise or previous knowledge of the navy. He succeeded because of different qualities. He was faceless ('with a smile so bland'). He was loyal ('always voted at my party's call'). He was submissive ('I thought so little.'). And he was devoted ('never thought of thinking of myself at all'). Added to these qualities were his ambition, his attention to detail ('so carefullee'), his accumulating wealth, and his proper political behaviour. He rose to the top of the tree by dint of his 'golden rule': 'Stick close by your desk and never go to sea/And you all may be Rulers of the Queen's Navee!' In short, he had all the virtues of an organisation man, and was adept at the tactics of bureaucratic politics.

For any who doubt that serious points can be made by jaunty songs, one might bring forward the big guns of scholarship to join the same attack. Marder, for example, has written of Jellicoe's disappointment that the new Navy high command did not include officers with recent sea experience.[2] Administrative arrangements within the Navy during the Great War were not throwing forward officers with practical experience, while *Pinafore*-like processes were having similar effects on the political leadership of the Navy:[3] as Jellicoe said of one First Lord, Sir Eric Geddes, he 'is of course profoundly ignorant of the Navy though good at a railway!' Much nearer to the present, one also recalls Gilbertian echoes in Crowe's comments about First Lords in the 1946-63 period: he wrote that

> The general pattern suggests that the typical First Lord is chosen for his political, and possibly social, connections and for his general knowledge of public affairs. There is no indication that he is selected because of abilities that particularly fit him to deal with the Navy.[4]

These introductory points are a reminder, if one was needed, that

127

navies are not clinical instruments in the hands of a political will: they are organisations (and like all organisations are good, bad or indifferent) and are made up of men (and like all groups of men contain the good, the bad and the indifferent). To attempt to understand naval happenings we need explore their organisational nature: we need to know about relevant players and processes.

Political scientists often talk about decisions being 'made'. Such a description is often no more than another example of the penchant of the social sciences for euphemism. The directives which emerge from decision-making bodies are often messy compromises or routine reactions: it cannot be assumed that they are rationally considered responses to the problem faced and the choices available. The processes through which decisions emerge and are implemented (or not) affect both the character of the actual decisions and the ultimate actions which take place: this fact is well recognised, if not always easy to describe. The study of such matters, however, has been pursued with great energy only in comparatively recent years. One of the earliest and most amusing books on the subject was Parkinson's famous contribution in 1958.[5] The aim of his book was to show that administration and bureaucracy were not rational, and that most books written about the subject should have been classified as fiction. Again, it is of some interest, if merely coincidental, that Parkinson was in part a maritime historian and was familiar with naval administration.[6] In the period since Parkinson's book there has been an outpouring of writing (unfortunately rarely as amusing as his) on the subject of administration and bureaucracy. It has added greatly to our knowledge of such matters. But it did not need an academic blitzkrieg, just an experience of affairs, to understand that 'camels are horses designed by a committee' and that 'where you stand depends upon where you sit', and that as Lord Salisbury put it, 'If you believe the doctors nothing is wholesome; if you believe the theologians, nothing is innocent; if you believe the soldiers, nothing is safe.' Such aphorisms are the stuff of the politics and processes of large organisations.

In recent years the behaviour and interplay between large organisations has attracted increasing attention from students of politics. 'Bureaucratic politics' and 'organisation theory' have been the focuses: only the former, however, has attracted any significant attention amongst those primarily interested in foreign policy. Since naval happenings in shipyards or at sea are the output of organisational behaviour, it behoves us to see what insights these new areas of study might contribute.

The idea of bureaucratic politics

Students of international politics have heard a great deal in recent years (too much for the liking of some) about the subject of bureaucratic politics. This idea is a reaction to the old habit of interpreting foreign and military policy in terms of the 'rational actor model'. In this formulation, policy was seen as an action-reaction process between unitary governments seeking to maximise something called 'national interests'. The 'government' is seen as a black box, and its actions are seen in terms of rational choice between goals and options. The 'bureaucratic politics model', on the other hand, is based on the idea that policy is best understood not as a product of inter-governmental action, but in terms of the interplay between the large organisations which make up 'government'. Governmental action is thus seen as an outcome of bureaucratic bargaining: it is not necessarily rational, and may even be an unintended outcome resulting from the 'pulling and hauling' which make up the bureaucratic 'game'. From this perspective the national government is seen not as a black box but as a conglomeration of organisations, in which bureaucratic players seek to maximise institutional as well as national interests: indeed, in some formulations the national interest is never seen as anything more than a rationalisation for narrow interests or even a cloak for special pleading. Stress in analysis is upon players in positions, with parochial priorities and perceptions, goals and interests, stakes and stands, deadlines in the face of issues, varied power, formal and informal action-channels, and patchily understood 'rules of the game'. From this perspective, foreign policy is bureaucratic politics writ large.[7]

The study of bureaucratic politics has had effect in many areas of political science, but only a limited effect in naval studies. However, it will become evident, even if documentary evidence is not available, that some of the 'shape', 'characteristics' and 'effort' of particular navies and their subdivisions will be in part at least the outcome of bureaucratic politics. That is, in the bargaining for the allocation of military missions and funds, the services (and relevant civilian departments) will pursue policies which conform well with Morgenthau's classification of foreign policy: they will follow a policy of the *status quo*, a policy of imperialism, or a policy of prestige. Organisations will be seeking to maintain, increase or demonstrate their power.

The rational policy idea is not enough. Sir John Fortescue was greatly exaggerating when he said that Admirals with their fleets were 'mere weapons wielded in the hands of statesmen'.[8] Until recently the possible impact of bureaucratic politics has been discounted. This tradition in naval studies has been strengthened by the heavy concentration of historical writings upon war at sea. In war, where people more or less tend to pull together, the simple action-reaction model is usually more appropriate than in peacetime. But even in war it is not entirely satisfactory: there is still plenty of pulling and hauling, and peacetime decisions often have a tremendous impact on wartime possibilities. To their regret, governments have often found that they cannot change strategic doctrines in midstream. They have to suffer the consequences of peacetime bureaucratic wranglings.

The idea of bureacratic politics is not without its drawbacks and dangers. There is often a shortage of hard data. Admirals are hardly likely to admit that they proposed a particular policy because it was 'good for the Navy' rather than being 'in the national interest'. Admirals do not have the freedom (or wish?) of trade union leaders to *say* that their primary responsibility is to those under them. Nor can an Admiral prudently proclaim that what is good for the navy is good for the country, even if he believes it (as he most surely will). In practice it is probably impossible to separate the various motivations and feelings of major actors. In all likelihood policy-makers are able to persuade themselves that a convenient harmony of interests is being achieved between national and organisational interests. With a shortage of information about bureaucratic politics, we are heavily dependent upon speculation. A second problem with the idea is that most of the existing work has focused on the United States; this means that there is a problem of comparability and transferability. Can the ideas developed in the US context be used to explain the decision-making processes of other countries? Obviously there will be differences, and care must be taken in transferring ideas. However, one spin-off from the rise of bureaucratic politics has been the encouragement of the study of organisational factors in the making and execution of Soviet naval policy.[9] These studies have shown that decisions affecting Soviet naval policy 'are made neither by a simple reaction to Western naval initiatives nor by a blind following of technological opportunity'. Rather, policy is formulated as a result of the inter-action of a number of groups and organisations, each with its own perception of the Western naval threat and of the limits of techno-logical possibility. These actors, 'of whom the navy is necessarily neither the most influential nor the most realistic' come together both formally and informally to create programmes and policies. The eventual decisions will sometimes lie 'not in purposeful strategic thought but in the organisational imperatives or bureaucratic machinations of the principal actors.'[10] Finally, there is a general danger in the bureaucratic politics emphasis. This is the possibility that the concept might end up as a political rag-bag, to be dipped into in a doctrinaire fashion, in order to patch up analyses when there is nothing else at hand. The aim should not be to throw out any of the existing conceptual models of the decision-making process, but to bring together the insights of all of them, as appropriate. None are exclusive.

The thrust of bureaucratic politics in the study of naval policy relates to the organisational behaviour of naval establishments and the other organisations with which they interact. This involves the study of organisational interests (missions, capabilities and influence; organisational essence; autonomy; organisational morale; budgets; organisational stands); the making of decisions (initiative; rules of the game; defining the issue; who is involved? who plans?; constraints on information and arguments; shared images; manoeuvres to affect information; relations with political authorities; staff skill; the ability to mobilise outside support); and the implementation of decisions (limits on faithful implementation; resistance; the struggle over implementation; field perspectives; evading instructions; action in the absence of decisions; stategies to gain compliance).[11]

At the heart of bureaucratic politics is the idea of 'organisational essence'; this is the view held by the dominant group in an organisation 'of what the missions and capabilities [of their organisation] should be ... [and their] convictions about what kinds of people with what expertise, experience and knowledge should be members of the organisation'.[12] All professions have an 'organisational essence'. The academic profession, for example, sees itself devoted to study, writing and teaching. Anything else is secondary. There is therefore almost a wilful neglect or mismanagement of tasks which are at best secondary, notably administration. Administration is not thought to be part of the academic's essence: to be overly associated with it, or to be good at it, is to risk a reputation for impurity. The same principle operates with naval professionals. The essence of the US Navy, for example, has been said to be the maintenance of combat ships 'whose primary mission must be to control the seas against potential enemies'.[13] Within the Navy, however, there have been traditional disputes between naval flyers, surface ship officers and submariners (and later Polaris submariners as a fourth group). While there may have been differences between these groups about which kind of force could best carry out the essential mission, there was an implicit agreement that the essence of the Navy did not lie in maritime transport. Consequently this function traditionally received little attention. Similarly, there was resistance from the carrier advocates, with the support of much of the rest of the Navy, to the Polaris programme; it was believed that Polaris would deprive the Navy of aircraft. When Kennedy and McNamara increased from three to ten the number of Polaris boats being authorised each year, senior naval officers in effect argued that the 'Polaris mission is not a traditional Navy mission and therefore should not be financed out of the Navy's share of the defense budget.'[14]

The classical example of the way a Navy's image of its essence affected its performance was the Royal Navy's attitude to convoys in the two world wars. One of the Admiralty's main objections to the convoy arose out of the cliché that patrolling was 'offensive', whereas convoy work was 'defensive'.[15] The prevailing image was that a naval officer's job was to 'seek out and destroy' the enemy U-boats, by 'offensive patrols' in 'hunting groups'. Similarly, the prevailing belief that navies existed to fight other navies in great battles resulted in the needs for such battles overwhelming all other pressures on resources. There was therefore a strong tendency to reserve destroyers and skilled personnel for the main fleet for the great battle, and to view the protection of shipping as a secondary (and much inferior) matter. In such ways the Navy was 'hypnotised by its past'.[16] In the pre-war years there had been much talk about the 'Nelson Touch' and the 'Nelson Tradition', and this, in the eyes of naval officers, meant that the Navy's principal *raison d'être* was to meet and annihilate the German High Seas Fleet in a second Trafalgar. The problems of the control of communications and the protection of merchant shipping were inevitably pushed into the background. As one Admiral put it, 'The tendency was to view maritime war merely as a kind of gladiatorial contest between two opposing fleets without ultimate aim or purpose, whereas its real object — control of passage by sea — was ignored.'[17] And in this latter task the truth was, as Marder succinctly put it: *'Sinking submarines is a bonus, not a necessity.'*[18] The Navy's view of its *aggressive* essence therefore encouraged a tendency to overlook the importance of the protection of shipping role; for a long time the Navy's traditional image of itself ruled out the adoption of what proved to be the most effective way of dealing with the problem of U-boats. The irony, as Marder points out, was that 'it does not appear to have been fully realised that lack of shipping could lose the war without a single major engagement at sea.'[19]

The implications of the naval essence can be seen in other respects. There is what Roskill called the 'fallacy of the dominant weapon'. This is the view that one weapon tends to be exalted (obviously the one most directly related to the main mission) and that this tends to undermine the importance of other weapons. Before and after the Great War the dominant weapon was the gun. One consequence of this was that other weapons were not given sufficient attention. Furthermore, the surest road to promotion tended to belong to those having expertise in the dominant weapon.[20] In fact, only four First Sea Lords between 1905 and 1945 were not chosen from a small section of ex-gunnery and torpedo specialists.[21] The implications of organisational essence are still with us, and at many levels. It can be seen, for example, in the way that naval officers believe that their job is essentially to run ships, and not to sit behind desks involved in paperwork or academic study. Junior officers in particular are certain that the latter is not the reason why they joined the Navy. This antipathy towards desk work and bureaucratic politics, which arises out of their ingrained image of what a naval officer *is*, can be easily understood. Individual and organisational image become somewhat degraded when the Whitehall or Pentagon warrior has to drive a desk rather than a ship, when he has to pass paper rather than orders, and when 'crossing the T' has a clerical rather than a Nelsonic connotation. Such biases are natural, but they have been detrimental in war, and they may not be helpful in steering the Navy's peacetime course between the shoals of bureaucrats and the reefs of politicians.

The idea of organisational processes

We live in an organisational world. As the realisation of this fact has dawned, an increasing amount of study has taken place within the field of organisation theory. For various reasons, however, this work has had minimal influence on the literature of foreign policy. This is surprising because, as Allison has put it, the happenings of international politics are in some 'critical' senses the results of organisational actions.[22] Foreign (and naval) policy actions are the outputs of organisations in a variety of ways: (i) the 'actual occurrences are organisational actions'; (ii) 'existing organisational routines for employing present physical capabilities constitute the effective options open to government leaders confronted with any problem'; (iii) 'organisational outputs structure the situation within the narrow constraints of which leaders must contribute their "decision" concerning an issue. Outputs raise the problem, provide the information, and make the initial moves that colour the face of the issue that is turned to the leaders.' In view of these types of impact, it is evident that the study of organisational processes should add to our understanding of naval happenings. The way in which weaponry is procured, for example, will always be determined by routine organisational behaviour, as well as rational strategic requirements.

The field of organisation theory is not an easy one. It is 'so large a subject, and still in many ways so dark, we should open upon it all the windows we can find'.[23] It is a field in which there are many problems to be considered, situations researched, and propositions developed concerning the culture and structure of particular organisations. It is a field in which, in Mackenzie's words, 'no single theory is necessarily the best theory even for a single situation.'[24] The field is wide. It encompasses data and propositions about planning, staffing, the human factor in general (especially 'motivations', 'group norms', discipline, 'cultural analysis'), directing, budgeting, co-ordination (including the relationship between organisational charts and real life), reporting (the quality and quantity of information), types of specialisation, the management (command) structure, interaction between levels in the hierarchy, and the adaptive ability of the organisation when faced by the demands put upon it from within and without. These are all interesting subjects and would appear to have relevance to students of navies.

'How much relevance?' is not immediately evident, because the students of organisational behaviour have directed their main attention to industrial and business firms. But the relevance of the study of non-military organisations to the study of navies is perhaps greater than might appear at first sight. Initially, it certainly would be well to stress the differences. For one thing, the discipline in the former is different in kind (in Western societies at least). Similarly, there are marked differences on matters such as group loyalty and codes of honour. However, while there are important cultural differences between the two types of organisation, there might be structural aspects which are more comparable. Furthermore, the two types of organisation may come to 'converge' rather more than hitherto. Armed forces, including navies, have become very much more technical: they have become more demanding of specialist skills and are very budgetary conscious; in addition, the tendency appears to be to move away from the traditional idea of 'leadership' towards a more industrial 'man-management' idea; the 'blood and thunder' approach has been giving way to more civilianised procedures.[25] One can go too far with the idea of

convergence, but the foregoing points suggest sufficient similarities
to encourage further speculation. With such trends as the replacement
of sea-dogs by technocrats, loyalty by 'human relations', and leadership by man-management — all within an increasingly technological
environment — the rewards for the student of navies of studying
the modern 'firm' might be expected to grow. For military professionals, there might be some useful practical lessons to be learned: for
academics seeking to understand navies there might be both useful
insights and new clues for the collection of data.

The organising concept of the organisation process approach is that
of a government as a *machine*, made up of sub-parts (organisations)
which each have their own machine-like behaviour.[26] These organisations, of which the Navy is one, must demonstrate competence in the
areas of responsibility which they have been allocated. They must not
make major mistakes or produce only a low measure of success. To do
this they seek to avoid uncertainty. This is done by preparing pre-
planned modes of behaviour: these so-called standard operating
procedures (SOPs) are intended to aid efficiency as well as reduce
the possible external sources of uncertainty. Organisations also have
their own 'culture' or 'living system', which results in the development
of certain preferred modes of behaviour; these might include the
avoidance of risk, strict hierarchy and loyalty. Special interest is
usually directed at the way organisations *process* information (the verb
itself is significant) and in the way they implement the decisions
handed to them. As a result of tales from the Vietnam War we have
become familiar in recent years with the idea that the information
which decision-makers receive might be highly structured or skewed
by organisational behaviour. In his important contribution *The
Nerves of Government*, Deutsch has shown how information passed
from any organisation to decision-makers bears the special stamp of
the information processing programmes of that organisation.

Organisations initially sort out their 'switchboard problem' (what
incoming messages go where) and until it is thought that the switchboard is unsatisfactory, incoming and outgoing information will be
fitted into the existing procedures; there will be a reluctance to face
the problems of re-creating the switchboard. In addition — a point
which is as important as it is obvious — the information which is
passed to decision-makers will rarely if ever be to the detriment of the
organisation from which it came. This is significant because while
subordinate organisations are not the final arbiters of policy, they do
provide a large amount of the information on which decisions are

based. Whether or not particular experts will be trusted, however, will also depend upon their reputation and upon the personality and scepticism of the relevant decision-makers.[27]

Conceptual models and naval happenings

Although it is certainly not alone in the field, Allison's study is the one single work which more than any other has encouraged (or taunted) students of international politics to think about bureaucratic politics and organisational processes. This work, like those of Halperin, Neustadt, Schilling, Hilsman and others is rich in hypotheses, and detailed studies of them would contribute a good deal to the student of naval policy, both directly and indirectly.

Allison's general argument is that professional analysts of foreign affairs (as well as laymen) think about the problems of foreign and military policy in terms of largely implicit conceptual models that have significant consequences for the content of their thought: 'Conceptual models not only fix the mesh of the nets that the analyst drags through the material in order to explain a particular action; they also direct him to cast his nets in selected ponds, at certain depths, in order to catch the fish he is after.'[28] Most analysts, he argues, explain (and predict) the behaviour of national governments in terms of one basic conceptual model, what he calls the 'rational actor' or 'classical model' ('the more or less purposive acts of unified national governments'). This 'Model I' mode of analysis has proved useful for many purposes, but it also obscures: in particular, it obscures the fact of bureaucracy ('the "maker" of government policy is not one calculating decision-maker but is rather a conglomerate of large organizations and political actions'). He therefore recommends that two other conceptual models be introduced to provide a base for improved evaluations and predictions; these are the 'organizational process ' model (Model II) and the 'governmental' (bureaucratic) politics' model (Model III), whose characteristics have just been discussed.

Allison's ideas have already been used as a basis for further studies in the area of public policy.[29] Certainly they seem to offer the basis for an improved explanation of happenings in international politics. The approach helps to uncover many previously underemphasised features; these may result in a variety of hypotheses about the causes of important outcomes.[30] Furthermore, the models are a complement to each other:

Model I fixes the broader context, the larger national patterns, and the shared images. Within this context, Model II illuminates the organizational routines that produce the information, alternatives, and action. Within the Model II context, Model III focusses in greater detail on the individual leaders of a government and the politics among them that determine major governmental choices. The best analysts of foreign policy manage to weave strands of each of the three conceptual models into their explanations.[31]

Much richer history should therefore be the result. Allison's own contribution to the understanding of the Cuban missile crisis is evidence of this. In showing what happened, he demonstrates that each model distinguished certain features as being the relevant determinants in explaining the central puzzle. Depending upon the model, different questions were asked, different information was searched for, different conclusions were drawn, and different lessons learned. 'The sources of the difference are the conceptual models each analyst employed.'[32] Furthermore, the self-conscious methodological approach should also be helpful in elucidating the 'lessons' of a particular episode. For example, in his own study of the Cuban missile crisis, Allison shows that the lessons an implicit Model I analyst draws concern the manageability of the crisis; that is, in situations involving the vital interests of the superpowers, the leaders of both nations will have little difficulty in thinking through the problem and its alternatives, finding limited actions that communicate resolve, and thus settling the issue. The lessons Model II and Model III analysts draw are rather different, however. They caution against confidence in the impossibility of nations stumbling — 'irrationally' — into a nuclear exchange, against confidence in the manageability of nuclear crises, and against confidence in our understanding of the ingredients of successful crisis management.[33] The value of a wider range of ideas about 'lessons' is particularly important in a field such as naval policy where most historical writings tend to become functional history in the hands of professionals and commentators. Forecasting might also be improved by a less hit-or-miss approach to foreign policy causation. Allison argues, for example, that the application of Model II and Model III speculation would have considerably modified predictions about the bomber and missile gaps.[34]

When faced by a problem, the character of the puzzle which different analysts see is therefore much affected by their conceptual lens. This lens affects the evidence which they assume to be relevant, and the concepts used to examine it. Different answers emerge to the key puzzles, because they are basically answering different questions. From this central theme Allison works towards a 'tentative, *ad hoc* working synthesis' of the models. He does it by considering the different questions that each model leads one to ask of a problem of explanation.

Allison's work is representative of a school of thought which provides the basis for better speculation about the interrelationships between navies and the making and execution of foreign policy. His work should be part of the intellectual equipment of all students of naval policy. However, several cautionary comments should be added. Firstly, as Allison himself admits,[35] the models are only tentative. They are not the last word. For one thing care must be taken about applying generalisations based on the US experience to other political cultures. Secondly, Allison's Cuban missile crisis case study distorts the actual importance of his bargaining and process model. His focusing on a crisis situation underplays the impact which these factors may have on policy in general. The rational policy model is in all likelihood at its most applicable in a crisis, when issues and options are clear, and when national governments tend to pull together. Thirdly, one must avoid the impression which might too easily be created by Allison and others that bureaucratic politics and organisational processes are synonymous with irrationality and foul-up. The processes of and interplay between organisations may or may not be synonymous with mistakes and messy policies. The picture given by the bureaucratic politics school is often very one-sided. As will be seen, one can certainly explain many failures in policy as a result of organisational processes, but one must never forget that when the instruments of policy work smoothly and successfully (e.g. when ships move efficiently to appointed places and discharge their missions), this too is the result of organisational processes. If one's mind is dominated by the idea of organisational foul-ups, it is well to remember the D-Day operation, surely one of the most complex military happenings ever devised and executed in so short a time. This 'happening' was also the result of the output of and interplay between different organisations. A final qualification concerns the possible danger of too doctrinaire an espousal of the bureaucratic politics approach. It might be satisfying to interpret all adversary actions in terms of bureaucratic interplay, but such a reading might be both inaccurate and dangerous. It is well to recall in this respect the comforting remarks made by William II to von Bulow, his Chancellor. He said that:

the alleged English agitation about our new [naval building] programme was simply bluff for reasons of English domestic policy.
Such is the opinion of Tirpitz, and His Majesty is in entire
agreement.[36]

The German leadership convinced itself that it could press on, secure
in the belief that British agitation was simply a matter of bureaucratic politics. The rational strategic element in British thinking,
meanwhile, was being increasingly convinced of German hostility, and
of the inevitability of a day of reckoning. Comforting bureaucratic
explanations can sometimes explode in the faces of those who espouse
them.

A bureaucratic politics cut

The literature on naval affairs is full of naval happenings which are
most appropriately explained by determinants other than 'rational
policy' or 'objective national interest'. Amongst happenings partly or
to an important extent explicable in terms of bureaucratic politics are
the following.

(1) *Supercarriers and B-36 bombers*

Hammond's famous study[37] demonstrated that the major strategic
purchases of the United States in the late 1940s were not seen (and therefore were not made) in foreign policy terms. Supercarriers were seen by
the Navy representatives as a guarantee of survival, by the Air Force representatives as a threat to their own monpoly of atomic delivery, and by the
Secretary of Defense as a very costly item when he was committed to
economy. The anti-supercarrier constellation was strong. The Secretary of
Defense scrapped the programme on 'professional military advice' and this
decision was accepted by the Director of the Bureau of the Budget and
President Truman. The latter was satisfied with the economising decision;
he also had a pro-Army orientation, and had not had good relations with
Forrestal.[38] The same constellation of 'players' faced up for the B-36
bomber question, and the decision was made to go ahead. Significantly,
the Navy representatives attacked both the bomber itself and the underlying concept of strategic bombing.

(2) *The incoherence of British strategy in the inter-war years*

For much of this period, the different services in Britain prepared to
fight different wars against different enemies. Each focused on the
enemy or potential enemy which best served its institutional interests.

The RAF, when its independent future was in doubt right at the start of the 1920s, based its needs on the alleged threat from France (which conveniently had the largest air force in Europe). With each service following its own plans, and putting most effort into favoured missions, this contributed to very poor co-ordination and distorted mission structures for the ultimate 'happening'. The RAF's fixation with the strategic bombing role contributed to a lack of effort in tactical co-operation on land and sea. The Army's preference for imperial policing contributed to a lack of effort for mechanised warfare in Europe. The Navy's concentration on the war at sea, the idea that navies exist to fight navies, helped to hinder co-operation in the development of amphibious operations. When war came, each of these neglected areas proved to be critical.

(3)   *'Broken-backed war'*

This idea, which gave shape to allied naval planning in the mid-1950s, posited a third Battle of the Atlantic: this long war scenario entailed the maintenance of large fleets. The validity of these assumptions was treated with scepticism by many (especially airmen) at a time when the idea of surprise nuclear attack and short war was coming into vogue. Since the role (and therefore funds) allocated to navies in a short-war scenario would be very limited, students of bureaucratic politics would not be surprised to discover that the Royal Navy advocated the long-war scenario, involving a 'broken-backed' phase, and prolonged naval operations. However, this should not be taken to mean that such ideas were necessarily strategically invalid when first promulgated.

(4)   *The Bureau of Aeronautics*

The creation of this Bureau in 1921 was not the result of rational calculations by the US Navy about strategic doctrine, but began 'merely as a political strategem designed to thwart Billy Mitchell's campaign'.[39] It was to show the invalidity of Mitchell's allegation that aviation was not receiving high priority in the Navy: the Navy was trying to show that aviation was an *inseparable* part of it. 'The ironic conclusion is that Mitchell's campaign to strip the Navy of its aviation units actually "spurred the development of naval air power".'[40] The consequence of the US Navy's involvement in naval air power does not need elaboration. In the Pacific theatre of World War Two it played a decisive role.

(5)   *The Gorshkov Series*

Perhaps the most discussed piece of naval writing in the last few years has been the eleven articles written by the Commander-in-Chief of the Soviet Navy. Most Western commentators believe that they are important, but they are not agreed on the reasons why.[41] A rational policy interpretation would conclude that Gorshkov was advocating more vigorous naval efforts in order to further Soviet 'national interests': he was advocating what he thought were the optimum means to further foreign policy objectives. A bureaucratic politics interpretation would focus on the inter-service situation, arguing that Gorshkov's main daily problem was not the US Navy but the Soviet Air Force and the Strategic Rocket Forces.[42] Thus large-scale exercises such as *Okean* might be designed to emit signals to the Politburo rather than Western navies. It is not unusual for services to spend most of their time worrying about their internal problems rather than their 'enemy'. As Davis said about his book on the US Navy:

> the primary purpose of this book — to analyze the forms of political activity of the naval officer corps after World War II — cannot be achieved without at least a rudimentary understanding of the Navy men's chief adversaries: the men of the Air Force.[43]

As he stated later, when armed services are espousing virtually identical strategies, their relationship takes on 'many of the aspects of a zero-sum game'.[44] Because of the importance of the resource allocation debates which take place within governments on military appropriations, it is not surprising that there is increased political activity by the services.

(6) *US ocean policy*

Lest it be thought that the armed services are unique or particularly self-interested in their pursuit of organisational interests, the bureaucratics of US ocean policy since the late 1960s is a reminder that this is not so. One recent study of this subject has shown that the most fruitful approach to understanding the formulation of ocean policy is that of bureaucratic politics:

> public officials and large bureaucracies [are] engaged in a continuous process of bargaining which is influenced throughout by domestic as well as foreign interests. The ocean policies that result are a product of contention . . . and not of a rational centralized decision-making process.[45]

The pulling and hauling involved is hardly surprising in view of the 'complex array of legal, political, military, economic, commercial, scientific, and ecological concerns' involved in this area of foreign policy.[46]

(7)   *The MLF*

Like all games, that of bureaucratic politics is affected by the skill, opportunism and resources of the players. Halperin and Kanter have pointed out that participants who do not have major responsibilities at any one moment, perhaps the members of planning staffs, can pick a single issue and devote substantial time and determination to it. Many observers believe that the proposal for multi-national ship crews drawn from a number of NATO countries got as far as it did because the State Department's Policy Planning Council was able to devote considerable time and effort to guiding the project through the bureaucracy, while its opponents were preoccupied with other, more pressing, responsibilities. Therefore 'time, determination, and the willingness to seek responsibility and to act are important attributes affecting the influence of a participant in any particular case.'[47]

(8)   *The US Navy's development of carriers for nuclear strike*

In his study of the US Navy's efforts after World War Two to develop a nuclear delivery capability, Davis has shown the importance of some of the bureaucratic skills and opportunities just described. Furthermore, this episode shows that important strategic decisions are sometimes made without serious attention to the international environment they will affect.[48]

The primary roles in this episode were played by Commander 'Dick' Ashworth and Commander 'Chick' Hayward. They were both naval aviators with wartime experience in the atomic field. They therefore had the background to persuade the Navy between 1945 and 1949 to press for the development of a nuclear delivery capability with carrier aircraft. It was believed that the proposal would have at least three benefits for the Navy: it would strengthen the Navy's existing capabilities; it would enhance the role of aviators within the service; and it would strengthen the Navy's case in its struggle with the Air Force. It was for the last of these reasons that senior officers were quickly won over to the naval nuclear strike mission. Significantly, all these pressures were *internal*:

There was little or no specific regard to any particular adversary in the thinking and arguments of the Ashworth-Hayward team

within the Navy . . . neither Hayward nor other naval officers argued
for this capability primarily or even secondarily in terms of a
response to the Soviet danger.[49]

But it was one thing to have the desire for the capability, and
another thing to receive the necessary approval from the President and
Congress. This was achieved by what Halperin and Kanter have called
'innovation by inadvertence', and by presenting the decision-makers
with a virtual *fait accompli*. Presidential attention was averted by
Secretary Forrestal deciding that the necessary aircraft modifications
did not require White House approval. Efforts were made to present
the issue to the President and Congress not as one of *creating* the
necessary capability but rather of merely *improving* an *already existing*
capability. Resources were made available from items then in the
inventory. It merely seemed that an incremental decision was necessary,
to improve an existing mission.[50]

(9) *The retarded development of amphibious operations*

In both the Royal Navy and the US Navy the doctrine and training for
amphibious operations were delayed because of bureaucratic factors
rather than the lack of objective ('rational') requirements. In the case
of the US Navy, amphibious warfare techniques were delayed because
of the Navy's view of its *essence*, namely that navies only exist to fight
navies.[51] In the case of the Royal Navy, the retarded development of
these techniques was related to the limited bureaucratic power of the
Royal Marines. The Commandant General was not a member of the
Board of Admiralty, and was not represented on the Naval Staff. The
Marines felt they were tolerated as long as they were 'tame soldiers,
not costing too much, not having ideas above their station.'[52]

(10) *Intra-service politics: Where you are allowed to sit might depend
upon where you are thought to stand*

The study of bureaucratic politics has tended to concentrate upon
inter-service or civilian-military interreactions. It should be borne in
mind, however, that the services themselves are made up of different
sub-organisations, and sub-interests, and that these are politically
important in settling service policy. Intra-service disputes have affected
the Royal Navy's policy at various times.[53] One is familiar with the
stresses and strains caused in an adaptive service between traditionalists
and technicians, generalists and engineers, submariners and surface
officers, gunnery experts and other specialists.[54] Intra-service politics

are also affected by the fact that senior personnel tend to gather around themselves men whom they believe are reliable and who will play the game as they want it: depending on the temperament and outlook of the senior officer concerned, this role might be one of a subservient will, a conscientious executor, or an institutional maverick. The classic example of 'where you are allowed to sit depends upon where you are thought to stand' occurred in the Royal Navy during the Fisher era. In this case Fisher was frequently accused of surrounding himself with 'yes-men', and of promoting his 'favourites and sycophants' while harassing those who did not belong to the so-called 'Fishpond'. Whatever the justification for this criticism, those who were not in the Fishpond spent a very uneasy period in the service. Marder's verdict on the Fishpond was that naval appointments and promotions before Fisher were largely matters of interest (family, service and political) and seniority, and not of merit. Fisher changed this, selecting on the basis of what he thought was merit rather than seniority and interest. However, the men who were pushed were men in sympathy with his own policies. 'But what was more natural than for a person in authority to gather around him able officers who were in sympathy with his ideas and reforms and would work as a team?'[55]

One will always get suspicions of such developments in large organisations, though they will rarely be as overt as the Fishpond. There are many examples in naval history. Lionel Halsey was appointed Third Sea Lord in 1917 because, in Beatty's words, he was 'a complaisant individual without much character or independent ideas'.[56] Khrushchev decided to support the 'younger cadres' in the Navy in the mid-1950s because their views were congenial to his own.[57] Gorshkov was elevated by Khrushchev twenty years ago, not because he was a powerful advocate of Soviet naval power but because he could be relied upon to carry out policies which were primarily designed to further Khrushchev's economising ideas.[58] No doubt many senior naval officers today could provide profiles of intra-service parochialism, and of promotion being affected by internal stands. Critics of navies would be wildly mistaken if they imagined that there was anything particularly unusual in this respect. All organisations tend to have their Fishponds. Fisher justified his policy with the aphorism: 'Favouritism is the secret of efficiency.'[59]

(11) *Civilian-Navy relations*

Bureaucratic politics in its various manifestations greatly affects the character and creativity (or otherwise) of the relationship between civilians (politicians and bureaucrats) and the military services. This relationship can affect a range of issues, including procurement, tactics and strategy, and so can importantly affect foreign policy outcomes. Many of the problems focus on the question of service autonomy.

Autonomy[60] refers to the way that the career officials in an organisation believe that they are in a better position than others to determine what capabilities their organisation should have, and how they should best fulfil their mission. In the case of service organisations, this means that the senior officers believe that they knew their job better than civilians, and so deserve a degree of autonomy. Thus senior officers attach a very high priority to controlling their own resources so that these can be used to support the essence of the organisation. Senior officers wish to be in a position to spend money allocated to them in the way they choose, to station their manpower as they choose, and to implement policy in their own fashion. They resist efforts by senior bureaucrats or politicians to obtain control of their activities.

History provides many examples of the quest for autonomy and of the service perspective dominating the thinking of its senior personnel. Crowe has described how the survival of the Royal Navy has been the basic objective of the Admiralty, and that defence issues are seen in this light. As one civil servant put it:

> The Admiralty always begins by asking what is the Navy's role in the defence posture. This is a misguided question. The basic query should be, 'what does the country need for its defence?' If the answer leaves the fleet with nothing to do, that is too bad, but every problem should still be approached in that fashion. Unfortunately, if you ask the wrong questions, you are bound to get the wrong answers.[61]

Perhaps this overstates the case, for as Crowe has shown, the Admiralty did manage to come up with the 'right' answers to many of the problems of the post-war decades, perhaps to a surprising extent. While showing a susceptibility to that inertia which characterises all large organisations, the Admiralty was relatively skilful in foreseeing technological trends, in interpreting the strategic environment, and in translating its recommendations into action.[62] In short, the Admiralty was an effective bureaucratic actor.

While the inclination for the services is to press for autonomy, the responsibility of the politician causes him to press for good advice and the effective implementation of decisions. In this respect the politicians of several countries have been disappointed by the performance of their senior naval officers. From the point of view of politicians, senior naval officers have always tended to appear stubborn. President Roosevelt summed up these troubles in a classic fashion. After complaining of the extreme difficulty of getting the desired actions from the Treasury and State Department, he said that

> the Treasury and the State Department put together are nothing compared with the Na-a-vy – To change anything in the Na-a-vy is like punching a feather bed. You punch it with your right and you punch it with your left until you are finally exhausted, and then you find the damn bed just as it was before you started punching.[63]

Churchill also had his troubles. He had disputes with Fisher in 1915, and he had trouble with the Admiralty between 1939 and 1943. During this later time there was not one Admiral in an important sea command whom Churchill did not attempt to have relieved. In each case this was largely because their appreciation of what needed to be done differed from Churchill's. He resisted Cunningham as First Sea Lord in 1943, telling A. V. Alexander, the First Lord: 'All right – you can have your Cunningham. But I warn you that if the Admiralty does not do as they are told I will bring them all down.'[64] Such civilian-naval problems are not the prerogatives of democracies, nor of states with great navies. In order to keep more securely in control of affairs, Stalin compartmentalised knowledge in World War Two. He would not discuss naval matters with his Defence Minister or Chief of the General Staff.[65] When he took power Khrushchev seems to have been surprised by the Navy's sense of independence. He records how Kuznetsov (the Commander-in-Chief before Gorshkov) felt that it was his responsibility to tell the Party leaders what to do, and for the Party leaders to approve his recommendations without any deliberation. Khrushchev records his feelings with a sense of challenged self-esteem. To have given into Kuznetsov would not have been decision by the government, but would have been a dictate by the Navy. Kuznetsov had no right, Khrushchev pedantically pointed out, to expect the Party leadership just to rubber-stamp his recommendations.[66] More recently, McNamara and Kennedy had trouble with their Navy. The Navy distrusted McNamara's military judgement and resented what they considered to be his intolerance to criticism.[67] The hostility which had been engendered in the Navy contributed to a certain amount of bickering and unresponsiveness in the face of what might be considered to have been a proper political 'meddling' by McNamara in their running of the operations during the Cuban missile crisis.[68] The consequences of this attitude might have been far-reaching. Despite a Presidential order, the Navy resisted the idea of moving the blockade line closer to Cuba. A closer line meant more risks to the ships from Cuban-based aircraft, but it also meant that the Soviet leadership would have more time 'to see, think, and blink'. The blockade line was slow in taking up its appointed position, and Allison alleges that at least one ship went through. As far as tactics were concerned, the Navy wanted to run the blockade — for which it understandably considered that it had unique professional expertise — in its own way. In addition, although the President gave no orders for US warships to attack Soviet submarines, the US Navy enjoyed impressing itself and its adversaries by its skill in forcing Soviet submarines in the area to surface.[69] It should be added, however, that the President had problems in the implementation of his orders from other organisations, and not just the Navy. Together, however, these cautionary illustrations are warnings against the simple image of the Cuban missile crisis as a case-book example of political command and control.

Because of such problems, it is hardly surprising that politicians have sometimes felt a degree of mistrust towards their service chiefs. Needless to say, this has been more than reciprocated by naval officers. The degree of mistrust at any one moment will depend upon many factors, including the personalities of the individuals concerned. The extent to which mistrust can develop is well illustrated by some swingeing comments by British naval officers about their political masters in World War One: 'Damn all these politicians to Hell. It is time we had a N.O. [naval officer] as Dictator!' '. . . with these slippery gentlemen [politicians] you never can tell what their real opinions are.' 'These politicians are all alike, a disgusting breed without real patriotism.' 'O, how I hate and loathe these politicians. Patriotism and the war they don't care about in reality. All they care for is votes and office.'[70] These comments have a very familiar and contemporary ring about them.

The difference of outlook, role and interest between political and military leaders has frequently affected naval policy. 'It is a sad fact of life, often remarked on by commanders-in-chief, that in war one spends a large part of one's time fighting one's own people.'[71] If this comment by Marder is valid for wartime, how much truer must it be in time of peace?

(12) *Inter-service rivalry*

When one thinks of bureaucratic politics there is a tendency to think automatically of inter-service rivalry and disputes. The general assumption about this phenomenon, evident in all political systems, is that it is necessarily undesirable; it results in the dissipation of money and effort. There is some truth in this, but it must also be pointed out that the effects of inter-service rivalry are not always negative. Crowe, for example, has questioned this assumption on the basis of the Royal Navy's experience.[72] He has shown that the Navy's 'rather desperate search for a new and meaningful role' in the mid-1950s resulted in a serious reappraisal which had several beneficial results. The outcome was the Navy's conversion to a limited war philosophy and the subsequent development of an appropriate fleet (the commando carrier, aircraft for troop support, afloat logistic support and so on). This development helped the Navy to survive as an important element in Britain's defence posture, and in Crowe's view this benefited not only the Navy, but also the country. It drew attention to Britain's overseas responsibilities, and how they should be fulfilled. Furthermore, support for Britain's commitment east of Suez grew, so that by the early 1960s it was supported 'by both parties, the public, and by most lay strategists'. While problems do arise as a result of inter-service rivalry, Crowe's examples show that this is not inevitably the case. Service rivalry may facilitate adjustment to changes and improve the quality of policy by injecting into the decision-making process a degree of competition and diversity. It assures that problems are looked at from different perspectives. It promotes fuller discussion and criticism, and it encourages the search for new roles and methods, thus offering the government a wider choice of options.[73] Governments may sometimes feel that they cannot afford inter-service rivalry, but sometimes they might be pleased by what emerges from it.

An organisational process cut

Amongst naval happenings in part or to an important extent explicable in terms of organisational outputs are the following.

(1) *The British Fleet at Jutland: 'There seems to be something wrong with our bloody ships today.'*

With these words at the height of the battle-cruiser phase of the Battle of Jutland, Beatty made a classic comment on the effect which organisational processes can have on naval happenings.[74] In this battle, organisational processes on the whole meant positive effects for the German fleet but negative effects on the British.

A great deal of the British disappointment about the course and outcome of Jutland is explicable in terms of standard operating procedures.[75] The following were some of the most prominent and significant failures: (i) *Poor training.* British gunnery was far from satisfactory. This was in part because battle-cruisers had not carried out practice at realistic speeds. There was a lack of tactical training amongst the destroyers. Jellicoe's staff used the latter for 'a myriad of odd jobs', which seriously limited their opportunities for training. Some did no torpedo or gunnery practice for months at a time. (ii) *Poor communication procedures.* There was a failure by British admirals and captains to make reports of the enemy ('action information'). This was 'a practically universal fault in the British Fleet at that time'.[76] During the night action at Jutland not a single report reached the C-in-C about any of the various important sightings to warn him that the enemy's battle fleet was crossing his stern. Another communication failure arose from mistakes and signalling errors by British ships (most of which could have been learned from earlier wartime engagements). This affected the details of the battle. On a broader scale there was an important lack of communication between the Operations Division in the Admiralty and 'Room 40' (the Admiralty's secret intelligence department). There was no camaraderie or genuine co-operation between the two. 'Operations did not consult Room 40 on, nor even make it aware of, signals which were sent to the C-in-C.'[77] Jellicoe became suspicious of intelligence sent by the Admiralty, and gave more weight to information from the fleet. This lulled the C-in-C into a false sense of security at the outset, and had 'disastrous consequences' at the time of the night action. Furthermore, in many cases the Admiralty was too long in passing messages about enemy positions to the fleet. They were often redundant before they arrived. (iii) *Poor command procedures.* The comment of Vice-Admiral Dewar sums up the feelings of many about the rigidity of British command procedures: 'The greatest opportunity in the history of the British Navy was lost through over-centralisation and lack of initiative.'[78] The three main conceptions dominating the Grand Fleet Battle Orders were: a subordination of the offensive spirit to defensive precautions, especially against the torpedo; the single line, parallel course and long range of the plan of battle; and centralised command. According to Bennett,[79] centuries of experience should have taught that such a plan of battle was seldom decisive, and that 'fighting instructions' must not be regarded as inflexible orders.[80] With his rigid standard operating procedures Jellicoe had 'put all his eggs into one basket', and a conservative and cautious one at that.[81] But as Marder has added, the stakes were high, the dangers of underwater weapons were largely unknown, and there had been no first-hand experience of a major sea-battle for a century.[82] One is not here concerned with attaching blame, merely in demonstrating the significance of SOPs worked out in peacetime on wartime naval actions. (iv) *Poor tactics.* Tactics are a special form of SOP. One important difference between the two fleets concerned their preparedness for night fighting. The German ships were trained and equipped for this contingency. The British were not: they even lacked satisfactory searchlights and starshells, and so were deprived of the opportunity of quickly adapting under duress. During the night action, Jellicoe rejected the idea of fighting while Scheer accepted the risks.[83] (v) *Poor organisational adaptivity.* Many of the British problems at Jutland (poor signalling has already been mentioned) were the result of an important failure to learn lessons from earlier engagements. Unlike their German counterparts, the relevant British organisations were not very adaptive. This was most evident in the failure to overcome design defects. The British did not learn from the *Seydlitz* at Dogger Bank, although they had the additional lesson of the *Kent* at the Falkland Islands. The Admiralty had not appreciated the importance of protecting magazines against cordite flash. This was a tragically costly failure. Some missed opportunities at Jutland resulted from the British shells breaking on impact, instead of piercing and detonating. This was largely the result of procurement procedures: shell design and production were not in the hands of the Navy; the shells were developed on an untested assumption about angle of impact; there were never any realistic trials; and the system for *proving* heavy naval armour-piercing shells was hopelessly chancy, permitting many dud shells to be accepted.[84] It should be recorded that the shell had been under suspicion after the Dogger Bank action It should also be recorded that this so called *proving* system remained in operation until the end of 1944.

To an important, and sometimes terrible extent, our lives are determined by the standard operating procedures of large organisations. When things go well, we have reason to congratulate them. When they go badly, especially in war, the consequences are always costly. The Jutland episode is a fruitful example of the value of making an explicit organisational process cut. But one did not have to be an academic,

writing many years later, to know the impact of organisational
failures on policy. Beatty, at the sharp end of it, summed it up as the
battle closed:

> In the afternoon (1 June 1916) Beatty came into the *Lion's*
> chart-house. Tired and depressed, he sat down on the settee, and
> settling himself in a corner he closed his eyes. Unable to hide his
> disappointment at the result of the battle, he repeated in a weary
> voice, 'There is something wrong with our ships', then opening his
> eyes and looking at the writer, he added, 'And something wrong
> with our system.'[85]

(2) *The organisational pathology of the Royal Navy in World War One*

Many of the weaknesses in the Navy's performance in World War One
resulted from various types of organisational weakness. Marder has
analysed these with insight and understanding in his masterly summary
of the Fisher Era.[86] He writes of the fundamental weaknesses of the
Naval Staff, which seriously hampered the efficient prosecution of the
war. There was a need for and lack of a proper 'thinking division'.[87]
There was overcentralisation and poor intra-staff co-operation; advis-
ory channels were weak and the organisations were not attuned to
learning from the changing environment. The staffing of organisations
was badly done: Marder makes the demoralising and debilitating point
that 'many senior officers had good brains, which they had never
been asked to use.' The system of promotion was not designed to
ensure that the best man for the job was invariably promoted. There
were weaknesses in officer selection procedures; there were square pegs
in round holes, and promotion was often a case of Buggin's turn.
There was an extreme reluctance to move men who had failed, and
little attempt was made to discover the aptitudes of officers and put
them to the best use. In general, officer training was not well adapted
to the problems of the day. There was an overconcentration on
technical matters to the exclusion of strategy and tactics (note
Churchill's famous comment: 'we had more captains of ships than
captains of war.'). Independent thought and 'intellect' in general
were viewed with suspicion. There was blind obedience to, and over-
confidence in, superiors. But even senior officers had little interest in
the higher aspects of war.[88] Equally strongly, Roskill considers 'beyond
doubt' that indifferent staff work was responsible for 'at any rate a

share' of the Gallipoli muddles, for the 'indecisiveness' of Jutland, and still more for the 'false views' propagated by the Admiralty with regard to the adoption of the escort-of-convoy strategy. The schisms produced by Fisher's leadership also took a long time to heal, and 'internal disunity in a fighting service must surely militate against efficient staff work and sound planning.' The war showed many brave individual efforts, but these 'can avail but little when the organization for the strategic direction of war is defective, and the staff work which should visualize, create, and exploit opportunities for decision leaves much to be desired.'[89]

(3)   *The impact of classification procedures*

An organisational procedure such as classification can affect policy in important ways. Two illustrations, one British and one Soviet, will show how such procedures can result in irrational policy.

The British mine barrage between the Orkneys and Scotland in the Second World War, called *Rosengarten* by the Germans, turned out to be an 'expensive folly'.[90] It consumed considerable resources and 'made no discernible difference to the passage of enemy surface ships or U-boats'. It resulted in the loss of ten Allied ships through navigational errors, and only one submarine. Gretton commented,

> The sad part of this story is that we had laid a similar type of mine barrier between Norway and Scotland in 1917-18 with similarly ineffective results. But, due to the misuse of the rules of secrecy, the planners of the second world war minefield were informed only of the claims of success magnified by war propaganda, and the true figures — three U-boat losses only — were kept in the 'top secret' safe. Thus, a decision to lay a second great anti-submarine barrier was taken on wholly inaccurate information.[91]

In his memoirs Khrushchev records a similar if less important example.[92] During his inspection of the staff manoeuvres of the Black Sea Fleet Khrushchev (as ever) intervened and said that the course of the exercise could not go as projected because of the air-to-surface missiles from US aircraft. The planners of the exercise had not taken such missiles into account because they had no knowledge of them. Khrushchev admitted that it was the Presidium's fault: 'All this information must be classified.' This seems to have caused Khrushchev to change the rules about letting commanders know 'both *what we have* and what the enemy has. Otherwise, in the event of war, they'll make crude miscalculations and get into big trouble.'[93] When the Presidium returned to Moscow, Khrushchev records that they 'decided to stop keeping everything secret from our military commanders.' In the light of revelations from the SALT talks, one has reason to doubt that this has gone far.

The dissemination of information is always a difficult problem in the military field. One writer on the subject has drawn attention to the 'disastrously inverted priorities' of security officials, and of their failure to learn from history. His deduction is that the operational rule seems to be 'when in doubt, classify or restrict circulation.' But his own recommendation was that history suggested that a better rule was: 'when in doubt, disseminate.'[94]

(4)   *Pipeline inertia*

The maximum extent of Soviet submarine building in the post-war years could in part be interpreted as the result of pipeline inertia rather than strategic doctrine.[95] The submarine branch has been relatively strong, and it is reasonable to assume that strong branches of the services will tend to overproduce equipment for their primary missions. A different type of inertia affected the different damage control capabilities of British and German dreadnoughts. This was in part because Fisher had refused to allocate naval funds for larger docks. British constructors had therefore to restrict the beam of their dreadnoughts to the width of the docks already available. Tirpitz, on the other hand, had built the docks which he needed to give his dreadnoughts the desired stability.[96]

(5)   *For the want of a nail: organisational factors and the sinking of the Bismarck*

The story of the sinking of the *Bismarck* is full of examples of the way that organisational routines (well or badly done) affected the course of the chase and its outcome. Three illustrations will show different aspects of this: (i) In March 1939, the Admiralty decided to undertake a major reconstruction of the *Hood*, including the fitting of additional horizontal and vertical armour. This was not carried out because of the outbreak of war.[97] The fate of the *Hood* has already been described. (ii) The *Luftwaffe*, having its own priorities and attitudes about what it should be doing, generally carried out sloppy work when detached on naval assignments. A reconnaissance flight failed to notice a changed situation at Scapa Flow at the outset of the episode, which would have basically affected the decisions of Admiral Lutjens.[98] (iii) Most important, and some might consider most mundane, was the question of oiling.[99] The *Bismarck* did not oil in Bergen harbour, although it had used over 1,000 tons since leaving Gotenhaven. This omission gave no margin for error or change of plan. It critically affected ensuing calculations of speed and course. With more fuel, Lutjens would have been able to outdistance some of his attackers, or to have taken a more circuitous route. In the event, the *Bismarck*'s lack of oil 'was the most direct cause of . . . defeat'. This mistake was the result of poor operational procedures, largely resulting from amateurish planning and a lack of experience of ocean warfare. In contrast, the Royal Navy's wartime rules stated that on reaching harbour, oiling took priority over everything else.

(6)   *Round pegs in round holes: the importance of selection procedures*

Everybody who has worked in any sort of organisation knows from experience how important leadership is, and how it can have manifold effects (good and bad) on the outputs of the organisation. Promotion procedures, whether they result in the rise of first-class men or men promoted beyond the level of their competence, have policy implications. It makes a difference if there are men such as Fisher or Forrestal at the top. Davis has identified the importance of the rise of a number of effective senior officers on the evolution of the US Navy.[100] The five volumes of Marder's work are a constant reminder of the importance of personality in the running of ships and shore-establishments, and in the shaping of plans.

Promotion patterns also affect the character of ideas which become accepted at the top, and are ultimately implemented. The development of an amphibious warfare capability by the Royal Navy after 1945 and the growth of the Fleet Air Arm (FAA) were both attributable to promotion patterns, as well as rational ideas. As was traditional, the Navy neglected amphibious warfare once the war was over. The proponents of amphibious warfare 'were continually improving their position', and in 1955 a new First Sea Lord sympathetic to their case assumed office. This change in staffing 'greatly facilitated the build up of an amphibious capability'.[101] World War Two had shown the value of fast mobile carriers, and Korea had shown the importance of the FAA contribution to operations. However, it was only really with a rise to responsible posts by officers who had flown in combat in World War Two that these lessons became more fully accepted by the Navy.

The FAA officers, including flag officers, had an increasingly strong voice in the affairs of the Navy, and they could cite Korea as an impressive precedent to confirm their arguments for a stronger and offensively minded FAA.[102] 'Throughout the mid-1950s the moves toward expanding the Fleet Air Arm's role were not only inspired by aviators, but were shepherded through the Admiralty, including the Board, by aviators.'[103]

(7)   *Co-ordination*

The manner in which the individual services co-ordinate with each other can have a major impact on policy outputs. Co-ordination involves not only the theory of administrative wire-diagrams but the practical enthusiasm which gives it life.

Parochial priorities and perceptions affect co-ordination in important ways. The quite watertight divisions between the services in Britain in the inter-war years are full of instructive examples. The siting of the airfields for the defence of Malaya was a classic case of non-existent co-ordination. Davis gives an equally clear indication of the 'bickering and confusion' between the US Army and Navy: there was mutual 'ignorance and distrust' of the possibilities and limitations of each other's service. The consequences were 'portentous' (e.g. in the expectations each service had of the capabilities of the other in the event of a war with Japan).[104] A similar bickering between the Army and Navy over strategic issues affected the British effort in World War One.[105]

The character of the co-ordination between the services and relevant civilians is also important. The absence of such regular contact delayed the US Navy's adoption of a nuclear capability. The US Navy's commitment to the 'scientific community' came only after World War Two. Previously its relations had been cool, certainly from the scientist's viewpoint. It was because of the Navy's cool attitude to civilian research carried out in the Office of Scientific Research and Development that led the latter's director, Dr Bush, to decide to assign the atomic bomb project to an Army agency rather than the Navy.[106]

(8)   *Tactics*

Fighting instructions are a basic standard operating procedure which have a direct influence on actions in war. Roskill has been particularly critical of the rigidity in battle which resulted from the Royal Navy's tactics up to and during World War One.[107] In lower-level maritime confrontations the rules of engagement are equally significant, as Hill has recently stressed.[108] Furthermore, McNamara's concern during the Cuban missile crisis that the standard operating procedures for blockade were all in order was one of the things which riled Admiral Anderson, the Chief of Naval Operations. One version describes that when Anderson waved the Manual of Navy Regulations in McNamara's face, shouting, 'It's all in there,' McNamara replied, 'I don't give a damn what John Paul Jones would have done; I want to know what you are going to do, now.'[109]

(9)   *The slow modernisation of Royal Navy weaponry*

The procurement of the optimum weaponry is right at the heart of a successful Navy's development. It is a business which is very much dominated by organisational routines, standard operating procedures, and parochial perceptions.

In his ever bombastic style, Divine in *The Blunted Sword* wrote a strong criticism of Admiralty procurement policy. He summed up the procurement consequences of both the organisation and outlook of the Admiralty in the following way:

> of the twenty major technological developments which lie between the first marine engine and the Polaris submarine, the Admiralty has discouraged, delayed, obstructed, or positively rejected seventeen. The eventual and necessary incorporation of these developments in the structure of modernization has been achieved by individual and sometimes undisciplined officers, by political and industrial pressures, or – and most frequently – by their successful adoption in rival navies.[110]

Divine's book is a general criticism of Britain's procurement policy. He asserts that the services have resisted change, and, by fighting off the future, have failed in one of their primary tasks, that of producing the best ships and other weapons to meet the challenges that arise. He argues that the defects have lain mainly in the constitution and procedures of the existing ministries (and especially their over-centralisation).

Similar criticisms of the Admiralty's opposition to reform have been made by other writers. Marder has discussed it before World War One,[111] and Roskill has endorsed the same criticism for the period before World War Two.[112] On the other hand, Crowe's study has shown that the post-1945 Navy generally overcame traditionalism and did as much as the country could have expected within its budgetary constraints.

A synthesis

The selection of episodes in the preceding two sections illustrates that important naval happenings can derive their primary cause not from the pursuing of what is sometimes thought of as an objective national interest, or of the rational selection of strategic choices, but from causes that lie in the many manifestations of organisational life. It is for this reason that an explicit conceptual net is desirable. The possession of such an instrument encourages the student to fish in places and in ways which he might otherwise ignore. However, it would be wrong to assume that these various nets are exclusive, or that there is no meaning to the idea of rational policy. A final illustration, synthesising the various approaches, will demonstrate the way the various nets combine to pull in a fuller explanation. The episode chosen is the demise of the British aircraft carrier in the mid-1960s.

In looking at the demise of the carrier on rational policy grounds, one would look at the tasks Britain had to perform in the declining years of its east of Suez posture, and use cost-benefit analysis to choose between land-based and sea-borne airpower. The Royal Navy stressed the uniqueness of the contribution of sea-borne aircraft, and argued that large carriers were not so expensive once the initial capital costs had been met. The RAF, on the other hand, stressed the relative cheapness of the land-based alternative, and the adequacy with which they could perform the necessary tasks. There were slight differences of emphasis, but in terms of rational policy this was very much a case of 'where you stand depends upon where you sit.'

From the bureaucratic perspective, it should go without saying that both the RAF and the Navy believed (or certainly persuaded themselves to believe) that they could do the job better than their competitor. They could both feel that the mission concerned was an essential part of their essence. Added spice was given to the debate because of Britain's weakening economic situation, and the consequent pressures on defence spending. Naturally the two services were keen for the mission in order to maintain their size and viability, and thus maintain the morale and prospects which go with being a thriving as opposed to a decaying organisation. Self-interest played a part, but how many human actions are free of this? Who could question their integrity when they argued (which they implicitly did) that 'what is good for my service is good for my country'? As it happened, the RAF in this debate seemed to have more prestige and tended to have more supporters in

Whitehall. Furthermore, they based their argument on cost, and this appealed to a Labour government which in the late 1960s was very economy-conscious and was also temperamentally inclined towards defence cuts. It can be argued that the government chose the RAF's advice not because it was necessarily the best *military* advice, but because the RAF had more political power than the Royal Navy and because the RAF's solution seemed to promise more financial savings. Of course, the public justification for the choice had to be based on the idea that land-based aircraft were best for the job.

What of the final cut, that of organisational processes? These considerations were by no means unimportant, although they never figured in the public debate at the time. Information is scanty, but three considerations might be relevant. Firstly, the RAF has been renowned for the amount and quality of effort put into matters of public relations. As an 'image-conscious' organisation, it would not be surprising if its promotion procedures encouraged the rise of officers who were not only well versed in such matters, but were themselves of a political rather than operational bent. The undermanned Royal Navy, having to keep its ships going in peace as well as war, continued to place a traditional emphasis on the sea-dog type. One might suppose that in Whitehall battles, the more politically conscious service would have the advantage. Secondly, the all-graduate entry system into the RAF (unlike the Navy, which had relatively few graduates) ensured a more 'civilian' influence in the officer corps. This in turn might have helped create an atmosphere in which politicians and bureaucrats felt that they 'spoke the same language' as the RAF. Thirdly, it appears that officer education in the two services placed different emphasis on paperwork. This is not a matter to be overlooked, for as one writer has put it: 'Armies move on their stomachs: governments on their memoranda.'[113] The art of the memorandum may often be a key tactic in bureaucratic manoeuvrings, and it seems to be a fact that the Royal Navy has traditionally failed to excel at paperwork. On the other hand, there is a general impression that the RAF does excel in this area. Many years ago a famous naval officer summed up his service's inadequacies in this respect as follows:

No encouragement has been given to officers to commit their thoughts to paper. On the contrary, every discouragement to the discussion of problems of the naval Service has been imposed, partly by Regulations, partly by consequences. This has had the direct effect of stifling thought and the power of discussion.

> Unaccustomed to reason or to write, uninstructed in the
> principles of naval war and policy, naval officers of high standing
> not infrequently find themselves in difficulty when they reach
> the responsible offices in administration in which they have to
> explain the reasons for the views they hold.[114]

No doubt the situation has improved somewhat since those words
were written. *How much* is another matter.

The conclusions which might be drawn from this brief synthesis
of interpretations are two-fold: firstly, the decision to end the carriers
was not necessarily based on what was in Britain's best *military*
interest (though there is never any way of knowing this, short of war
itself); and secondly, the decision is best explained by the determination of the RAF to have the dominant role in the projection of air
power east of Suez, by its being better organised and more powerful
in the bureaucratic game than its rival, and because the RAF's proposals
conformed with the Labour government's immediate domestic
priorities and developing foreign policy perspectives.

Naval organisation man

Naval studies have often been lacking in comprehensive modes of
analysis. Like poor clothes which 'fit where they touch' (covering but
not embellishing what lies beneath), history without a rich theory
fits reality only where the documents allow it to touch. This often
means that there is a tendency to overlook other explanations, such as
considerations arising out of 'organisational essence' or standard
operating procedures. Many books seem to present such episodes as
aberrations, as if the norm was a perfect correspondence between
theory and practice. It is as if the norm was that decisions were made
by *Naval Man*, who had a coherent set of objectives in the naval field
which were calculated to maximise national interests, and that the
implementation of these best-laid plans would then be unaffected
by the frictions of life in organisations. *Naval Man* does not exist:
there is only a bundle of organisations, although obviously the
character of bureaucratic politics or the suitability of organisational
processes at any one point will be affected by the qualities of the
individuals making up those organisations. But this rider does not
detract from the main point. Organisational opportunities and
frictions are not aberrations. They are an inescapable part of life.

The student of contemporary naval affairs faces a difficult task in
trying to understand the particular organisation in which he is

interested. It is probably necessary, as Davis has suggested, to 'go native' in the course of such research. This is not likely to be easy. But he and Crowe in particular have shown what can be achieved in this field. Unfortunately, perhaps the only country where much progress is possible is the United States, though MccGwire's interpretation of the Gorshkov series shows what can be done with informed speculation and systematic analysis even about a closed society. But it is difficult to imagine that *The Admiral's Lobby* could have been written about the Royal Navy. In general, the British services have been more careful (and touchy?) about academic intrusion into their inner workings. (Or is it that British academics are less dynamic than their US counterparts?) In the absence of easily available data, it might be worthwhile for the services themselves, as well as onlookers, to encourage retiring officers to write more; if a flood of full memoirs would be too much, at least vignettes in naval journals on aspects on their careers would be useful. In particular, much of benefit might emerge in terms of folk wisdom about the running of various types of units, ashore and at sea. It would mean that valuable experience would not be lost, and it would add immeasurably to our knowledge of naval organisational man.

With more methodological self-consciousness and the investment of more intellectual effort, richer studies of past and present naval policy should surely come. Further development needs a more fruitful interchange between academics and professionals, in order to shape research strategies, discover more information, and work towards developing further insights into the organisational and bureaucratic aspects of naval policy. Through the development and application of more theoretical approaches, naval analysis might move on to a new stage of development. It might at last leave the adolescence of the 'classical school' to a post-Mahanite sophistication, characterised by methodological self-consciousness, systematic analysis, academic respectability and professional relevance.

Notes

1.   For the background to the song, and other aspects of *HMS Pinafore* satirising the contemporary navy, see Leslie Bailey, *The Gilbert & Sullivan Book* (London: Cassell, 1956), pp. 151-68.
2.   Arthur J. Marder, *From the Dreadnought to Scapa Flow*, Vol. 2 (London: Oxford University Press, 1965), p. 302.
3.   Ibid., Vol. 4, pp. 53, 176, 213.

4. W. J. Crowe, *The Policy Roots of the Modern Royal Navy, 1946-1963,* Princeton University Ph.D., 1965 (University Microfilms, Inc., Ann Arbor, Michigan, 1970), p. 353.

5. C. Northcote Parkinson, *Parkinson's Law or the pursuit of progress* (London: Murray, 1958).

6. His naval related books include: *Edward Pellew, Viscount Exmouth, Admiral of the Red* (London: Methuen, 1934); *Portsmouth Point: the Navy in fiction, 1793-1815* (London: Hodder and Stoughton, 1948); *Life and Times of Horatio Hornblower* (London: Michael Joseph, 1970).

7. The preceding paragraph is based on Graham T. Allison's models of the decision-making process. His contribution to this area of the subject has been of major importance. See his 'Conceptual Models and the Cuban Missile Crisis', *APSR*, 63, No. 3, September 1969, pp. 689-718 and *Essence of Decision: Explaining the Cuban Missile Crisis* (Boston: Little, Brown, 1971). See also Morton H. Halperin, *Bureaucratic Politics and Foreign Policy* (Washington, D.C.: The Brookings Institution, 1974).

8. Quoted by G. S. Graham, *The Politics of Naval Supremacy* (Cambridge: Cambridge University Press, 1965), p. vii.

9. James A. Barry, 'Institutional Factors in Soviet Naval Policy', Paper prepared for the Third Annual Seminar on Soviet Naval Developments, Dalhousie University, 8-11 September 1974, p. 41; John Erickson, 'Soviet Defence Policies and Naval Interests', Chapter 4 in Michael MccGwire, Ken Booth and John McDonnell, *Soviet Naval Policy. Objectives and Constraints* (New York: Praeger, 1975).

10. These are Barry's conclusions, ibid., pp. 40-1.

11. This check-list of factors is based on some of the chapter headings and subsections of Halperin, op. cit.

12. Ibid., p. 28.

13. Ibid., p. 32.

14. Alain C. Enthoven and K. Wayne Smith, *How Much is Enough? Shaping the Defense Program, 1961-1969* (New York: Harper and Row, 1971), pp. 16-17, quoted by Halperin, p. 34.

15. See Marder, *From the Dreadnought to Scapa Flow*, Vol. 4, pp. 125-6 and Chapter IV; Vol. 5, Chapter IV.

16. Ibid., Vol. 5, p. 305.

17. Ibid.

18. Ibid., p. 103.

19. Ibid., Vol. 4, p. 128. The Navy was not alone in its misconception of what navies should do. Its blockade and convoy tactics were later criticised by the press for being 'defensive' and 'passive'. Ibid., pp. 323-4.

20. Ibid., Vol. 1, p. 413.

21. Ibid., Vol. 5, p. 4.

22. Allison, *APSR*, p. 699.

23. Dwight Waldo, *Perspectives on Administration*, p. 49, quoted by W. J. M. Mackenzie, *Politics and Social Science* (Harmondsworth: Penguin Books, 1971), p. 244.

24. Ibid., p. 246.

25. Even varieties of trade union activity exist within the armed forces of a few countries.

26. This summary is based on Harvey Starr, 'Organisation Process as an Influence on National Security Policy', *International Relations*, Vol. IV (2), November 1972, pp. 176-86.

27. Compare Presidents Kennedy and Johnson in this respect. See the comments of Bernard Brodie, *War and Politics* (London: Cassell, 1973),

Ch. 5.

28.   Allison, *Essence of Decision*, p. 4.
29.   Ibid., p. 272. Joseph Frankel has suggested its relevance for a study of Britain and the EEC in his *Contemporary International Theory and the Behaviour of States* (London: Oxford University Press, 1973), p. 111.
30.   Allison, *Essence of Decision*, p. 245.
31.   Ibid., pp. 258-9.
32.   Ibid., p. 245.
33.   Ibid., p. 259.
34.   Ibid., p. 265.
35.   Ibid., pp. 7-9.
36.   Geoffrey Bennett, *The Battle of Jutland* (London: Batsford, 1964), p. 35.
37.   Paul Y. Hammond, 'Super Carriers and B-36 Bombers: Appropriations, Strategy and Politics', pp. 465-568 in Harold Stein (ed.), *American Civil-Military Decisions. A Book of Case Studies* (Birmingham: University of Alabama Press, 1963).
38.   Vincent Davis, *The Admirals' Lobby* (Chapel Hill: University of North Carolina Press, 1967), pp. 185-6.
39.   Ibid., pp. 78-9.
40.   Ibid., p. 79.
41.   For three important assessments, see *Admiral Gorshkov on 'Navies in War and Peace'*, (CNA, CRC 257, September 1974).
42.   See, for example, John Erickson, 'Soviet Defence Policies and Naval Interests', Chapter 4 in MccGwire, Booth and McDonnell, op. cit.
43.   Davis, op. cit., p. 191.
44.   Ibid., p. 211.
45.   Ann L. Hollick and Robert E. Osgood, *New Era of Ocean Politics* (Baltimore: The Johns Hopkins University Press, 1974), p. 7.
46.   Ibid., p. vii.
47.   Morton H. Halperin and Arnold Kanter (eds.), *Readings in American Forei Foreign Policy: A Bureaucratic Perspective* (Boston: Little, Brown, 1973), p. 29. See Kissinger's comments, p. 88.
48.   Vincent Davis, 'The Development of a Capability to Deliver Nuclear Weapons by Carrier-Based Aircraft', reprinted and abridged from his *The Politics of Innovation: Patterns in Navy Cases*, (Monograph No. 3, Monograph Series in World Affairs, Denver: The University of Denver, 1971); Halperin and Kanter, op. cit., pp. 262-75.
49.   Ibid., p. 274.
50.   See the editor's comments, ibid., pp. 261-2.
51.   Davis, op. cit., p. 135.
52.   Sir Lesie Chasemore Hollis, *One Marine's Tale* (London: Andre Deutsch, 1956), p. 3.
53.   See, for example, Captain S. W. Roskill, *Naval Policy Between the Wars* (London: Collins, 1968), p. 140.
54.   See, for example, Crowe, op. cit., p. 331.
55.   Marder, *From the Dreadnought to Scapa Flow*, Vol. 1, pp. 79, 83-4, 87.
56.   Ibid., Vol. 4, p. 174.
57.   Strobe Talbott (translator and editor), *Khrushchev Remembers. The Last Testament* (London: Andre Deutsch, 1974), p. 30.
58.   See note 41: MccGwire's comments, pp. 21-70.
59.   Quoted by Marder, *From the Dreadnought to Scapa Flow*, Vol. 1, p. 84.
60.   This paragraph is based on Halperin, op. cit., pp. 51-4.
61.   Quoted by Crowe, op. cit., p. 324.
62.   Ibid., Chapter VIII.

63. Marriner Eccles, *Beckoning Frontiers* (New York, 1951) p. 336. Quoted by Allison, *APSR*, p. 702.

64. S. W. Roskill, 'Marder, Churchill and the Admiralty 1939-42', *RUSIJ*, December 1972, pp. 50, 53.

65. Ronald Hingley, *Joseph Stalin: man and legend* (London: Hutchinson, 1974), p. 329.

66. Talbott, op. cit., pp. 25-6.

67. Davis, op. cit., pp. 236-7.

68. Allison, *APSR*, p. 707.

69. Halperin, op. cit., p. 280.

70. They were made, respectively, by Wemyss, Wemyss, Beatty and Admiral Sir Stanley Colville (C-in-C, Portsmouth). Quoted by Marder, *From the Dreadnought to Scapa Flow*, Vol. 5, p. 341.

71. Ibid., p. 341.

72. Crowe, op. cit., pp. 324-31.

73. Ibid., pp. 328-9. Inter-service rivalry played a critical role in the development of the Polaris programme in the United States in the second half of the 1950s. Amongst other things, the determination of the Navy leaders to get the system operational before the Air Force's *Thor* caused them deliberately to reduce the strike power of Polaris in terms of range and accuracy. See Richard G. Hewlett and Francis Duncan, *Nuclear Navy* (Chicago: Chicago University Press, 1974), pp. 307-15.

74. Quoted by Marder, *From the Dreadnought to Scapa Flow*, Vol. 3, p. 60.

75. These comments are largely based on the evaluations of Bennett, op. cit., and Marder, ibid.

76. Marder, ibid., p. 159.

77. Ibid., p. 42.

78. Ibid., p. 165.

79. Bennett, op. cit., p. 168.

80. Compare the comments after the Dogger Bank action in 1915, ibid., p. 46.

81. Marder, *From the Dreadnought to Scapa Flow*, Vol. 3, p. 32.

82. Ibid.

83. Ibid., Chapter IV; Bennett, op. cit., Chapter 5.

84. Marder, *From the Dreadnought to Scapa Flow*, Vol. 3, pp. 169-71.

85. From W. S. Chalmers, *The Life and Letters of David Beatty*, quoted by Marder, ibid., p. 165.

86. Marder, *From the Dreadnought to Scapa Flow*, Vol. 5, pp. 313-30.

87. Ibid., Vol. 4, pp. 180, 195. Roskill agrees, op. cit., pp. 139-40.

88. On pre-war attitudes see Marder, *From the Dreadnought to Scapa Flow*, Vol. 1, pp. 28-31, 402-6, 412.

89. Roskill, op. cit., pp. 103-4.

90. Vice-Admiral Sir Peter Gretton, *Maritime Strategy: A Study of British Defence Problems* (London: Cassell, 1965), p. 118.

91. Ibid., pp. 118-19.

92. Talbott, op. cit., pp. 28-9.

93. My italics.

94. Harry Howe Ransom, *Strategic Intelligence* (Morristown, N.J.: General Learning Corporation, 1973), p. 11.

95. Martin, op. cit., p. 96.

96. Bennett, op. cit., pp. 156-8.

97. Ludovic Kennedy, *Pursuit: the chase and sinking of the Bismarck* (London: Collins, 1974), p. 231.

98. Ibid., p. 51.

99. Ibid., *passim.*

100. Davis, op. cit., pp. 43-4, 276.
101. Crowe, op. cit., pp. 389-90. Note also the importance of Admiral Rickover, demonstrating 'the effectiveness of a highly personalized approach to technological innovation' in Hewlett and Duncan, op. cit., p. 341.
102. Ibid., pp. 128-31.
103. Ibid., p. 389.
104. Davis, op. cit., pp. 132-3.
105. Roskill, *The Strategy of Sea Power*, p. 140.
106. Letters from Dr Bush, quoted by Davis, op. cit., pp. 174-5.
107. Roskill, op. cit., pp. 46-7, 80-1, 108-9, 246-8.
108. Hill, op. cit., p. 31.
109. Elie Abel, *The Missiles of October: Twelve Days to World War Three* (London: Macgibbon and Kee, 1969), p. 109.
110. David Divine, *The Blunted Sword* (London: Hutchinson, 1964), p. 19.
111. Marder, *From the Dreadnought to Scapa Flow*, Vol. 1, p. 78; Vol. 2, pp. 70, 77-81; Vol. 4, pp. 23-4, 331; Vol. 5, pp. 308-13.
112. Roskill, op. cit., pp. 103-4.
113. Joseph Porter Clark Jnr., 'The Art of the Memorandum', reprinted from *The Washington Monthly*, 1, 2 (March 1969), in Halperin and Kanter, op. cit., pp. 236-9. This is an amusing and insightful essay.
114. Sir Herbert Richmond to Lord Haldane, 15 February 1919, quoted by Marder, *From the Dreadnought to Scapa Flow*, Vol. 5, p. 319.

PART TWO: NAVAL POLICY:
THE PERMANENTLY OPERATING FACTORS

7 NAVAL CAPABILITIES

In order to comprehend the interrelationships between navies and the making and execution of foreign policy, it is necessary to understand a wide range of variables. These have been grouped under three headings. In this chapter the focus is *naval capabilities*, that is the technical, physical, doctrinal and human variables related to the potential or actual operational performance of the units of naval power. In the following chapter the focus is on the *domestic sources* of policy, that is the internal variables which affect the general size, effort and character of a country's military policy in general and naval effort in particular. Finally, in Chapter Nine, the subject is the *international context*, that is the variables in the external arena which affect the roles and usability of warships in the support of foreign policy.

Appreciations of the potential or actual performance of naval units, whether they be implicit or explicit, underlie much of the debate about naval policy. Indeed many commentators regard capabilities as the only reliable key to the strategist's dilemma. It is frequently asserted that a nation's *intentions* 'can change overnight with changing circumstances': it is therefore argued that it is more prudent to base one's own policies on the 'capabilities given to countries to threaten to pursue or pursue courses of action'.[1] But what, precisely, are naval *capabilities*? What is involved in assessing them? Reference books such as *Jane's Fighting Ships* and a number of others[2] provide full national inventories of ships and weapons, but is that enough? What do such inventories reveal about the naval 'balance', or imbalance? What do they reveal about the missions for which ships have presumably been built? Clearly, understanding capabilities must go much deeper than looking at inventories, however well researched and conceived. What starts as a relatively (but not very) straightforward numbers game, develops into the problem of shuffling various human, material and geographical factors in dynamic situations. By the end it merges into the broadest and most elusive questions of national policy.

The numbers game

Counting chunks of hardware is the first task. Although there is a great

167

deal of basic quantitative information at hand, the literature is surprisingly unhelpful in assisting its non-specialised readers to understand hardware in a dynamic rather than a static sense. There are plenty of sources to provide more or less accurate raw data about the numbers, types and armament of ships; this is useful, but it does not go far enough. How is the non-specialist to begin to assess it all? Raw numbers themselves are not much of a guide. This comment has been made by many naval spokesmen in a variety of countries.[3] What, for example, is a reader to make of an assertion that the Soviet squadron in the Mediterranean can 'outgun' its NATO counterpart? What should he know about in order to make a reasonable appreciation of such an assertion? Certainly a simple list of numbers of ships and types of weapons is not enough. We have all seen too many Westerns to know that there is much more to a shoot-out than the number and type of the opponents' guns.

Those wanting enlightenment on contemporary comparative naval forces face a most difficult problem, and one which is probably getting more rather than less complicated.[4] But even readers of naval history will often find themselves disappointed. Although the problem of comparative capabilities is always present, it is usually dismissed rather summarily, either because it is not thought very important, because 'laymen' are not likely to understand it or find it interesting, or because skimming over it is the lazy way out. None of these comments imply that the writers guilty of over-simplification do not have precise knowledge; rather it is an expression of surprise that they choose not to deploy it, especially as so much usually hinges on the various aspects of the numbers game. Marder's work is an exception, with his thorough comparisons of men and material on the eve of great events.[5] In contrast, Roskill's comparison of the British and German navies at the outbreak of World War One is abrupt to the point of meaninglessness. He was merely satisfied to say that one of the 'solid advantages' of the Royal Navy was its 'superior numerical strength', though he added that this was to a 'considerable extent offset' by its world-wide responsibility for commerce protection.[6] But how much is a 'considerable extent'? This is the crux of the question − or might have been. Furthermore, in the example quoted, the writer had earlier discussed the effects of tactics, technology and training on Britain's readiness for war. This is useful analytical material, but without any comparison with the enemy, its usefulness is restricted. Similarly, Roskill's one-volume history of the Second World War provides a minimum of scene-setting.[7] Elsewhere, however, Roskill's work is more helpful in this respect. His first volume of the Official History of the Second World War provides a comprehensive picture of the naval situation on the eve of war.[8] In contrast, the introduction to Morison's 'semi-official' histories of US naval operations in World War Two slip over the question of comparative capabilities. This is frustrating for any reader who wants to be fully in the picture. The introductory chapter on the US Navy between the wars has tables with the tonnage of completed ships down to the last thousand ton, but there is no detailed expert analysis of these figures, except the comment:

> Since we had to fight in the Atlantic as well as in the Pacific, and because of our great inferiority in overseas bases, the Japanese Navy was then substantially superior to ours for operations in the central and Western Pacific Oceans.[9]

Again, what is 'substantially superior'? This is what we want to know. The concerned reader wants to feel the pressures felt by the political leaders and naval commanders.

At least these distinguished sources are not misleading: they are only incomplete. Some commentators today present numbers which, by accident or design, are very misleading to those who have had little or no contact with naval analysis. Tables are sometimes shown in the press purporting to compare Soviet and Western naval 'strengths'. They will typically consist of simple lists of numbers of submarines. Rarely, if ever, is there anything about deployment patterns, type and function, operational availability and relative capabilities in the fullest sense (that is, against the units which they would have to face in war). The reader is presumably expected simply to draw the conclusion that the extent of the submarine 'threat' is in 'direct proportion to the excess of Soviet submarines over NATO submarines'.[10] Such fallacious arguments continue to be put forward.

Appreciating comparative naval capabilities is a difficult activity. Unfortunately, the literature gives relatively little guidance to non-specialists on how to turn cold numbers into hot reality.

The order-of-battle

The initial object of the numbers game is to draw up an order-of-battle (OOB).[11] On the basis of the raw numbers in the analyst's possession, he then works out an OOB in the light of such factors as deployment patterns, operational availability, types, missions, time on station and so on. While warships are the primary interest, the potential military role of some merchant ships should not be ignored. For most observers, acceptably accurate numbers are available from a number of sources, such as *Jane's Fighting Ships* or even the more basic IISS *Military Balance*. What is less easily available, though, is any detailed discussion of matters such as transit times, and other factors affecting deployment cycles (e.g. submarine habitability). Few analysts present their readers with a detailed OOB, and some indication of how it was arrived at. MccGwire was probably the only analyst in the early part of the Soviet naval debate who presented his readers with anything comprehensive and coherent in this respect. Interestingly, his original critique of establishment interpretations of Soviet naval policy seems to have resulted in the latter improving somewhat the level of its presentation. In addition, one has noted a development in newspaper articles, from the generalisations and traditional clichés of 1967-8 to the rather more professional approach of recent years.

Critical maritime operations

Having drawn up an OOB it is then necessary to examine the critical maritime operations. This is a very difficult task even for the most directly involved professionals. It involves assessments of the weapons balance, performance characteristics, tactics, likely effectiveness and so on. Because of the sensitivity of intelligence about such matters it will not be possible for the outsider to go very far: classified information and expert interpretation dominate this area of the subject. However, if the outsider is to have any feel for naval matters it is both necessary (and possible) to acquire some basic principles concerning the critical maritime operations. The most up-to-date intelligence will always be unobtainable, but that is rarely a disqualification for sensible comment.

While tactics are obviously a sensitive subject, one knows enough in theory and from historical examples to be aware of the decisive impact which they can have on naval engagements between opponents whose size and performance characteristics may differ widely. Knowledge of tactics will help observers to assess with at least a little perspective some of the unqualified propositions made about such matters as the tracking of submarines and the vulnerability of ships to missiles. A comprehensive picture of critical maritime operations at sea should be part of the knowledge of the 'interested public' in this field; it is not easy to come by, though there are a handful of basic introductions.[12] Only a close reading of the professional literature over a long period can fill in details and give an impression of developing trends.

A weapons inventory is static. Furthermore, an understanding of the critical maritime operations will underline the point that ship-to-ship comparisons are less valid.[13] As time has passed, a growing variety of instruments, based under and above the surface of the sea, as well as on it, and also projected from the land, have had to be taken into consideration in the preparation and execution of a war at sea, whatever its level.

While assembling knowledge on these matters may not provide outsiders with answers to the great naval questions of the day, it should help them to speculate more fruitfully and to confront insiders with more perceptive questions. Knowledge of the principles of critical maritime operations, however, is only a starting point in the task of making dynamic appreciations of a naval balance. Many qualitative human factors have to be taken into consideration, as well as many specific contextual factors. Matters such as which side has the initiative and details of local prepositioning might be critical in war. Furthermore, relative tactical abilities have to be weighed into the account, although this is obviously a highly classified area. How much of the curtain can be safely lifted is a difficult question, but what are outsiders to make of a statement concerning 'outgunning' without reference to tactics and the relevant contextual factors? When navalists assert that their ships can be 'outgunned', the import of their message is that they need better if not bigger, and certainly more ships. But 'outgunning', as measured in crude static terms, can be overcome by better training, better vigilance, and better tactics.

It is understandable why discussions about naval balances focus on the readily quantifiable aspects. Furthermore, the prudent assumption is always that Neptune is on the side of the big battleships. But the many qualitative factors in a naval balance cannot be left out of account, although the complexity of these issues is such that it has become increasingly difficult to settle which are the 'big battalions' in modern naval warfare. For one thing, so many of the determinants of *performance* are hidden. What can outsiders (or insiders) know about relative capabilities in sonar, electronics and the other hidden features which make modern warships what they are? All these difficulties have been reflected in the prolonged debate about the 'balance' or 'imbalance' (which way?) between the Sixth Fleet and the Soviet *eskadra* in the Mediterranean, or the many viewpoints concerning the 'balance' or 'imbalance' (which way?) between submarine and anti-submarine systems.

Two further comments are necessary when considering relative effectiveness in the critical maritime operations. Firstly, the maritime confrontation between the chief naval powers has changed its character. Straight comparisons of the main battle fleets for decisive wartime engagements are no longer as politically meaningful as in previous eras, since major war would now represent a catastrophic breakdown of all political effort. In assessments of the naval balance, 'the showdown' is not as meaningful as hitherto, although it remains the chief determinant in the design of major warships. The answer to the question 'capability for what?' is not as clear as formerly, when phrases such as 'another Trafalgar' or 'the destruction of enemy commerce' were perfectly adequate. Today, warships are more. than ever concerned with deterring the ultimate showdown and with manipulation short of war. But if the showdown is to be avoided at almost all costs, then the traditional yardstick must steadily lose its meaning. But by what other standard is 'the balance' to be measured? Secondly, the problem of assessing a naval balance is not simplified if attention is focused on specific scenarios. Many unpredictable circumstances and factors can arise in the course of an engagement — weather or a failure of nerve — as well as 'real time learning', that is the relative adaptability of the combatants to the new and invariably surprising realities of conflict. As with all scenarios, there is a danger that an advocate of a certain course is apt to postulate the scenario which most aptly supports his position, 'disregarding the fact that his scenario will constitute but one of several hundred combinations of opposing forces, tactics and experimental conditions'.[14] Despite all the problems, appreciations of relative capabilities for local engagements or localised campaigns must be made: this leads on to one of the chief contextual factors, namely geographical considerations in naval operations.

Geographical factors

Theodore Ropp has described geography as 'the bones of strategy'.[15] Naval strategy, and the capabilities mobilised in support of it, are incomprehensible without close attention to maps and other revealers of geographical factors. The numbers game cannot be properly played without its appropriate map board: 'what is deployed where?' is a first important question.

A country's maritime policy will be affected by the nature of its geographical characteristics in several ways. Geography will affect such matters as whether its fleets have to be separated, whether and where it has good harbours, its location relative to important narrow waters, its location in relation to its potential allies and enemies, its distance from its responsibilities and the configuration of the land and the seas in between. The geography under the surface of the sea is ⋅ essential knowledge for submariners and their opponents: in this respect the growing importance of oceanography has been reflected in the attention invested in it by the world's major maritime countries.

Distance is a fundamental consideration in all strategy. It has political implications, and it also has operational importance in terms of transit times, time-on-station, and logistic constraints. These factors are often skimmed over. The Soviet threat to the Cape route, for example, is often asserted without any reference to the resupply problems which Soviet units would face in any sustained campaign against Western shipping in that distant area. Obviously, these constraints would be less significant if the campaign were one of individual submarine terrorism against occasional targets; a more systematic campaign would certainly involve the need for the replenishment of ammunition, change of crew and so on. Inverting a map, so that Murmansk is at the bottom and Cape Town at the top, gives one a better impression of how the problem of the interdiction of the Cape Route might appear from the perspective of Moscow. It shows the physical constraints, and it also suggests that if Soviet leaders believed that it was in their interests to disrupt the flow of Western oil, then the most rational action would neither be in the vicinity of the Cape nor involve the sinking of supertankers. It would be a disruption at source. As well as imposing constraints on objectives, operating at a distance also increases the significance of the number of warships. This was evident in the British support of the Beira patrol,[16] and in the Soviet proposal in the SALT II negotiations that the longer transit-times for their SSBNs (when compared with their forward-based US equivalents) justified a claim for twice the number, in order to keep the same number on station. Distance also affects strategy and tactics. While quicker communications have effectively reduced the immensity of the sea, its sheer size is still a factor of considerable significance. In particular, the alarmists who warn us of the imminence of the detection of nuclear submarines seem to pay no attention to the freedom of SSBNs offered by a combination of clever tactics and the watery character of two-thirds of the earth's surface, more than half of which is deeper than 10,000 feet.

The significance of geographical factors can be vividly illustrated by an examination of British naval history. The relative advantages of Britain in its wars against Holland, France and Germany are well known: as Fisher put it, 'Providence has arranged England as a sort of huge breakwater.'[17] Britain's location also bestowed it with advantages for the air war over the sea in World War Two.[18] But geography bestows disadvantages as well as advantages, as Japan found in World War Two.[19] These disadvantages remain today. Japan's future as an industrial power depends upon maritime transport, and a significant part of this (nearly 90 per cent of its oil is from the Gulf) passes through the Indonesian archipelago. Potentially, therefore, Indonesia has a hand on Japan's lifeline.[20] The impact of geographical factors on the Soviet Navy, historically and today, is well known, although the daily headache which this causes Soviet naval planners is perhaps not sufficiently felt by Western commentators. Geography means that Soviet SSBN operations have to strain if they seek to maintain a parity in readiness with their forward-based US counterparts. More significantly, naval geography means that the country needs four widely separated fleets, and contact between them is hindered by the vastness of the distances and problems of climate. The exits of three of the Soviet fleet areas are controlled by potentially hostile states, while even the Northern Fleet access zone is vulnerable to interdiction, certainly for surface units. The lack of 'waterfront real estate' is disadvantageous as far as Soviet ASW operations are concerned.

Geographical factors are both obvious and crucial to the naval practitioner: they affect his basic calculations of time, space and available force. For the archetypal armchair strategist, be he academic (in the pejorative sense) or politician, these constraining facts of life are too easily relegated to the sidelines. It is well to remember the World War One jingle which went: 'Big fingers, little maps, means lots of deaths for the chaps.'

Logistics

The author of the just-quoted jingle knew that geographical factors, and specifically distance, greatly affected logistical possibilities. Non-practitioners tend not to notice this less glamorous aspect of military operations, though it is a vital underpinner of a navy's strategy. In considering any navy, but especially one with a 'blue water' strategy, the problem of logistics — primarily maintenance and replenishment — is of major importance. Whether it is a navy in forward deployment in peacetime, or fighting in a war, the 'fleet train' is a critical constraining and/or permissive factor. US naval operations in the Pacific War of 1944 and 1945 are the classic wartime illustration of the importance of an effective fleet train, while the maintenance of the Sixth Fleet in the

Mediterranean has been its most prominent modern peacetime accomplishment.

In any consideration of capabilities, it is necessary to examine the possible constraints imposed on operations by a country's capacity for logistic support. Two alternative answers exist: forward bases (or facilities) or afloat support. An individual country will weigh the relative costs, practicability and reliability of each. Increasingly, modern developments in afloat support have improved the sea-keeping qualities of naval forces. The political difficulties associated with bases have grown. Together these factors have caused a shift in favour of afloat support, though this is a technique which does not come without much time and cost, and this has undoubtedly been a factor in the Soviet hesitancy in this regard.[21] The requirements for a fully efficient fleet train are demanding. It requires fast general purpose replenishment ships and tankers, able to keep up with the operating warships, and it requires a supporting force of victualling ships, stores ships, ammunition ships and tankers to keep the faster ships topped up. It requires repair ships for surface ships, for helicopters and possibly for aircraft, and maintenance ships for submarines, minesweepers and frigates and other small ships. A mobile floating dock is essential for the repair of hull damage.[22] And for all these requirements, the greater the operating distance, the greater the demand on numbers and operational performance.

In considering logistics, the naval-related use which a country can make of its merchant ships should be considered.[23] Certainly it is essential as far as wartime situations are concerned; the inestimable value of a merchant fleet has been written about very effectively by Roskill.[24] Logistic possibilities are also affected by air staging and transit rights.

For most people logistics is not a compulsive subject. Operationally, however, it is of fundamental account. Few commentators give it proper attention. The effort required to maintain the unsung Beira Patrol has not been given the recognition which its practitioners know it deserved.[25] Equally, the debate about the Soviet threat to Western shipping in the Indian Ocean is often carried on with little reference to the logistical problems which units of the Soviet Navy would face operating in a hostile environment, remote from their bases, and with inadequate afloat support. Logistics remain as important (and unfashionable) a factor today as they did when a writer made the following still-relevant comment about World War Two:

Everybody likes to talk about and analyze *strategy*. Some 'mystic' quality about strategy and strategic planning and strategic decisions seem to arouse the spirits of all to a sense of intellectual contest. But World War II turned out to be less a game of strategy than of logistics. There were certain choices, but more often than not the choice hinged on the logistical factors and implications rather than upon some abstract gamesmanship.[26]

Procurement

Just as foreign policy outputs are affected by the nature of the processes of their creation, so naval capabilities need to be understood in relation to the processes of their procurement. It is a very sensitive area of national policy, and it is difficult to know whether outsiders can go very far. However, its importance remains: the 'research and development balance' is one of the factors which affect perceptions of the overall naval balance, and an understanding of 'procurement philosophies' is a significant input in the forecasting of naval programmes.

Procurement is an area of military policy where information is both elusive and difficult. Its study requires the co-operation of the detective-minded researcher and somebody with relevant technical expertise. To build up a picture of the naval procurement policies of a particular country, we need to know about its shipbuilding industry, its yards, its technical sophistication, its characteristic problems and ways of dealing with them, its general procurement philosophy, patterns of shipbuilding programmes, practices and procedures, and lead-times. The current state of the art needs to be assessed, and the particular country's hardware measured against it.

Some understanding of the procurement process is important in various ways. Knowledge of lead-times is important in analysing intentions; knowledge of lead-times can contribute to a more precise dating of when particular programmes were decided upon. This knowledge will therefore minimise untutored discussion and gross errors of linkage between particular decisions and events. It would appear from a close scrutiny of lead-times that the experience of the Cuban missile crisis was not as decisive in the evolution of Soviet naval policy as many commentators have stressed. Because of lead-times it can be argued that the hardware decisions to support Soviet naval expansion pre-dated Cuba. If this is true, the most that can be said about the experience of October 1962 is that it *confirmed* a growing appreciation of naval power.

An appreciation of procurement philosophies and naval shipbuilding industries assists forecasting and underlines the misconception of crude ship-to-ship comparisons. Comparable types of ships will perform differently because of possibly very different design priorities. As Admiral Holloway, the US Chief of Naval Operations simply put it: 'We don't build ships the same way the Soviets do, because we intend them for different purposes.'[27]

The elusiveness of the subject of naval procurement is attested to by the scarcity of works on the subject. Indeed for some reason the scholarly studies in the procurement field have invariably concentrated on aircraft. It may be that naval procurement has been relatively more successful, and has therefore not attracted the same attention. Its secrecy and complexity is another deterrent to study. Procurement is a political and technical snakes-and-ladders game which few within any military service would claim to fully understand. It is something they suffer rather than control. It involves the interplay between scientists, design teams, industries, armed forces, economic departments and politicians. The process allows an opportunity for a number of institutional interests to be followed. The 'game' therefore involves plenty of hard bargaining on all sides. The regular pressures are the external threat, economic constraints and the urge to modernise.

Procurement is an important building-brick which needs to be incorporated within the edifice of naval policy. It is another field in which outsiders are dependent upon a few people with a high degree of specialised knowledge and expertise. Despite the importance of the 'hardware approach', there have been few step-by-step analyses. Brodie's book starts well in his discussion of the 'tools' of naval power: but his content is now outdated and in any case did not go far enough. Unlike Brodie, Martin has very little of the fighting-ships-at-sea approach. He does offer insights into some of the problems of procurement, however, discussing such problems as balancing sophistication against cost. MccGwire's writings have perhaps been most useful of all in lifting up part of the curtain on the hardware approach, dealing with matters such as time and space, procurement, the drawing up of an OOB, the construction of a model of the shipbuilding industry, and the measuring of capabilities against critical maritime operations.[28]

Doctrine

Military doctrine incorporates the bundle of ideas by which capabilities are translated into military action relevant to the fulfilment of goals. It includes ideas about the nature of future war, and how the forces plan to fight it. Doctrine reveals something of a country's conception of the 'threat' it faces, and how it prepares to deal with it. It affects and is affected by the procurement process: each is a necessary, but not sufficient factor for the understanding of the other. Because of what doctrine might reveal about perceptions and intentions, and because it guides hardware into action, it is a crucial consideration for the naval analyst. However, an almost exclusive concentration on 'software' gives an incomplete explanation of a country's naval policy.

As a result of publicised exercises, and writings in military journals, there is often relatively more about doctrine than other aspects of a country's military posture. Too much should not be read into it. Many commentators are misled about the threat presented by a particular country because of too narrow a reading of doctrine, without taking a broader view of the country's whole posture and interests in international politics, or the internal and external reasons why particular statements might have been made. After attempting to unravel the possible tactical nature of military declarations, it is also necessary to give attention to the 'levels-of-analysis' problem and its possible impact on threat assessment.[29] An analysis of doctrine is at best only a partial indicator of a country's 'threat' in a strategic sense. As is suggested in the old maxim 'attack is the best form of defence', a country's aggressiveness in the event of war is not necessarily incompatible with an overall strategy which is war-avoiding.

Together, a picture of a country's doctrine and hardware will help to reveal how well its planners have married their technological capacities with their strategic environment. It will give a picture of how they plan to operate their forces in war or short of war. Their understanding of these factors depends, in turn, on the quality and quantity of their information.

It is one of the simplest but most important maxims of the social sciences that behaviour is based not on objective reality, but on what participants believe to be true. The importance of congruity between image and reality in military affairs, because of the violent potential, is more urgent than in many aspects of public policy. Short of access to a particular navy's top-secret files, however, it is impossible to know with great accuracy how it perceives its potential enemies. Nevertheless, this is a subject for serious speculation. In particular, attempting to understand an adversary's perceptions is a first step towards understanding his behaviour. Seeing the world from what, in a naval context, might be called 'the other side of the horizon' is a difficult task; it involves problems of information, as well as the fogs of culture-bound thinking. In their efforts to reveal the nature of Soviet naval strategy from the *Soviet* viewpoint, the pioneering work of Herrick and MccGwire was outstanding in this respect. It was also instrumental in opening up the great Soviet naval debate to serious discussion: other participants in the debate owe them a great deal, whether or not they agree with their conclusions, as many indeed do not.[30]

Capabilities and mission flexibility

On the basis of a careful evaluation of a navy's OOB and its doctrine, it should be possible to speculate with some profit about its likely missions in both peace and war, and its level of capability for discharging them. Naval missions must be considered in a naval balance, as well as ships, because capabilities can only be fully comprehended in terms of *what they are for*. It is meaningless to compare the Soviet capability for intervention from the sea against the same US capability, because they are not conceived as being against each other: rather, they need to be considered against relevant defensive forces. Equally, in analysing historical engagements, one cannot properly assess 'success' and 'failure' apart from the mission structure of the respective fleets. Many of the misjudgements about the Battle of Jutland have arisen out of the failure to bear in mind the different strategic aims of the rival fleets.[31]

Amongst the questions to be asked about a particular navy are: What are its missions? What is their priority? What capability is needed to discharge them satisfactorily? How much can be afforded? How critical is the shortfall? What degree of interchangeability is there between missions? Such problems are teasing enough for those at the core of naval intelligence. The answers are the more elusive in practice because 'flexibility' is often the result of improvisation: 'How do I know what I can do until I see what my orders are?' might be a naval commander's comment.

There is often a considerable disagreement about questions of mission flexibility. The character of the disagreement often reflects the backgrounds of the proponents. Those with professional naval backgrounds tend to be more cautious. Clearly, there is a wide margin for error when estimating whether a particular state has the requisite equipment to discharge a particular mission. There are many complications. One is never sure about mission priority. Different navies have different ways of approaching similar missions. Those navies which are relatively powerful within their own system will tend to overinsure.

It was traditionally maintained by British naval authorities that exigencies of deployment made it necessary to assess the number of ships required not only against the number and quality of opposing ships but also against the 'absolute' requirements of particular tasks, such as patrolling and maintaining a presence.[32]

The problem of mission flexibility has been highlighted in recent years by the debate about the capabilities and mission structure of the Soviet Navy. There are those who have argued that the priority missions of the Soviet Navy have been and are structured by the perceived maritime threat from the West.[33] The general war tasks which have developed from this perceived threat have basically established the priorities of the Soviet Navy's missions, and set limits to their inter-changeability. Using Sokolovskii to support his point, MccGwire has written:

> For the time being, the Soviet Navy lacks any such a deployable surplus of capability over requirements. Its three primary tasks, of countering Polaris and the aircraft carrier, and deploying its own SSBN, are concerned with deterrence and strategic defense, and the Soviet Navy's flexibility of action is severely circumscribed. Naval forces deployed to these roles cannot be diverted to tasks that are likely to increase tension with the West, since it is at times of crisis that the Soviet Union's concern for the security of the homeland becomes most acute.[34]

The idea of *surplus* is central to MccGwire's thesis. He argues that flexibility is really a function of surplus, and that the Soviet Navy, unlike the US Navy, lacks 'surplus'. However, he does not consider that this lack of surplus has prevented or will prevent the Soviet Navy from exploiting the peacetime uses of naval power: but he has argued that it will impose a severe inhibition against any possibility that a Soviet leadership would deliberately use force at sea.[35] While con-temporary attention is naturally drawn to Soviet and US naval strategy, some of the clearest illustrations of the impact and value of the flexibility which surplus bestows come from British naval history. This was evident in the convergence of British warships in the hunting of the *Bismarck*, when the advantages of numbers were present 'not for the first time but almost the last'.[36] One historical illustration conforming with MccGwire's thesis was the despatch of British forces to Gibraltar in 1940 to replace the lost French force in the Mediterranean. This division of force was possible without weakening the Home Fleet,

the irreducible minimum of national defence. It was the strength of
the Home Fleet which one First Lord described as 'the mainspring
from which all offensive operations must proceed'.[37] If states are
rational and cautious they will not embark on risky behaviour in distant
waters if that action might increase the dangers to the homeland, and
if the diversion of forces will weaken their ability to limit any ensuing
damage.

MccGwire's general view about the imperative of navy-to-navy
general war tasks has been contested by Martin and Cable (amongst
others). His critics have argued that a greater interchangeability of
missions is feasible, and that the OOB for general war, and preoccupation with it, will not necessarily inhibit the Soviet Navy from undertaking a more activist policy if the leadership considers that it is in
Soviet interests. Cable's position[38] is that 'the motives for which warships are built seldom foreshadow the actual nature of their employment, even in war, and are almost irrelevant to their utility in time of
peace.' This argument leads in a useful direction. A distinction can
be made between the primary and collateral objectives of warships.
The basic character of the most powerful warships is determined by
their role for major war. Like river dikes, warships must be able to cope
with the worst situations, however infrequently they occur. It is
pointless to build them strong enough to deal only with normal
everyday problems. By being designed to withstand the flood, they
should be able to deal with the ordinary tide. In developing this argument about the peacetime utilities of Soviet warships, Cable asked
himself the negative question:

> Is there a peace-time role of which they (Soviet warships) are
> technically incapable or from which they are manifestly debarred
> by the need to maintain instant readiness for nuclear war? If this
> analysis reveals the existence of useful warships not irretrievably
> committed in time of peace, it will then be necessary . . . to
> examine the kind of contingencies in which the use of limited
> naval force might seem politically feasible to the Soviet Govern-
> ment.

Later, he argued that commitment to strategic defence need not be
'absolute' because, unlike coastal defence, its chances of success are
'too small even if maximum strength is available' to discourage the
Soviet Navy from deploying ocean-going warships for other purposes
in times of peace. Certainly the commitment to strategic defence *need*

not be absolute, but that phrase does not tell the reader anything about the actual Soviet commitment to it. Against this side-stepping of the issue it is important to point out the importance traditionally attached by the Soviet Union to damage limitation efforts, even if the chances for *absolute* success may have been small. Cable's next point is more telling: 'it does not necessarily follow that the Soviet Government will always regard every peacetime use of warships as automatically entailing the risk of general war.' It would be difficult to disagree with this observation. For such peacetime uses, he reckoned that in 1971 it was already possible to assume that the Soviet Navy could spare 'at least a dozen ocean-going warships'.[39] While one might question the number stated (a 'dozen' of what? where? in what circumstances? for what purpose?) his reminders about the flexibility of mission structures is very pertinent.[40]

Most ships are multi-purpose. Above all, the aircraft carrier is the pinnacle of operational flexibility. Its primary mission can change between air defence, strike against surface ships, hunting submarines, to projecting power ashore. It is unique amongst warships in the versatility if its wartime roles, while also being capable of performing all the short-of-war activities, from the most social to the most harassing aspects of coercive diplomacy. Naval flexibility is no longer an Anglo-American prerogative. Admiral Gorshkov has been a notable publicist on behalf of the flexibility of warships, arising out of their many modes of employment *in addition* to their primary wartime tasks.[41] The ageing *Sverdlovs* are good illustrations. Designed originally as traditional cruisers, their present potential purposes are wide. Is their maintenance simply for training? Is it because of the possible political impact of their size and impressive appearance? Is it part of the Russian habit of 'overinsuring' in numerical terms? Is it for ceremonial occasions? Is it inertia? Is it for supporting action in a conflict with China or NATO? Is it that they believe they have been sufficiently modernised to meet general war contingencies? Whatever purpose is presently in the minds of Soviet naval planners, future employment will depend upon the thrust of events. This has often destroyed the hopes of coherent planning. Despite the ostensible rationality of the British battle-cruiser concept, it sometimes happened, to their cost, that they had to be deployed in circumstances for which they were badly designed.[42] Improvisation is a norm of naval employment: rare has been the warship which has been kept in the manner to which its original designer thought it would be accustomed. Because of their life-span of twenty to thirty years, this is hardly surprising.

Some of the arguments about flexibility in the great Soviet naval debate have been bogus. Between the proponents of the so-called 'defensive' and 'activist' interpretations of Soviet naval strategy there is more common ground than might appear at first sight. There is nothing in Cable's activist argument that 'it does not necessarily follow that the Soviet Government will always regard every peacetime use of warships as automatically entailing the risk of general war' with anything which has been written by MccGwire, the most prominent of the misleadingly called 'defensive' school. However, Cable and others would evidently consider such a comment to be a telling contrary point. An examination of MccGwire's work shows his recognition of the potential of Soviet warships for the purposes of increasing 'prestige and influence'.[43] The difference between the two emphases can be most clearly seen by comparing the writings of MccGwire and Weinland, who has made the most solid contribution to the 'activist' school.[44] The gap between them is quite narrow. There is a consensus regarding the initial impulse behind the building of the modern Soviet Navy and for its pattern of progressively widening deployment. The difference about present trends is one of degree rather than kind, and as far as the problem facing Western navies is concerned, their conclusions would be broadly similar. The MccGwire thesis is that the Soviet Navy has invariably lagged far behind in its efforts to meet the threat represented by the US Navy: it is doubtful, even with the improvement in the last few years, whether the Soviet Navy is satisfied with its damage-limiting potential. This primary general war orientation continues to establish the shape of Soviet naval efforts. It imposes constraints upon it: it does not allow a 'disposable surplus' for activities riskier than attempting to increase prestige and influence, activities which require 'the protection of peace'. Weinland's thesis accepts that defence of the homeland against attack from the sea remains the Soviet Navy's primary mission, but he argues that there has been a significant modification of the Navy's mission structure. It now has the additional responsibility for the 'protection of the State interests of the USSR on the seas and oceans'. Whether one is drawn to the activist interpretation pointing to experimentation and the creation of options, or to the determinism of the navy-to-navy confrontation, there is an important area of common agreement. In order to fulfil its foreign policy tasks the Soviet Navy needs maritime stability. Clashing with Western navies, and particularly that of the United States, would take away that freedom and would perceptibly increase the risk of escalation. For these reasons, it is argued by all the serious

commentators, be they of the 'activist' or 'defensive' emphasis, that
the Soviet Navy is unlikely to risk using force at and from the sea
where it might involve a clash with the United States. To a large extent
the difference of emphasis is not about the Soviet Navy as such, but
about the likelihood of militancy in Soviet foreign policy. There is
little disagreement about the possible range of Soviet naval behaviour:
the difference is more over the range of *probable* behaviour, as determined by the makers of Soviet foreign policy.

All these problems involve the juggling of capabilities and intentions.
At their base is a perennial and important question: to what extent
does 'hardware analysis' reveal the underlying intentions of naval
policy? MccGwire, who has written most consistently about this, has
argued that from the evidence of ship types, operational activity
and patterns of deployment, it should be possible to work out a 'reasonably clear outline of the underlying naval policy'.[45] His approach is
followed through to the finer details of naval policy: 'To a varying
extent, it is possible to deduce the primary role(s) for which a class of
warship was *designed* by reference to its characteristics.'[46] Furthermore,
shipbuilding programmes and operational evidence provides 'a reasonably factual matrix' against which to evaluate Soviet pronouncements.[47]
His conclusion is that hardware analysis

> is not a panacea. But because it rests on a firm foundation of
> physical data, it does provide a relatively concrete form of
> reference against which to evaluate and interpret other types
> of evidence.[48]

Hardware analysis of Soviet naval policy has been attempted most
comprehensively by MccGwire. Hill attempted to put a sharper edge
on it by looking at tactical weapons as indicators, though he admits
that the picture presented is a complex one.[49]

The hardware analysis approach has been criticised by Cable. He
revealed his scepticism early in his book: 'Warships . . . are such
flexible instruments of coercion . . . Changes in the order of battle
of the world's navies thus offer only partial indications of their
prospective employment.'[50] His view is that what matters is the *existence* of ships, not the role for which they were created, possibly many
years before.[51] Again, the debate is a little false. What is a 'partial
indication'? Nobody, including MccGwire, claims that hardware
analysis is a full indicator, only the most reliable one at hand. Nor does
MccGwire's thesis rule out the possibility that factors other than general

war employment might affect the character and shape of warships. Design inertia or a compromise between different requirements are amongst the additional complicating factors.

The difference of view between Cable and MccGwire is partly a matter of degree, but it is also based on a basic difference of opinion about naval strategy, and may in turn be a reflection of different backgrounds. Is the 'flexibility' of naval units a function of their versatile nature, as Cable argues, or of their number (surplus) in relation to their tasks, as MccGwire argues? Cable's thesis tends to ignore the extent to which warships are rationally built for extreme cases and the extent to which their primary missions affect their daily routines. MccGwire, on the other hand, is in danger of underestimating political pressures for improvisation, the way ships are sometimes matched to tasks in an ill-fitting way, and the scope for 'activism' which is possible in local areas before significant fears arise of general war, an eventuality which all seem agreed is steadily more remote in the perceptions of the leaders of the superpowers.

The debate about capabilities and the flexibility of mission structure will go on. For the contingency planner, concerned to understand the potential threat in terms of what an adversary *can* do, it is an exercise which should be carried out with imagination as well as thoroughness. Surprise, after all, is a constant feature in everybody's principles of war.

The human factor

Whatever comparative technologies and mission structures are on show, the competence of sailors and the skill of their commanders can make all the difference between success and failure. However, assessing the 'human factor' is often the most elusive of all the elements in the balance.

Even the most professional assessments are likely to be vague. Observation and interpretation of training routines, exercises, seamanship, performance under stress, maintenance ability, morale and so on are difficult enough problems for naval intelligence organisations. Historians, with the advantage of hindsight and as much evidence as there is, have not been able to go very far. It is impossible to achieve more than generalisations; and the import of these, in any particular case, is difficult to assess and so weigh in the balance.[52] Because the human factor is elusive, it is often left out of account: *Jane's* provides no guidance as to the skill with which all those impressive amounts of steel and shell which it portrays may be utilised.

Despite the difficulties, the human factor ('form' in military parlance)
is one which continues to be stressed by military practitioners.
While this stress on the human factor by senior officers has an obvious
morale-boosting element, it is evident that in many situations the
'form' of the crew will make a big difference in the effectiveness of
an operation. The importance of the commander himself goes almost
without saying.[53] The whole movement of the ship depends upon his
skill. In some ways, however, his task is easier than that of a commander
of infantrymen. Unlike an infantryman, an ordinary sailor, however
wobbly his knees, cannot opt out of the move chosen by his commander. But that does not mean that his morale is of no effect. At a
moment of crisis in the denouement of the *Bismarck* drama, Admiral
Lutjens gave a speech which eroded the spirit of his crew.[54] Strategically, this was not significant as long as he continued to make rational
decisions and his orders were obeyed: tactically, by taking away the
will to fight, it could have been decisive. The 'form' of the commander
is of great account strategically, as is evident with the allegations that
Admirals Jellicoe and Halsey were too cautious, and so missed
important opportunities, or that Admiral Pound interfered too much in
the running of decisions, so that when he was 'off form' disaster might
be the outcome; this was possibly the case with the destruction of
Convoy PQ17.

Traditionally, the practitioners of the art of war have stressed the
importance of the 'moral' over the 'material'. Although the 'moral'
cannot really be quantified (though some have tried), it is usually
thought to be something worth weighing in the balance.[55] The impact
of expertise and training is evident in ASW or convoy work, not to
mention some of the more flamboyant aspects of naval action.[56]
In modern conditions there are many occasions in which 'form' will
show itself, for instance in low-level maritime confrontations.[57] The
importance of form was evident in the discipline and command-
and-control arrangements of the US carrier commanders during the
June War.[58] It was not evident in the low readiness of the crew of the
Israeli destroyer *Eilat*, sunk by *Styx* missiles from Alexandria in
1967.[59] But times change: in the Yom Kippur War six years later, not
a single Israeli vessel was sunk although 52 missiles were fired from
Egyptian and Syrian vessels.[60]

The preference remains for counting hardware rather than speculating about intangibles. Nevertheless, practitioners continue to point to
the significance of the human element. In his first press conference
as Chief of Naval Operations, Admiral James L. Holloway stressed the

importance of his men and their experience. In comparing US and
Soviet naval strengths he said,

> Finally, I think probably one of our greatest assets is I feel that
> our people are better. They are more imaginative, [have] greater
> resourcefulness, and we have veterans. We have pilots who have
> flown over 200 missions in combat. We have destroyer skippers who
> have spent four and five years on the gunline in Vietnam exercising
> their equipment. We have an awful lot of combat veterans in the
> United States Navy.[61]

Ultimately, it is only those who have seen action who can really know,
who can subjectively feel, how important it is to have the right men
alongside them.

In the past it has often been true that 'form' was basically a matter
of personality as well as skill. Ability, strategy and tactics, and
panache could overcome material factors. Hawke's boast that 'It is a
matter of indifference whether I fight the enemy with an equal number,
one ship more, or one less' was characteristic of the swashbuckling age
of strategy at sea. In an electronic age it might be argued that narrow
technical specialisation is more important than courage and personality.
Whether the increased technocratisation of war will undermine the
traditional stress on the moral over the material remains to be seen,
but the human factor, in one way or another, remains critical. It is
different qualities which demand our attention.

Although skill has been most commonly associated with fighting
ability in war, we should also today consider the diplomatic skill
surrounding the political use of naval force in situations short of
war. In some circumstances ensuring that naval signals are properly
perceived is partly a diplomat's responsibility.

People are often said to prefer myths to reality. One social
historian has said that myths 'give identity, purpose and meaning . . .
They shape the attitudes and determine the outlooks of its adherents.'[62]
Studying the mythology surrounding different national officer corps
gives some insight into the human element. Self-image affects
behaviour. It played some part in the predisposition of British naval
officers in favour of the aggressive 'hunting group' or 'offensive patrol',
and it played its part in the preference of some British officers for the
excitement and glory of the east of Suez role. To British seamen, being
a naval officer meant seeing the seven distant seas, not just the contiguous one, as has been the lot of his counterpart in most of the

world's navies. Naval mythology also plays its part in establishing the prestige with which the naval profession is invested in different countries: this in turn affects the quality and quantity of recruits. The mythology is reflected and built up by the way navies are treated in films, literature and drama.

When considering the human element it is well to be reminded of the importance of accident and chance. 'Friction' was the term which Clausewitz gave to the process by which plans fell short of the mark as a result of human frailty or external agencies such as the weather. The role of chance is one of the themes of military history. One estimate put the chances of a hit on *Bismarck*'s rudders from *Ark Royal's Swordfish* at 1:100,000.[63] One does not record it with astonishment: *c'est la guerre*. In naval affairs the unexpected can take many forms, and can result from human or non-human factors: weather can always upset plans, as can enemy intentions. In this respect it is well to remember that 'surprise' is one of the most hallowed of the principles of war. Despite careful appreciations, practitioners have often been overcome by 'behavioural' or 'technical' surprises.[64] Lord Carrington, the British Minister of Defence, admitted with disarming candour that an analysis of 45 engagements of British forces between 1945 and 1959 revealed that on no single occasion had the engagement been foreseen.[65] Given the pattern of operational success this speaks volumes about British skill in improvising, though it must be a uniquely bad forecasting record.

Land, sea and air forces: their interconnectedness

Naval operations are hardly ever isolated activities. Not only do naval acts have their meaning elsewhere than on the sea space on which they take place, but many considerations apart from naval factors have to be taken into account when assessing capabilities. Indeed it is hardly valid today to talk about a 'naval balance': there are too many related capabilities involved.

The interdependence between naval affairs and military and political affairs on land has always been complete in terms of politics,[66] and has become increasingly so in terms of the use of armed forces. A small but significant milestone in this evolution was the coming into use of the adjective 'maritime' in association with nouns such as 'power' and 'strategy' in World War Two, as a result of the need to co-locate the command and control of aircraft which were being used for naval purposes with that of the associated warships: these shore-based RAF aircraft were known as 'maritime patrol' aircraft, and they were

directed from a 'Maritime Headquarters'.[67] In the last thirty years
the concept of maritime strategy has expanded further, involving as it
does many complex interrelationships. Land-based aircraft and
missiles can cover the oceans: carrier-borne aircraft and submarine-
launched missiles can cover the land. Activity on the sea has also
become involved with another dimension as a result of the space
satellite: communication, navigation and surveillance at sea have all
been affected by this invention. In particular conflict situations, naval
balances have no meaning apart from local army and air force balances:
these in turn are affected by matters such as alliance potential and
division of labour, and air staging and transit rights.

These brief points underline the fact that the concept of strategy
cannot be easily compartmentalised. The distinction between 'land'
and 'naval' strategy is both more complicated and less meaningful than
ever before. A mark of this change has been the development of the
ballistic missile-firing submarine. This weapons system has little to do
with naval strategy as such, having no role in relation to hostile warships
other than evading them: but it does have a critical role in relation to
the decision-making which goes on in capital cities which may lie
deeply inland. Warships have lost their almost exclusive proprietorship
of naval strategy, but they have maintained their stake in limited
international conflicts, and they have become one of the most important components of the central strategic balance.

Allies and treaties

Treaties of various types can affect the character and operations of
particular navies. In the inter-war years the Washington Treaties
affected ship types and size, as well as the fortification and disposition
of naval bases. Although this type of agreement no longer affects naval
behaviour, various treaty provisions do affect naval policy: they define
the allies and responsibilities of some navies; they impose some constraints on movement, as with the Montreux Convention governing the
Turkish Straits; they place numerical limitations on some types of
warship, as with the Protocol of the SALT I Treaty of May 1972;
and they remove some areas from the arms race, as with the Seabed
Treaty of 1970. While naval arms control has been a non-starter in most
respects since World War Two, it nevertheless remains amongst the
objectives of several states, and if successful would affect naval planning.
Some countries bordering the Mediterranean Sea and Indian Ocean have
called for an agreement to end the superpower naval confrontations
there, and there is good reason to suppose that the Soviet leaders have

conceived arms control to be a potentially useful tactic in its naval confrontation with the United States.[68]

The help which a particular navy might receive from allies is obviously an important factor in any assessment of capabilities. Foreign assistance affects a navy's 'disposable surplus' for urgent tasks. In this respect the Royal Navy has had a sometimes passive importance in US naval policy which it did not fully appreciate.[69] In addition, an alliance affects the worst case forecasting of adversaries. It was hardly surprising that Soviet authorities during the SALT II negotiations proposed the inclusion of the total SSBN potential of Britain, France and the United States on the assumption that they would act in concert in a major war. In addition, an integrated alliance such as NATO allows a degree of specialisation in naval tasks, though rarely does the impulse of national independence allow this to proceed very far.

Finally, the so-called 'progressive development of international law' affects naval planning in many important respects.[70] As O'Connell has pointed out, it impinges upon naval planning through the tactical use of ASW in times of political tension, the choice of areas in which operations are to be mounted or ships or devices deployed, and even procurement policy in cases where weapons or their launching vehicles would be of doubtful legality in any situation that can be envisaged. Administrative structures have to be adjusted to meet these problems, so that 'the lawyers and the seamen' can work closely together, and, it is hoped, understand each other's problems. Some progress has already been made along these lines in the US Navy and Royal Australian Navy, but this is not the case in many navies, 'although it is evident that any crisis would immediately reveal areas of confusion and indecision because the forward thinking about legal policy and rules of the game was lacking.' In sum, *the influence of law upon sea power* is of growing importance.

Conclusion

Assessing naval capabilities is an immensely complex task, involving far more than counting and classifying 'the warships of the nations'. Hardware is not everything, for 'capabilities' also consist of many non-material facets: however, a discussion of hardware in its static and dynamic aspects remains at the heart of the matter. For this reason interested observers depend for their education upon the direct assistance of those with professional experience: they alone can effectively provide the necessary specialised knowledge, technical awareness and professional expertise.

Notes

1. Captain John E. Moore, *Jane's Fighting Ships 1973-74* (London: Sampson, Low, Marston and Co. Ltd., 1973), Editor's Foreword, p. 78.
2. Other widely used sources are *Les Flottes de Combat* (Paris), *The Military Balance* (London), and *Weyers Taschenbuch der Kriegsflotten bzw. Flottentaschenbuch* (Munich).
3. Including Admiral Gorshkov. Quoted by B. Thomas Trout, 'Naval Strategy and Naval Politics: Peacetime Uses of a Wartime Naval Force', *NWCR*, Jul.-Aug. 1974, p. 11.
4. For a general discussion of the problem, and one of the few sophisticated public presentations of this subject, see Nigel D. Brodeur, 'Comparative Capabilities of Soviet and Western Weapons Systems', in Michael MccGwire, Ken Booth and John McDonnell, *Soviet Naval Policy. Objectives and Constraints* (New York: Praeger, 1975), pp. 452-68.
5. For example, on the eve of the outbreak of World War One, in Chapter XIII of *From the Dreadnought to Scapa Flow* (Arthur J. Marder, Oxford University Press, 1961), Vol. 1, and on the eve of Jutland in Chapter XVII of ibid., Vol. 2, and Chapter I of ibid., Vol. 3.
6. Captain S. W. Roskill, *The Strategy of Sea Power. Its Development and Application* (London: Collins, 1962), pp. 109-10.
7. See Captain S. W. Roskill, *The Navy at War. 1939-1945* (London: Collins, 1960).
8. Captain S. W. Roskill, *The War at Sea, 1939-1945*, Vol. 1, *The Defensive* (London: HMSO, 1954), History of the Second World War, UK Military Series, Chs. I-IV.
9. S. E. Morison, *History of United States Naval Operations in World War I* (London: Oxford University Press, 1948). See Vol. 1 (1948), p. ix. The Introduction was written by Commodore Dudley W. Knox USN (Retd.).
10. Given the fearsome picture of the Soviet submarine threat to Western shipping in the post-war years, raising as it did the spectre of another Battle of the Atlantic, it is salutary to be reminded that, however chilling the absolute total of Soviet submarines, only 9 per cent of the total was based in the Northern Fleet, with ready access to the main shipping routes. See R. W. Herrick, *Soviet Naval Strategy: Fifty Years of Theory and Practice* (US Naval Institute, Annapolis, 1968), p. 131.
11. Order-of-Battle is not a traditional naval term, but it is one which seems to be gaining increasing usage, and it is descriptive.
12. See, for example, the Annex 'The Technology of Maritime Warfare', pp. 45-54 in J. L. Moulton, *British Maritime Strategy in the 1970s* (London: RUSI, 1969); Laurence Martin, *Arms and Strategy* (London: Weidenfeld and Nicolson, 1973), Chapter 5, 'The Maritime Battle', p. 14. Factual summaries of trends have been provided by Vice-Admiral B. B. Schofield's regular 'Developments in Maritime Forces', in *Brassey's Annual* (London: William Clowes). The Editor's introduction to *Jane's* is usually awaited for its pungent comments on trends in naval developments.
13. Brodeur, op. cit., pp. 452-4. See also Gorshkov's comments, quoted by Thomas Trout, op. cit.
14. Brodeur, ibid., p. 461.

15.   Theodore Ropp, *War in the Modern World* (New York: Collier Books, 1971), p. 5.
16.   See James Cable, *Gunboat Diplomacy. Political Applications of Limited Naval Force* (London: Chatto and Windus for the ISS, 1971), pp. 107ff.
17.   Quoted by Roskill, *The Strategy of Sea Power*, p. 110. See also Roskill's own pertinent comments, and Marder, *From the Dreadnought to Scapa Flow*, Vol. 1, pp. 379, 431.
18.   Bernard Brodie, *A Guide to Naval Strategy* (New York: Praeger, 1965, 5th ed.), pp. 89-90.
19.   Ibid., p. 101.
20.   See Captain Richard W. Miller USN, 'Indonesia's Archipelago Doctrine and Japan's Jugular', *USNIPs*, Vol. 98, No. 10/836, October 1972, pp. 26-30.
21.   MccGwire, Booth and McDonnell, op. cit., p. 540.
22.   See Vice-Admiral Sir Peter Gretton, *Maritime Strategy: A Study of British Defence Problems* (London: Cassell, 1965), pp. 148-50. Those who are unfamiliar with the range of requirements might dwell with some awe on the photographs and specifications of the US Navy's capability in this regard, as presented annually in *Jane's*.
23.   Gretton, op. cit., p. 67.
24.   Roskill, *The Strategy of Sea Power*, pp. 231-2.
25.   For a short commentary on aspects of this operation, see F.E.C. Gregory, 'The Beira Patrol', *JRUSI*, Vol. CXIV, No. 656, December 1969, pp. 75-7.
26.   James A. Huston, 'A History of US Army Logistics, 1775-1953', Part IV, quoted by Henry E. Eccles, *Military Concepts and Philosophy* (New Brunswick, N.J.: Rutgers UP, 1965), p. 67.
27.   Press conference of 30 October 1974, quoted in *The Defence Monitor*, Vol. 3, No. 10, December 1974, p. 6.
28.   See, for example, the picture of Soviet naval procurement which emerges from Michael MccGwire, *Soviet Naval Developments* (New York: Praeger, 1973), Chs. 11, 12, 13, 14, 16.
29.   This problem is discussed more fully in ibid., pp. 1-5, 31-3.
30.   Herrick, op. cit. MccGwire's first entries into the public debate were: 'The Background to Russian Naval Policy', pp. 141-58 in *Brassey's Annual. The Armed Forces Year-Book, 1968* (London: Wm. Clowes and Sons, 1968), and 'Soviet Naval Capabilities and Intentions' and 'Soviet Naval Procurement', pp. 33-51, 74-87 in *The Soviet Union in Europe and the Near East: Her Capabilities and Intentions* (London: RUSI, 1970). The work and findings of these former naval officers attracted substantial disapproval from Western naval establishments. (Note the 'Publisher's Preface' to Herrick's book, pp. xi-xii.) However, within five years or so their interpretation of the basic motives for the expanding deployment of Soviet naval forces in the 1960s had become the generally accepted one.
31.   Geoffrey Bennett, *The Battle of Jutland* (London: Batsford, 1964), pp. 57-8.
32.   Martin, op. cit., p. 116.
33.   Notably MccGwire, though this viewpoint now commands great support amongst specialists on the Soviet Navy. For a comprehensive presentation of MccGwire's approach, see 'The Evolution of Soviet Naval Policy: 1960-74', Ch. 28 in MccGwire, Booth and McDonnell, op. cit.
34.   MccGwire, *Soviet Naval Developments*, p. 501.
35.   Ibid., pp. 502-12.
36.   Ludovic Kennedy, *Pursuit: the chase and sinking of the Bismarck* (London: Collins, 1974), pp. 101-2.

37.   Said by Lord Barnham, First Lord of the Admiralty during the Trafalgar campaign: quoted by Roskill, *The War at Sea*, Vol. 1, p. 8.
38.   Cable, op. cit., pp. 131-2.
39.   Ibid., pp. 140-1.
40.   Ibid. See also p. 12.
41.   Gorshkov's views are discussed by Trout, op. cit., p. 11.
42.   Kennedy, op. cit., p. 232.
43.   E.g. MccGwire, *Soviet Naval Developments*, pp. 502-8.
44.   For Weinland's work see ibid., Ch. 22, and MccGwire, Booth and McDonnell, op. cit., Ch. 20.
45.   MccGwire, *Soviet Naval Developments*, p. 176.
46.   Ibid., p. 184.
47.   Ibid., p. 187.
48.   Ibid., p. 207.
49.   Captain J. R. Hill RN, 'Developments in Soviet Maritime Tactical Weapon Systems' (unpublished paper, presented to the seminar on Soviet Naval Developments, Dalhousie University, October 1973).
50.   Cable, op. cit., p. 12.
51.   Ibid., p. 131.
52.   Marder is particularly good on the human factor. See *From the Dreadnought Dreadnought to Scapa Flow*, Vols. 1-5, *passim*. On a more general plane see Brodie's 'The Men Behind the Guns', Ch. 10 in his *Guide to Naval Strategy*.
53.   On the character of leadership, see Brodie, op. cit., pp. 249-51; S. W. Roskill's extended essay, *The Art of Leadership* (London: Collins, 1964); and Marder's comments, *From the Dreadnought to Scapa Flow*, Vol. 5, pp. 338-41.
54.   Kennedy, op. cit., pp. 179-80.
55.   Roskill, *The Strategy of Sea Power*, p. 110.
56.   Note the glamour and interest focusing on wartime submarine commanders, the Richtofens of the deep. The importance of ability and enterprise was reflected partly in disparity in 'kills'. For World War One, see Marder, *From the Dreadnought to Scapa Flow*, Vol. 5, p. 83.
57.   Hill, 'Maritime Forces in Confrontation', *Brassey's Annual, 1972* (London: Wm. Clowes and Sons, Ltd., 1972), p. 36.
58.   Jonathan Trumbull Howe, *Multicrises. Sea Power and Global Politics in the Missile Age* (Cambridge, Mass.: The MIT Press, 1971), Ch. 5.
59.   For a much less comforting picture, see Robert D. Colvin, 'Aftermath of the Elath', *Survival*, Vol. XII, No. 1, January 1970, pp. 7-12 (reprinted from *USNIPs*, October 1969).
60.   Chaim Herzog, *The War of Atonement* (London: Weidenfeld and Nicolson, 1975), p. 269.
61.   Quoted in *The Defence Monitor*, Vol. 3, No. 10, December 1974, p. 6.
62.   Jeffrey Richards, *Visions of Yesterday* (London: Routledge and Kegan Paul, 1973), p. xv.
63.   Kennedy, op. cit., p. 228.
64.   This useful distinction is explained by Klaus Knorr, 'Failures in National Intelligence Estimates: The Case of the Cuban Missiles', *World Politics*, XVI, 3 (April 1964), pp. 455-67;
65.   *The Listener*, 7 January 1971.
66.   This is one of the themes of G. S. Graham, *The Politics of Naval Supremacy* (Cambridge: Cambridge University Press, 1965).
67.   This information was supplied by Vice-Admiral Sir Ian McGeogh.
68.   See Barry M. Blechman, 'Soviet Interests in Naval Arms Control: Prospects for Disengagement in the Mediterranean', Ch. 35 in MccGwire, *Soviet*

Naval Developments, and Franklin Griffiths, 'The Tactical Uses of Naval Arms Control', Ch. 34 in MccGwire, Booth and McDonnell, op. cit.

69.   See Howe, op. cit., p. 333.

70.   D. P. O'Connell, 'Naval Policy and International Law and International Relations', in *Britain and the Sea*, The Collected Papers and Records of the Conference held at the Royal Naval College Greenwich, 12-14 September 1973. The only book-length study of the problems that contemporary international law poses for naval planning is in O'Connell's excellent *The Influence of Law on Sea Power* (Manchester: Manchester University Press, 1975).

8 THE DOMESTIC SOURCES

Foreign policy cannot be properly understood apart from the domestic context of the country concerned: 'foreign policy is domestic policy writ large' has increasingly become the theme in area studies and in writings about economic and military relationships.[1] If governments have to concentrate more on internal pressures, if societies continue to turn 'inwards', if the acceptability of military force declines further, and if economic security continues to be the primary daily concern for governments, then the domestic sources of naval policy will demand a novel attention from the students of the subject.

Domestic factors 'may be of considerable significance even if they are not primary sources of foreign policy, and on some issues they may well be dominant'.[2] Few are likely to disagree with this: however, it is much easier to state this general proposition than to identify precise linkages: 'the links between the domestic sources and the resulting behaviour — foreign policy — are not easily observed and are thus especially resistant to coherent analysis.'[3] The aim must be to be specific. As has been written about the domestic sources of policy in another and more deeply worked context:

> *Which* factors have *what kind of* influence under *what* conditions during *which* time periods are empirical questions, albeit difficult ones. Informed observers, in efforts to identify and confirm these relationships, can and do differ. But one cannot meaningfully analyse 'the' influence of domestic politics on international behaviour.[4]

The relevance of this comment should be evident. In this chapter, however, the aim is merely to provide a reminder of the types of domestic factor which might affect naval policy.

A reminder is certainly needed. Relatively little work has been done on the domestic sources of naval policy, although domestic factors affect the size of the slice of the national budgetary cake which a particular navy is given, and through this naval procurement and the quality and quantity of its manpower will be affected. The economic factor is the most obvious and direct domestic constraint, but how this operates on a navy in practice is, in turn, affected by other domestic sources of policy, such as public opinion. The domestic sources of naval policy might be elusive and resistant to coherent analysis, but they exist. Nevertheless, few if any books or articles have this relationship as a major theme. Exceptions sometimes occur in works which study navies in peacetime. Marder's first book, for example, has a useful section on public opinion,[5] while Crowe's study attempts to make what it can of the significance of the policy process.[6] Such efforts are all too infrequent and all too brief.

Most writers on naval matters ignore the domestic sources of naval policy. Mahan gave it a rather simplistic and deterministic glance.[7] Others have dealt with it even more cursorily. Most writers have conceived 'policy' too narrowly. By 'policy' they refer almost entirely to foreign policy. It is significant, for example, that the indexes of the major works of Roskill and Schofield show no acknowledgement of the domestic sources of naval policy as major concepts or organising categories for their enquiries.[8] For writers to whom 'naval strategy' is the name of the game, the political and economic constraints faced by policy-makers are either ignored or treated as unchangeable givens. Schofield's *British Sea Power* is a dirge on the theme of the parsimony of successive British governments, and its deleterious effects on naval vitality, but the book does not consider the reasons why British governments assessed their priorities in the way they did. Much writing about naval matters is concerned with the size and shape of particular maritime forces, but few naval writers have been concerned to explain with any sophistication why the navy's slice of the cake is almost always smaller than they would deem desirable. With expertise and detailed analysis they deal with naval strategy and technology, but they are much less good at explaining why naval establishments failed to persuade their political leaders of the need for a penny or so on the income tax for naval purposes.

Naval policy is only one demand on the time and effort of governments. Governments, above all things, have to make their countries *work,*[9] and this involves a far wider range of considerations than naval policy. Naval policy has to be understood in this wider context, which will affect naval efforts not only in the release of all-important man-power and money, but also through attitudes towards the country's role in international affairs. This is especially relevant for countries wanting to exercise military power overseas, for here national self-confidence and domestic consensus are critical factors. The domestic sources of policy transform what is strategically desirable from the perspective of *Naval Man* into what is politically possible from the perspective of the actual policy-maker.

Economic factors

Of all the domestic sources of military policy, the economic factor is the one which most immediately and most persistently demands attention. The importance of 'defence economics' is increasingly recognised, but the subject can find few exponents, and fewer still with both political expertise and the ability to communicate with laymen.

(1) *Capacity and insurance*

A nation's ability to mobilise and deploy military forces is determined in large part by its capacity to produce various goods and services (its labour force, raw materials, financial resources and so on) and by its technological resources.[10] Its capacity depends on the size and structure of the population, the nation's territory with its land, water and mineral resources, the economic productivity of its labour force, its capital equipment, and the stage of its economic and technological development.

Within a given nation's capacity the tantalising question is: how much is enough? The traditional answer was obvious if a clear military threat was perceived. 'Enough' meant striving to have the ability to defeat enemy forces in war. In periods of peace, with no clearly defined threat, or as we now are in a nuclear deterrent situation, the answer is not so obvious. How much is enough for a general insurance against an improbable event? John Garnett has suggested two rules of thumb which restrain the defence expenditure of democratic governments. Firstly, in peacetime the defence budget should not be so high that it damages the economy as a whole. Secondly, the pursuit of national security should not be allowed to undermine the achievement of other values in society, such as health, education and housing. Having identified those operating norms, he then added the warning that

> governments which allow their defence policies to be determined solely by internal political and economic considerations may find themselves hamstrung with a defence policy they can afford and which is electorally popular, but which bears no relationship to the external threat it is designed to counter.[11]

The influence which economic factors have on the size and shape of armies, navies and air forces is often decisive. Indeed, it is often said that the military policies of countries such as Britain are conditioned more by the country's economy than by the external 'threat'. Certainly economic considerations played a major part in the British decision to withdraw from east of Suez, a development which changed the shape of decades of British naval policy. Many critics of the way democratic governments settle their military policy argue that their level of military spending is more often a function of what they think the electorate is willing to support rather than what it can objectively afford on defence, or what it 'should' afford in terms of an optimum military posture. As Garnett has succinctly put it: 'Governments are always tempted to design defence policies to counter threats which they can afford rather than those which may actually exist.'[12] One important implication of this has been that Western governments have tended to base their strategic planning on enemy *intentions* rather more explicitly than ever before. This shift was recognised by NATO in 1967. From a professional military viewpoint it is never as satisfactory to base policy on intentions: a policy based on enemy capabilities will provide more military insurance.

(2)   *Economic factors and operational efficiency*

Economic factors impinge upon naval policy in manifold ways. At a low level, in training (and possibly pay) naval officers are made to feel increasingly conscious of the cost element. More important, the economic factor determines the size of the national cake from which the leadership determines the slice which can be allocated to its navy. This in turn will affect whether it can discharge its responsibilities satisfactorily. In this respect strain is a more common historical characteristic than surplus. This is especially true today. It can be argued that the economic factor is of no small importance in Soviet thinking about its more widely deployed navy.[13] The decline of foreign bases has increased the economic costs of forward deployment and thus the general burden which it represents. Costly auxiliaries of the right type and in the right number have to be acquired, manned and operated. Economic considerations can also seriously affect govern-ment policy when contemplating naval responses to a crisis.[14] In some cases, notably the British intervention over the Suez affair in 1956, concern about economic effects and direct economic pressure can cause a government to halt an operation in which it has become in-volved. The country thus gets the worst of all worlds: for those who could so conceive it, an important opportunity was lost; certainly men and money were squandered.

(3)   *Opportunity costs*

The real economic costs of maintaining and using armed forces are the other goods and services whose use is forgone.[15] The burden of a particular navy can only be understood in terms of the economy as a whole, and this involves matters such as the structure of the economy, balance of payments questions, the nature of industry, and research and development potential. The precise impact of a navy on the national economy (what demands in the way of supplies, equipment, services and other requirements have to be met in the construction and upkeep of a fleet) remains an elusive and underworked problem.[16] The opportunity costs are in three fields: military, civilian and foreign policy. What other military options are forgone for particular naval spending? What values are sacrificed in the civilian sector? And could the money spent on warships have been spent more usefully on altern-ative instruments of foreign policy, such as aid or propaganda?

A significant illustration of opportunity costs within the military sector is provided by the French Navy. The research and development of SSBNs and their missiles, the provision of highly trained crews, and the diversion of effort to provide the necessary support – all these have been very taxing to the French naval effort. The result of this emphasis has been that other tasks have been forgone. In Cable's words: 'The expense, actual and prospective, of the naval contribution to the *Force de Frappe* has already compelled France to abandon her *Force Amphibie d'Intervention*.'[17] The sacrifice of French naval effort at the altar of nuclear deterrence is also reflected in the fact that up to 40 per cent of the French Navy has been tied up for periods of six months in supervising the country's nuclear tests in the Pacific.[18] Other branches of the services have had to forgo equipment modernisation on the scale desired.

The burden of defence on the civilian sector is a familiar theme in Western public affairs, and scarcely needs reiterating. It is therefore of more interest to be reminded of the importance of economic constraints in other societies. In this respect Mr Khrushchev's memoirs are reveal-ing, for one section of them is pervaded by comments concerning the financial problems of building warships. The section is punctuated by phrases such as 'an enormous amount of money to keep afloat', 'huge cost', 'terribly expensive', and 'simply beyond our means'.[19] Khrush-chev acknowledged the valid reasons for building warships but he was very conscious of economic considerations. His concerns were evident in a discussion of the proposed building of new cruisers and destroyers: he said that

> It involved diverting huge sums of money from the development of other more necessary and more reliable forms of warfare, not to mention the funds it diverted from our overwhelming non-military needs.[20]

This was Khrushchev's view, an opinion which Western naval officers have frequently heard from the mouths of their own politicians. In the period since Khrushchev's fall, domestic needs in the Soviet Union have not ceased to be overwhelming.

Professional naval writers naturally take pride in the efficiacy of their chosen instrument. However, analysts should always consider whether a country's foreign policy aims might be pursued more effectively and at less cost by investing money in diplomats, businessmen and military advisers rather than in frigates and lieutenants. It is always necessary to ask whether the political and strategic advantages of forward naval deployment outweigh the economic costs, and whether its objectives could be more satisfactorily achieved by an alternative instrument.[21] As time has passed, most governments have come to favour non-military over military instruments.

(4)   *The domestic aspect of naval spending*

The economic factor in naval policy might not be a matter solely of external affairs. Naval policy might sometimes be a function of domestic policy, to keep people in particular areas and with particular skills in work, both afloat and ashore.

Certainly some localities in many countries are heavily dependent for their prosperity on government spending on naval weapons. This fact is sometimes used by governments to 'sell' naval spending to groups which otherwise would disapprove of military spending as such. In a British defence debate in December 1974, Labour Party left-wingers strongly criticised the government because the defence cuts did not go far enough for their liking. A government spokesman defended the policy, especially the naval spending involved, not on grounds of an ostensible naval threat, but on the grounds of the redundancies which would result if the cuts went further.[22]

(5)   *Economic power and naval potential*

Above all things the economic factor is the basis for dividing the relatively weak from the relatively strong. Although this cannot in any simple way determine success or failure in international politics, it is a basic consideration. As far as navies are concerned, disparity in economic strength means that as time goes on fewer and fewer countries are able to compete in the production of the most advanced equipment. Furthermore, the populations of many countries would rather use their resources for something other than competing in advanced naval hardware. As far as costs are concerned, as Martin has said, there may now be two answers in the naval field: one for the Americans, and one for the rest of the world.[23] The drift of his remark is valid, even if it failed to foresee the extent of Soviet exertions. The projection of this trend in future will mean that governments wanting the most modern military equipment will be faced with two alternatives: either they will have to forgo important domestic expectations, or they will have to purchase weapons from the United States or the Soviet Union, and so risk a degree of dependence. Both alternatives have drawbacks, but the pressures for weapons modernisation seem irresistible. There is a vicious circle in the pressure for modernisation.[24] On the one hand there is an urge in all navies, even small ones, to secure the most sophisticated systems; the pattern of naval transfers shows a 'hungry demand' for high quality. On the other hand, this improving quality of the smaller navies pushes up the requirements of the rest.

Financial considerations must inevitably be a major determinant of the future of navies. Traditional considerations are exacerbated by the continuing sharp rise in costs, the increase in social demands, and the ever-growing variety of weapons systems competing for military resources. In Martin's opinion the military use of the sea is likely to remain important for the nations that can afford it, but navies will be one indicator of the growing disparity between the truly great and the medium powers.[25]

With the pressure for modernisation comes the problem of obsolescence: 'if it works it is obsolete' is a true but unavoidable feature of modern weapons procurement. This problem is further compounded by the spiralling cost of weaponry.[26] With civilian pressures to halt or reduce defence spending, inflation means quantitative though not necessarily qualitative reductions in deployed effort. When financial stringency bites, this also usually means that research and development efforts are constrained: this in turn will increase the pressures to opt out of commitments or to 'buy off the shelf' from another country. The former degrades a country's international significance; the latter

degrades some of its independence. Within an alliance, financial stringency will intensify pressures for weapons standardisation, and this
may make the problem of standardisation a political issue beyond its
objective military importance. These are difficult questions. They have
been reflected in political irritation amongst the members of NATO,
where arguments about the logic of military efficiency have threatened
the political cohesion of the members.[27] Problems of standardisation
affect naval as well as other weapons, though by no means as prominently.

Financial questions are not always the most important determinants
of defence policy, but they often are. But even in the British case it
has been argued that strategic factors 'are often of equal, if not greater,
importance'.[28] As a general proposition, however, it appears that
strategic factors are of chief significance in allocating priorities *within*
an overall defence budget which has been increasingly shaped by
economic and political rather than strategic appraisals.

Human factors

The human factor as a source of naval policy can include many things,
such as size of population, age balance, distribution, technical skill and
so on. A nation with a strong tradition of seafaring, with an important
investment in maritime affairs, with a large number of people deriving
pleasure or profit from the sea, and with a technically minded
population, would seem destined to produce better sailors than a nation
lacking these elements. The regularity and effectiveness of the servicing
of equipment — a critical if unglamorous part of naval life — will bear
some relationship to the machine-mindedness of the society as a whole.
For present purposes, the possible significance of three sets of human
factors will be suggested: the personality of the leaders, ideological
considerations and social factors.

(1) *The personality of the leaders*

Personalities can affect naval policy or individual naval happenings in a
variety of ways. It is therefore necessary to speculate, in so far as it is
possible, about the personal beliefs and values of the relevant leaders,
their character and temperament, their image of the world and their
country's role in it, the alternatives which they consider feasible, the
style with which they implement decisions, the way key policy-makers
conceive their role, and whether they are burdened by it, seek to en-
large it, or simply make full and proper use of it. Personalities do affect
the running of naval organisations,[29] and so it is important to try to

discover when and how.

The attitudes of political leaders to naval matters has varied considerably, and this has been a matter of some strategic significance. Hitler's failure to understand naval strategy was significant in the course of the Second World War. The unease felt by this otherwise self-confident and self-appointed man of destiny was summed up by his own classic statement that he was a 'lion' on land, but a 'lamb' at sea. In Britain, the impact of individual personalities on defence decision-making has varied in importance, but it has always mattered. Interestingly, Ramsay MacDonald, perhaps Britain's most pacifistically-minded Prime Minister, was thought nevertheless to have taken care of his Navy. On the other hand, Winston Churchill, as First Lord and Prime Minister, revelled in naval matters for half-a-century, though not always profitably. In more recent times the role of personality remains significant because of the special characteristics of defence policy-making in Britain. The relatively minor role of Parliament and public in the formulation of defence policy inflates the significance of the personalities of a small number of key individuals, especially the Prime Minister and Minister of Defence.[30] Duncan Sandys, the Minister of Defence from 1956 to 1959, was an important illustration of this. He took a number of important military decisions on his own initiative, with little consultation among the services, and despite the strenuous objections of the military. It was said that he treated the Chiefs of Staff 'like schoolboys'. One consequence of this was that he earned the distrust of the Admiralty. The latter became reluctant to make recommendations or to argue with Sandys unless forced to. This resulted in the Admiralty deciding to delay its campaign for a new carrier until after his departure. Furthermore, because of the Minister's dogmatic attitude towards finance, the Admiralty was reluctant to accept responsibility for Polaris, despite its evident significance: they were convinced that under Sandys they would not receive extra funds for taking on this additional responsibility.[31] Thus the effect of Sandys' personality was partially to remove the Admiralty from the defence policy process. In contrast, there had been a happier conjunction of personality and problems from the Royal Navy's viewpoint with the appointment of Admiral Lord Louis Mountbatten as First Sea Lord in 1955. Although not overly popular in some naval circles, his 'enviable combination of political know-how, influential connections, inter-Service experience, and a mind unusually receptive to new ideas' played an important part in leading the Royal Navy out of a difficult period of uncertainty.[32]

In the United States one might contrast the different attitudes to naval affairs of Presidents Truman and Kennedy. The former had a pro-Army orientation, while the latter had a background and understanding of naval matters. Below the President, the personality of the Secretary of Defense might be significant, as was the case with the incumbency of James Forrestal.[33]

In the Soviet Union the impact of different leaders on naval policy has often been more pronounced than in the West. It is clear from Khrushchev's memoirs that he was obviously very interested in naval matters: he had his own opinions and was 'pushy'.[34] He had strong ideas about the impact of nuclear weapons and of air-to-surface missiles on the future of the surface fleet. These opinions, reinforced by his concern for internal economic developments, led him to see large parts of the surface navy as no more than 'metal-eaters'. As one study brings out, Soviet naval programmes have been characterised by alternating cycles of 'radical change and incremental improvement', and the former have been generally attributable to new ideas imposed from the top. The study concludes that personalities have had a significant impact on Soviet naval policy.[35]

(2)   *Ideological considerations*

Ideological factors include such influences as the perceptions of those involved in shaping policy, and of their cluster of beliefs about their state's aims and interests in the outside world. The impact of 'ideology' or 'outlooks' on foreign policy varies from state to state, but it is important for naval policy in the way it might affect perceptions of likely enemies, threats and roles; it may affect alliance formation and other sorts of international affiliation. Decision-makers are 'part and parcel' of domestic politics: they internalise the values of domestic society; they partake in the national culture and characteristics; and they are constantly exposed to the influences and pressures in the play of domestic politics.[36]

Ideology is usually assumed to have most significance for countries such as the USSR. However, it is worth adding that ideological considerations can also affect the policies, and even the naval policies, of countries which are as ostensibly pragmatic as Britain. In June 1975, for example, the agreement with South Africa over the Simonstown base was ended by the British Labour government. From an operational viewpoint the decision could hardly be defended. The reason for the government's decision, according to its critics, was its wish to placate the left wing of the Labour Party, which had focused attention on the

Simonstown issue and had insisted that the continuance of the agreement represented an endorsement of *apartheid*. The government's critics saw the decision as an 'empty gesture', which weakened Britain's naval efforts in an area through which large amounts of vital British shipping passed: they alleged that the agreement could have been kept, for even the black African states made relatively little of the issue. Despite the strong operational argument, the Labour government did not change its mind. It had more considerations to weigh in the balance than naval operations in the vicinity of the Cape Route: for one thing the Labour government depended upon the support of its left wing for the fulfilment of some of the crucial economic programmes which were aimed at making the country work more effectively. Like all governments, British Labour governments are descended more from the genus *Domestic Political Man* than *Strategic Man*.

(3)   *Social factors*

Knorr has cogently argued that a 'broader approach' to military potential is more necessary than hitherto. As he puts it,

> The daunting fact is that there are few characteristics in a society which do or may not affect, directly or indirectly, its ability to generate and employ military power. Its political system, social structure and culture patterns are as relevant, though not necessarily as weighty, as its economic and technological resources and sheer numbers or population.[37]

Historically the very different naval potential of the maritime countries of Japan and Indonesia was partly explicable in terms of different social, cultural and political factors. One could not imagine Japanese warships being 'non-operational', like some of those of the Indonesian Navy today. An investigation of social factors should provide some insights into manning and recruitment problems, relations between officers and non-officers, the quality of leadership at different levels, the level of skilled manpower, the acceptability and effectiveness of conscription, morale, group cohesion, discipline, normal levels of administrative competence, technical skill and so on. Social questions are therefore relevant to naval performance in a number of ways. The attention paid by naval establishments to projecting improved public images, and to overcoming personnel problems (such as those involved in mixed-race groups) are testimonies to the importance of these questions. Social factors may also affect role conception, bureaucratic success and

general competence. In his study of the post-war Admiralty, Crowe has
shown the bureaucratic significance of the common social background
shared by senior British civilian and naval officials; it is important in
shaping their values, in their formulation of interests, and in giving
them access (through what used to be called the 'old boy's network')
to other élite groupings.[38] His researches suggested that the homogen-
eity of the educational and social background of the Admiralty's civil
servants may have inhibited change in the not-too-distant past through
a mixture of conservatism and a tendency to look down upon engineers
and scientists.[39]

Most major military establishments have been worrying for some
time about the problems of running their services. Changing social
attitudes can create many strains in the smooth running of military
machines.[40] The Soviet Navy today is by no means short of manning
problems.[41] While some of these matters might seem insignificant when
compared with the traditional indices of geopolitics, such as iron ore
production or size of population, they all may play their part in
determining 'form' in the final account. Information is difficult to
gather on many of these questions, but in assessing naval performance
it would be unwise to assume that that which was unmeasurable was
unimportant.

The policy process

Economic factors determine what *can* be afforded on defence: political
considerations affect what *will* be afforded, and the shape and nature
of the allocations. The relevant considerations include the nature of
the political system, the role within it of the organisations responsible
for making and executing naval policy, and the objectives and
constraints established by what, for the want of a better term, is usually
called 'public opinion'.

(1) *The governmental system*

The governmental system is important in the development of a
country's naval policy because its structure affects the way the political
community identifies its interests, conceives its policies, develops its
resources, sees its threats, exploits its opportunities, allocates its resources and ultimately meets its challenges. Invariably, examinations of
the 'system' turn out to be exercises in political pathology: but as was
pointed out in an earlier chapter, there is also room to remember that
when things go right, this is also the result of the outputs of large
political organisations.

In Britain, it is striking how far defence policy is removed from everyday political pressures.[42] The Cabinet has tight control over policy, and defence policy is largely the result of a dialogue between politicians in government and the relevant departments of state. Parliament deliberates and debates in the background, but major strategic decisions may be taken without it being informed, let alone consulted. In the United States, on the other hand, defence policy is an issue which is very much in the political arena. Congress can (and increasingly does) make independent judgements on the money and manpower of the services: it legislates in a more positive way than the British Parliament. One of the many implications of this difference concerns the role of pressure groups. While pressure groups have a place in the British system, this is less so in defence than in many other important areas of public policy. The government's powerful position, the nature of the channels of influence, and the confidential character of military problems gives the British government considerable control over, and immunity from, those groups which do act on defence issues. The impact of pressure groups is severely restricted compared with the United States. Power is more diffused in the latter, so that pressure groups enjoy numerous channels for attempting to influence policy. They can sometimes secure decisions on defence matters which are opposed to the administration's desires: this is rarely if ever the case in Britain. Interest groups seem to have had a miniscule importance in the formulation of British naval policy: the post-war impact of the Navy League and economic groups interested in naval matters has been negligible.[43]

The policy process in the Soviet Union is obviously very different again.[44] In that country there is no tradition of public debate on defence issues in the media, the academic world, or in elected political bodies. Interest group activity is more restricted: there are no private 'lobbyists' for competing arms firms on the US pattern. Decision-making powers on security matters rest firmly with the Politburo. In the last ten years, however, resulting from a mixture of international pressures, the impact of particular personalities, institutional pressures, and the increasing complexity of defence issues, military 'influence' has grown: the Politburo has been more predisposed to seek and perhaps listen to professional advice.[45] What is particularly significant from the Soviet Navy's viewpoint is the traditional dominance of the Army. Neither in prestige nor institutional prominence has the Soviet Navy been the 'Senior Service'. Taken together, this means that if the Navy finds its requests obstructed by the Army-

dominated apparatus, its only court of appeal is the political leadership itself. Soviet defence decision-making is relatively insulated from
extraneous influences; it is dominated by a relatively small number of
senior politicians and (mainly Army) officers. The latter, the youngest
officer corps in the world at the end of World War Two, had become
the oldest twenty years later.[46] The process through which Soviet naval
policy is made therefore involves a smaller, more inbred and more
professionally committed group than is the case with the Washington
model. Amongst other things, this process means that to a far greater
extent than occurs in Britain and the United States, the Soviet Navy's
hopes have to be acceptable to *soldiers* before they can be translated
into operational programmes.

(2)   *Admiralties/Navy Departments*

Within the policy process the role played by the Admiralty or Navy
Department will always be of particular interest. A researcher is
interested in finding out about the system's ability to select the
'best' men for responsible positions, its record in forecasting and
meeting strategic and tactical developments, the relevance and success
of its research and development, and also its ability to formulate its
requirements into packages which are militarily sensible, politically
acceptable, and financially viable.

In examining a Navy Department's role and impact, Crowe has
provided us with a useful framework for analysis. His examination of
the British Admiralty is in two parts.[47] Firstly he looked at the
decision-makers. This provides a picture of specific personalities, social
profiles, and the characteristics of the three professional groups
involved (the political leaders, naval officers and civil servants). In the
second place he examined the Admiralty's performance over a number
of years from three different perspectives, namely its bureaucratic
competence, its scientific and technical competence, and its strategic
competence. The result of his efforts was an interesting analysis, with
insights and thoughtful generalisations on what is a dark corner in the
subject of navies and foreign policy.

In the light of the discussion in Chapter Six, the significance of
organisational processes does not require labouring further; it merely
remains to stress the importance of patterns of co-ordination between
a navy department and other departments of state. The huge feat of
organisation and co-ordination which led to the epic amphibious
operations in Normandy in June 1944 stand out in the whole of
military history. Usually, though, it is the problems and failures of

co-ordination which attract attention. It has been argued that the failure to reappraise British defence policy after India became inde- pendent in 1947, an event which changed many of the assumptions of British policy east of Suez, was partly the result of institutional weaknesses.[48] On a lower but not insignificant level another writer has pointed to the organisational limitations and failure of co-ordination between the Service and Overseas Departments in the 1950s. In the case of Singapore, for example, the Service Departments were planning on the assumption of base sovereignty and control over internal security, while the Colonial Office was going ahead with its own plans for self- government.[49] In each of these cases the process of co-ordination — or lack of it — affected the policy and the efficiency of the military and naval effort.

It is common to hear naval officers talk about 'driving desks' instead of ships. It is always said in a derisive way, and for those with salt in their veins it is an understandable prejudice. But it is a potentially dangerous one. The politico-bureaucratic skill required to translate recommendations into practical policy is as important as technical or leadership expertise. How many important ideas have been lost through the absence of the crucial if not heroic skill of bureaucratic manipula- tion? A close examination of the policy process will show that fierce engagements at sea are only the last act in a drama which begins with restrained confrontations in far-off corridors of power.

(3) *Public opinion*

This is not the place to begin an explanation of the difficult questions concerning 'public opinion'. What is it? How can it be measured? How can its political impact be identified? It is sufficient to note that how- ever public opinion is conceived, it is usually regarded as an important factor in the formulation of defence policy. While public opinion is certainly difficult to analyse, and in Britain such evidence as exists confirms a view of general apathy,[50] it remains important, if only in a negative sense. When a few pence extra on income tax might make a considerable difference in terms of ships, weapons and manpower, fine judgements by politicians of 'what the public will stand' are clearly matters of major significance.

Relevant information is scanty. This point is underlined by the fact that Crowe spends less than three pages (out of 427) discussing public opinion, and out of his six paragraphs on the subject only one is specifically on naval as opposed to general defence questions. How- ever, perhaps the small space he gives to the subject is justified by his view that public attitudes present few limitations on decision-makers on defence in Britain. He found that the government enjoyed considerable independence in making strategic judgements and in formulating defence policy. Significantly, his general impression was that the British public was sympathetic to the Navy, but he could find no instance of public affection helping the Navy in its struggles.[51] In other words, the British public admires its Navy, but is reluctant to demonstrate on its behalf, either financially or otherwise.

Public opinion may not play a direct and positive role in the formulation of defence policy in general and naval policy in particular, even in an open political system. However, in open systems and perhaps closed systems too, what Almond has called 'the mood' does help shape policy in general terms. The 'climate' of public opinion can exercise an important negative influence: it narrows the choice within which decision-makers operate. The 'interested' or 'attentive' public might sometimes have a positive influence, but in most countries this is rare. As far as naval policy is concerned, the negative influence of public opinion can be felt in three main ways. Firstly, it affects the amount of money allowed to be spent on defence as against other public demands. Secondly, it affects the way the armed forces are used, through the 'acceptability' of the use of force. In Western societies this has meant that public opinion has contributed towards the erasing of policy objectives (such as overseas intervention) in which navies formerly had an important supportive function. Public opinion represents the political foundations of a nation's military power, its 'basic mobilizability for purposes of sustaining and using military strength internationally'.[52] Vietnam is the most potent modern illustration of a war in which the necessary degree of domestic support was lacking. But this is not a modern phenomenon: it was also evident in the wilting of the British intervention in Russia between 1918 and 1920.[53] Attention today is frequently drawn to the alleged 'declining self-confidence' of the United States concerning its role in the world;[54] this sense of confidence will obviously have implications for the way its government chooses to use its military instrument. Thirdly, public attitudes also play a part in determining the quality and quantity of recruits to the naval service. This in turn affects 'form' and morale, as well as quantitative strength.

While public opinion is usually conceived in terms of constraints on defence spending, it is often possible for governments to achieve a stronger degree of consensus on defence questions than on many others. National security is a 'gut' issue. People tend to be supportive of governmental action: outlooks in many countries are perhaps more traditionalist than many would credit. People may grumble about paying taxes, but few doubt their country's need for some naval forces.

The efforts of governments are both constrained and supported by public opinion. In addition, governments themselves have to influence public opinion on what they conceive to be proper courses of action. On defence matters this invariably involves what Lord Vansittart neatly called the problem of 'how to induce the unwilling to accept the unavoidable'.[55] It is a commonplace to report that this traditional problem has become increasingly difficult in Western societies. Military forces will only be acceptable if the population is helped to understand their continuing external functions: as Hoffman has put it,

> What is necessary, and has not sufficiently been followed through by most governments, is to give a rational and clear explanation of the . . . functions which force still performs. If force today is misunderstood, it is partly because it is too oblique, but also partly because the change in role has not been well explained.[56]

Admittedly this is a difficult task, especially as the practitioners themselves are not certain about their changed environment. Parenthetically, it might be added that it is not only members of the general public who need informing about naval matters in Western countries: some junior officers are also uncertain about their Service's role, and are in need of having it explained in understandable terms. Paranoia on the part of politicians and senior officers is likely to be counter-productive: inflating external threats is likely only to inflate scepticism. For those who are unsure about the role of a navy in the modern world it is necessary to couch explanations of the changing maritime environment and the naval instruments needed to operate within it in terms which are convincing to people with a rather different set of attitudes than was common a generation ago. Outdated phraseology must be avoided, as must once glorious but now hackneyed clichés. Furthermore, as far as the general public is concerned, it is probably true that 'the more force is wrapped in political calculations and constraints, the less the citizenry understands or approves its use'.[57] Since, by common consent, naval strategy is now more *political* in its meaning than ever before, the task of educating the interested public, 'without either confusion or hyperbole', is one of the main challenges.

facing naval commentators today.

Military critics and civilian scapegoats

Domestic constraints, be they economic, social or political, are invariably political appraisals. As the conclusion of the last section suggested, there is some scope for changing attitudes: if the interested public is sceptical about the role of a navy, some of the blame at least must lie with naval commentators and spokesmen. Too often, however, the latter rest content with grumbling about civilian parsimony and misunderstanding. If there is a military failure, there is often a tendency to search for civilian scapegoats, and to overlook faults that are the result of the service's own lack of imagination, vitality and determination. Two examples will suffice, one from Britain and the other from the United States.

In the British context the discussion surrounding the impact of the Ten Year Rule in the inter-war years is a classic illustration of military critics overlooking the domestic sources of policy, searching for civilian scapegoats, and failing to stress their own inadequacies. Through the years almost all writers[58] have used the Rule as the basic explanation for Britain's poor military performance at the outbreak of World War Two. The Rule is ritually paraded as the main reason why British forces lacked the weapons and doctrine to enable them to be the fighting force which the test initially required. However, the military critics and their supporters overlook at least three important considerations. Firstly, they do not attempt to explain the rationality of the Rule from the perspective of its framers, nor do they explain that while it was in operation, and certainly for the first ten years, it represented an accurate assessment of the strategic environment, and so a reasonable basis for planning. Secondly, they do not stress the range of domestic problems facing British governments, which resulted in the strong belief that the country's economic problems were more pressing than its military problems. This was a valid appraisal (the Rule was cancelled in 1932). Nor do they explain why other countries facing similar or worse problems nevertheless made a much better effort with their military resources. It is too simple to explain Britain's military failings on the basis of the Ten Year Rule. The cause and effect relationship is not so clear. Inter-war civilian scapegoats are readily at hand; there were anti-war sentiments, weak governments and limited funds, but neither these nor the Ten Year Rule can be held responsible for some of the great military mistakes of the period. Often, responsibility for these mistakes rested in the quality and organisation of the services

concerned, inadequacies which resulted in strategic and tactical
doctrines and weaponry which proved to be ill-suited for the eventual
task. Whatever else might be said about civilian constraints, they can
hardly be said to be responsible for the armed services' technological
short-sightedness, doctrinal conservatism, poor planning, unfruitful
inter-service rivalries, weak and unco-ordinated programmes, the
ignoring of those with different (and in the event) valid ideas, the lack
of testing of operational hypotheses, and their unwillingness and/or
inability to learn some of the main 'lessons' of World War One. Can the
Ten Year Rule be held responsible for the Navy's passion for the
smartness of its ships and the quality of its ceremonial functions while
perpetuating tactical sterility, as evidenced in its failure to think about
amphibious operations? Can the Rule be held responsible for the
fact that the naval establishment did not think it worth while to have
one exercise in the protection of a slow mercantile convoy against
submarine or air attack between 1919 and 1939?[59]

Brodie has pointed to a more specific example of the same
phenomenon from the United States: this concerns the virtual absence
of anti-aircraft defences on US battleships on the day of Pearl
Harbor.[60] In explaining this critical shortcoming, Navy spokesmen
during and since the war frequently placed the main blame on
Congress, for failing to appropriate sufficient funds. In Brodie's view
this criticism does not withstand the test of the record. His researches
found little evidence that the Navy as a whole, and particularly the
Bureau of Ships, came anything near to predicting the needs of the war
in that category of weapon, or that any concerted effort was made to
persuade Congress of the urgency of the problem. The governing Navy
doctrine was that offensive strength should not be sacrificed for greater
defensive strength. Brodie could find little to indicate that the Navy
was eager to sacrifice other less necessary things accorded it by Congress, in order to remedy the glaring deficiency. This episode, and
Brodie's comments, are a pointed reminder to contemporary naval
establishments.

Military critics often complain that civilians want 'defence on the
cheap'. This is usually true: humans would be different animals if they
did not prefer things 'on the cheap'. Money is certainly important, but
it is not everything. There is sometimes a tendency for military
establishments to hide their inadequacies behind the phrase: 'If only
we had more money . . .' But money is not a guarantee of success.
Indeed, relative poverty can be a spur to innovation. Historically,
while the fat naval cats have languished, the smaller naval powers have

often been the great innovators in tactics and weaponry. Thus, in addressing the parsimonious civilian scapegoat the 'big navy' advocates may be misdirecting their attentions. Admiral Fisher recognised this perfectly well seventy years ago: he denied that

> fighting efficiency is inalienably associated with the Estimates! The exact opposite is the real truth! Lavish naval expenditure, like human high-living, leads to the development of latent parasitical bacilli which prey on and diminish the vitality of the belligerent force whether in the human body or in the fighting ship![61]

The extravagant impotence of the US military effort in Vietnam will be seen as a general monument to Fisher's trenchant words.

Notes

1.   Note James N. Rosenau, *Domestic Sources of Foreign Policy* (New York: Free Press, 1967), p. 2.
2.   Ibid., p. 4.
3.   Ibid., p. 2.
4.   Erik P. Hoffman and Frederick J. Fleron (eds.), *The Conduct of Soviet Foreign Policy* (Chicago: Aldine, Atherton, 1971), p. 31.
5.   A. J. Marder, *Anatomy of British Sea Power* (London: Frank Cass, 1964), Chapter IV, 'Public Opinion and the Navy'.
6.   W. J. Crowe, *The Policy Roots of the Modern Royal Navy, 1946-1963*, Princeton University Ph.D., 1965 (University Microfilms, Inc., Ann Arbor, Michigan, 1970), Ch. VII, 'Policy Process'.
7.   Alfred Thayer Mahan, *The Influence of Sea Power upon History, 1660-1783* (London: Methuen, 1965. First published in Boston by Little, Brown and Co., 1890), pp. 44-88.
8.   Roskill, *The Strategy of Sea Power*, op. cit.; B. B. Schofield, *British Sea Power: Naval Policy in the Twentieth Century* (London: Batsford, 1967). Apart from a vague one-line reference on page 253, Roskill does not hint at domestic constraints in his review of the 'Perspectives and Prospects' of British naval strategy, though these constraints would prevent Britain from doing in the naval field many of the things which Roskill was recommending (see pp. 248-65).
9.   In this respect see the perceptive comment of Edward Crankshaw in his Foreword to *Khrushchev's Russia* (Harmondsworth: Penguin Books, revised edition, 1962).
10.   See Klaus Knorr, *Military Power and Potential* (Lexington, Mass.: D.C. Heath, 1970), Chapters 2 and 3 are useful general introductions to the concepts of military potential and economic capacity.
11.   John C. Garnett, 'Defence Against What?', *JRUSI*, December 1970, No. 660, Vol. CXV, p. 26.
12.   Ibid., p. 26.

13.   Michael MccGwire, *Soviet Naval Developments* (New York: Praeger, 1973), p. 228ff.
14.   See Jonathan Trumbull Howe, *Multicrises. Sea Power and Global Politics in the Missile Age* (Cambridge, Mass.: The MIT Press, 1971), *passim.*
15.   See Chapter Nine. One small historical illustration of naval opportunity costs measured in terms of manpower can be seen in the case of a rule-of-thumb used in German shipbuilding before World War Two: 'One ton of warship represents the year's labour of one German worker. Thus to construct a battleship of 35,000 tons requires the labour of 10,000 workers for three years and a half, even if working to a well thought-out and precisely applied blueprint.' Cajus Bekker, *Hitler's Naval War* (London: Macdonald, 1974), p. 33.
16.   An imaginative model for looking at this question, and a useful reminder of the detailed naval demands on an economy is provided by Raymond Hutchings in his 'The Economic Burden of the Soviet Navy', Chapter 17 in MccGwire, *Soviet Naval Developments.*
17.   James Cable, *Gunboat Diplomacy. Political Applications of Limited Naval Force* (London: Chatto and Windus for the ISS, 1971), p. 119.
18.   Ibid., pp. 118-20.
19.   Strobe Talbott (translator and editor), *Khrushchev Remembers. The Last Testament* (London: Andre Deutsch, 1974), especially pp. 20, 31.
20.   Ibid., p. 20.
21.   For a discussion of this in the Soviet case, see MccGwire, *Soviet Naval Developments*, Parts IV-VII.
22.   *The Times*, 17 December 1974.
23.   L. W. Martin, *The Sea in Modern Strategy* (London: Chatto and Windus for the ISS, 1967), p. 12.
24.   See ibid., pp. 118-21.
25.   Ibid., pp. 170-1.
26.   For some examples of the spiralling costs see Martin, op. cit., p. 114; Crowe, op. cit., p. 140; Phillip Darby, *British Defence Policy East of Suez* (Oxford: Oxford University Press for RIIA, 1973), pp. 249-50; A. Cecil Hampshire, *The Royal Navy since 1945. Its transition to the nuclear age* (London: William Kimber, 1976), p. 113. For the costs of the Kuwait operation (£1 million) see Darby, op. cit., pp. 254-5; and for confrontation with Indonesia (£250 million) see C. J. Bartlett, *The Long Retreat: a short history of British defence policy, 1945-1970* (London: Macmillan, 1972), p. 186.
27.   Ken Booth, 'Security Makes Strange Bedfellows: The Problems of NATO from a Minimalist Perspective', *JRUSI*, Vol. 120, No. 4, December 1975, pp. 3-14.
28.   John Baylis, 'Defence Decision-making in Britain and the Determinants of Defence Policy', *JRUSI*, Vol. 120, No. 1, March 1975, p. 46.
29.   Marder's detailed account of the running of the Royal Navy between 1904 and 1919 brings this out very clearly; and it also makes fascinating reading.
30.   Baylis, op. cit., p. 42.
31.   Crowe, op. cit., pp. 339-41, cf. Darby, op. cit., p. 108.
32.   Crowe, op. cit., pp. 386-7.
33.   Davis, op. cit., pp. 256-7.
34.   Talbott, op. cit., pp. 19-34.
35.   James A. Barry, 'Institutional Factors in Soviet Naval Policy', Paper prepared for the Third Annual Seminar on Soviet Naval Developments, Dalhousie University, 8-11 September 1974, p. 41.
36.   Joseph Frankel, *The Making of Foreign Policy* (New York: Oxford

University Press, 1968), p. 70.
37.   Knorr, *Military Power and Potential*, pp. 24-5.
38.   Crowe, op. cit., pp. 351-60.
39.   Ibid., pp. 363-4.
40.   E.g., see the changing public attitudes in the United States revealed by
       Charles C. Moskos, *Public Opinion and the Military Establishment*
       (Beverly Hills, California: Sage Publications, 1971). For a brief picture
       of the US Navy's problems of adjusting to a changing society see Cmdr.
       George Thibault USN, 'The Naval Profession in the United States',
       JRUSI, June 1975, Vol. 120, No. 2, pp. 51-5.
41.   See Captain John E. Moore, *The Soviet Navy Today* (London: Macdonald
       and Janes, 1975), pp. 45-8. Harsh conditions and relatively poor pay
       mean that few conscripts seek a permanent career in the Navy. There is a
       severe lack of senior technical ratings. This picture of an overstretched
       Soviet Navy is all the more interesting in the light of a small 'mutiny'
       reported in the Baltic in January 1976.
42.   The comments below are based on Crowe, op. cit., Ch. VII.
43.   Ibid., pp. 307-10.
44.   This paragraph is based on Geoffrey Jukes, 'The Military Approach to
       Deterrence and Defence', Ch. 26 in Michael MccGwire, Ken Booth and
       John McDonnell, *Soviet Naval Policy. Objectives and Constraints* (New
       York: Praeger, 1975).
45.   E.g., Malcolm Mackintosh, 'The Soviet Military's Influence on Foreign
       Policy', ibid., Ch. 2.
46.   John Erickson, 'The Army, the Party, and the People', *JRUSI*, No. 669,
       Vol. CVX, September 1970, pp. 27-31 and No. 670, December 1970,
       pp. 45-7.
47.   Crowe, op. cit., Ch. VIII.
48.   Darby, op. cit., pp. 10-31.
49.   Baylis, op. cit., p. 44.
50.   Ibid., pp. 45-6.
51.   Crowe, op. cit., pp. 310-12.
52.   Knorr, *Military Power and Potential*, pp. 27-30.
53.   Captain S. W. Roskill, *Naval Policy Between the Wars* (London: Collins,
       1968), pp. 131-80.
54.   E.g., P. Wiles, 'Declining Self-Confidence', *International Affairs*, Vol. 47,
       No. 2, April 1971, pp. 289-301.
55.   Lord Vansittart, *The Mist Procession: the autobiography of Lord
       Vansittart* (London: Hutchinson, 1958), p. 63.
56.   Hoffman, op. cit., pp. 11-12.
57.   Ibid., p. 6.
58.   See, for example, Peter Silverman, 'The Ten Year Rule', *JRUSI*, No. 661,
       March 1971, Vol. CXVI, pp. 42-5. A contrary view is provided in my
       'The Ten-Year Rule — An Unfinished Debate', *JRUSI*, No. 663, September
       1971, Vol. CXVI, pp. 58-63.
59.   On this lack of training see Roskill, *Naval Policy Between the Wars*, Ch.
       XV, and esp. p. 336.
60.   Brodie, 'Strategy as Science', *World Politics*, Vol. 1 (No. 4), July 1949,
       p. 483.
61.   Quoted by A. J. Marder, *From the Dreadnought to Scapa Flow*, Vol. 1
       (London: Oxford University Press, 1961), p. 24.

9 THE INTERNATIONAL CONTEXT

In the perspective of the rational policy model, the international context has been the chief focus of attention for those wishing to understand the dynamics of military behaviour. In suggesting that the rational policy model is not completely satisfactory,[1] however, we should take care that we do not throw out the baby as well as the bath-water. The international context remains a major variable in any analysis of military behaviour: 'international context' includes not only contingent situations, but also the essential characteristics of a particular period.

The historian's view that all periods are transitional is a familiar one. Certainly the environment within which naval activity has been taking place over the last few years has been marked by change, and the promise of more, in many of its political, economic, ideological, socio-logical and technological aspects. It is a mark of this changeableness that hardly anybody in the 1950s would have imagined the salience of maritime affairs in the mid-1970s. Today, the sea is once more a major headline in politics among nations. This change would seem to promise a revived significance for navies, but it has occurred against a back-ground in which the traditional roles of armed forces have been increasingly questioned, in the Western world at least.

The questioning of the traditional utility of armed forces has been one of the characteristic features of strategic discourse in the last decade or so. The doubts began sooner and were felt more deeply amongst those concerned with navies than amongst those concerned with other branches of military service. This uncertainty tended to encourage a rush to extremes. Too many of those professionally committed tried to oversell the usefulness of navies: they talked in nineteenth-century terms about 'the defence of trade routes' and the need for bases, and they discussed the Soviet naval threat in a way which sounded like an ersatz version of the German challenge of seventy years before. But there were equally glib statements made on the other side: too many commentators were quick to dismiss the contribution which warships could make to the support of policy in peace and war, off-handedly implying that because some of the traditional usages of warships seemed improbable, that navies were therefore useless.

In the light of these opening remarks, it is obvious that the provision of satisfactory frameworks for assessing the utility of warships is one of the most pressing tasks for students of naval affairs. The subsequent discussion of this problem is based on the belief that the role of navies cannot be properly understood apart from the other elements of a country's military inventory, the changing (or unchanging) utility of armed forces in general, and the interests subjectively perceived by politically important groups in different countries.

Armed forces and the concept of utility

The idea of utility in the study of politics is derived from economics, on the assumption that much political behaviour and choice is comparable to economic behaviour and choice. As it is generally understood, 'utility is the capacity of a good or service to give satisfaction by meeting a want or ministering to a purpose'. Of particular interest are: (1) the *marginal purchase*: this is the point at which a consumer must balance the satisfaction to be gained from one or more units of the good or service against that to be gained from an alternative use of his money; it is assumed that a point is reached where a consumer prefers to spend his money on an alternative good or service; (2) the idea of *opportunity cost*: that is, the real cost of meeting one want or ministering to one purpose is ultimately the cost of not meeting other wants or ministering to other purposes. The relevance of such concepts to the problems associated with the development and use of a country's military potential for the satisfaction of such wants as security, influence and prestige should be readily apparent.

The concept of utility cannot be applied with any precision, for it involves a number of analytical difficulties. [2] These may be summarised as follows. (1) The concept is entirely subjective. It is an appraisal by an individual or group with reference to the scale of values of that individual or group. Assessing values is always difficult: there are always problems of information and culture-boundedness. Comparisons between national groups will always be tentative. (2) Utility is contextual. Circumstances alter appraisals of values and costs: even for the same government the capacity of A to minister to purpose X may vary in different times and situations. (3) Utility involves the consideration of a complex of phenomena, encompassing a wide range of possible costs and values. (4) The most convenient concept for understanding a government's purposes remains the 'national interest', although this concept is much criticised and of limited value. (5) Utility is not measurable. Numerical values cannot be ascribed to 'political goods' such as prestige or security. It is only possible to say (and therefore it is sufficient to say) that the utility of A is greater than B, in the eyes of government C for purpose X. (6) It will always be easier to assess utility in a specific rather than in a general sense. In sum, one cannot approach any discussion of the utility of naval forces with any confidence of clear-cut answers. Utility is in the eye of the beholder.

The utility which a government or group derives from the maintenance and use of military power depends on the satisfaction of certain values and the accrual of certain costs: utility is the difference between aggregate values and aggregate costs.[3] The types of cost and value involved must be the starting point of discussion.

The range of costs involved in the maintenance and use of armed forces is considerable, and they confront societies with profound dilemmas. (1) Direct economic and financial burdens are the most obvious cost. Armed forces involve the use of fabulous amounts of capital, and enormous quantities of manpower, human ingenuity and skill, and they place considerable demands on scarce raw materials and land. (2) Opportunity costs are the real meaning of the direct burdens. The real cost to society of using its scarce resources for military purposes is the forgoing of their use for other purposes. What could that society achieve if its resources and skills were invested differently? (3) For some people there are important social costs involved in the very existence of armed forces. The regimentation and discipline involved are seen as threats to liberal values. (4) There are similar ethical costs. While military force which is used 'justly' might be defendable on the grounds of the lesser evil, it is nevertheless invariably regarded as an evil. (5) Armed forces can involve heavy internal political costs. They represent, or can represent, a threat to legitimate authority, for they hold the weapons and are the physically most powerful group within a state. All governments have feared 'the man on horseback', and it is a norm in the modern world that governments are more likely to be toppled by their own armed forces than by external attack. (6) The maintenance and use of armed forces, and especially their misuse, can incur many external political costs: the action-reaction phenomenon might provoke an arms race; exposure might result in a loss of prestige; war might result in defeat; victory might generate hatred.

The costs involved in the maintenance and use of armed forces are immediate and significant. However, the values which they are said to protect and promote are equally impressive. (1) The provision of basic physical security (territorial integrity) has been the first obligation of governments, and armed forces have been the traditional means for achieving this. Without a satisfactory degree of security, societies cannot hope to achieve their other objectives. (2) Physical security involves internal order. In this respect, military aid to the civil authority has always been a basic role. It involves the preservation of order against challenges, thereby creating the conditions for the enjoyment of social, economic and political development. (3) For some societies, especially those of new or unstable countries, armed forces perform a variety of nation-building roles. They are a badge of sovereignty, immediately minted by all new states. They can be a force for domestic unification and can strengthen national purpose by carrying out political indoctrination and socialising functions, and by contributing to civic action schemes such as educational programmes and economic development. They may be important symbols of national unity, by providing psychological reassurance about past glories or present hopes. Furthermore, the military values which are criticised by some Western liberals may be warmly embraced in some countries as being socially desirable; such attitudes might favour a degree of youth control or the espousing of the full militarist ethos. (4) In addition to providing for basic territorial defence, the armed forces of many countries have been used to extend deterrent and defensive capabilities to allies and associates. (5) The possession of armed forces enables states to deal with others from a position of some power ('to negotiate from strength'). A government may be able to use its armed forces (either as a backdrop or explicitly in the foreground) to support diplomacy by a range of bargaining techniques. (6) Armed forces have often been used directly for acquisitive purposes, to take by brute force what could not otherwise be obtained. (7) Historically, armed forces have had an important role in establishing and maintaining international status, enabling their possessors to enjoy the deference, respect and political leverage which flows from this attribution. (8) The safest guarantee of international order has usually been thought to be a balance of power system, in which military power was an essential ingredient. The willingness of groups to fight and defend their patch of territory has established the basic framework for whatever degree of order and society exists in international relations.

Before turning to the utility of naval forces, it is necessary at the outset to state some assumptions about the balance of these various values and costs as they affect the thinking of different types of country. Subsequent discussion will be based on these assumptions.[4]

The costs of maintaining and using armed forces have risen, whatever the society. Direct economic costs have soared: even authoritarian societies are more aware of civilian expectations. There is a clear consciousness of opportunity costs: skills and resources are in demand for many public needs, be they the solving of the problems of industrial societies or the pushing along of the development of new countries. In the Western world there has been increasing opposition to the social and ethical implications of force, particularly amongst the more vocal and flamboyant sections of Western 'youth culture'. But the majority of the world is neither Western nor developed: in the rest of the world the social and ethical objections scarcely raise their head. In many countries, in fact, armed forces are cultivated for their nation-building and modernising roles, although this often entails the threat of political intervention. Because of the prevalence of the latter, it is clear that the internal political costs involved in the maintenance of armed forces have risen. This is also the case with external political costs. Certainly, the 'aggressive' use of force has less legitimacy, though in any particular situation any definition of 'aggressive' is likely to be based on political expediency rather than on abstract ideals or legal definition. There is a general perception that the costs of territorial conquest have risen, certainly for the Western industrial nations. This is because the Davids fight with more vigour and more sophisticated weaponry, and thereby seriously increase the direct costs of using force against them, while the benefits of conquest have declined for the major industrialised powers; the latter see national success and prosperity lying in internal investment and development rather than in fighting for the control of markets and raw materials. But for some countries territorial conquest is still worth the candle, and for the most old-fashioned of motives. For all states, including the major industrialised powers, few are likely to disagree with Knorr's verdict that the deterrent role of armed forces retains its traditional utility; it is only that the usability of force for compellant purposes has somewhat declined.[5]

Turning to the values which armed forces can promote, a more variegated picture is present. Since basic territorial integrity remains of supreme value, and since armed forces retain their effectiveness for deterrent and defensive purposes, this function remains as important as ever. Furthermore, through extended deterrence and defence armed forces can play a crucial role in attempting to preserve a 'compatible' world of allies and associates. In terms of the most basic value of all, physical security, armed forces therefore remain an important instrument for all types of states. The same is true for internal security, especially in a world where problems of 'governability' have arisen in many countries. In both developed and developing countries armed forces have been increasingly drawn into politics to aid the civil power. By contributing to order and nation-building, armed forces play an integral part in the development of their states. Equally, all governments retain a belief in the importance of force and the threat of force as a preserver of a degree of international order: to judge by actions rather than words, the security of all states rests on military power, not disarmament. However, the military element is not as prominent as formerly as a contributor to international prestige: but military considerations are not insignificant, particularly in some local 'balances'. From these general comments it can be seen that while armed forces do not contribute as importantly as in the past to the promotion of *some* national values, they are believed to be critical in the protection of some of the most important.

The main question-mark is over the usability and acceptability of armed forces for the advanced Western countries. In the rest of the world, opinions about the utility of armed forces have not changed very much. In the Soviet Union, for example, there has been no overt opposition to all things military: indeed, the military instrument has proved itself to be important in the discharging of a variety of vital tasks, and the experience of the Soviet leaders has confirmed that their armed forces are not only a necessary but also an effective instrument of policy. Nevertheless, most commentators accept the thesis of the restricted 'usability' of military power in the contemporary setting, especially for the major powers: compared with former times, there are certain circumstances and certain objectives in and for which armed force cannot be threatened as credibly as hitherto. Changed attitudes to war, various domestic pressures, rising costs and declining benefits, the end of colonialism, and the dangers of escalation to nuclear war all add inhibitions to the use of military power by and certainly between the major powers. Such inhibitions have been felt most strongly in Western democratic societies, where there has been a perceptible decline in the *acceptability* of military force.[6] Hoffman has convincingly argued that this decline (as evidenced in the abandonment of the draft in the United States, and the unpopularity of conscription in Western Europe) has been the result of a 'concatenation' of purely accidental circumstances and more sweeping and fundamental explanations. Of the former he lists the post-Vietnam reaction in the United States, the post-colonial reaction in Europe, the residues of the impact

of World War Two in West Germany and Japan, and a general fatigue
following a quarter-century of cold war. Of the more basic explanations
he lists such cultural and political changes as the revolt of the young
against imposed discipline, conformity and deference, an associated
'humanistic horror of violence', and political attitudes which are far
removed from military virtues. In addition, force has declined in
acceptability partly as a result of the growing acceptability of such
non-military instruments of policy as propaganda, diplomatic bargaining, economic aid and pressure. Changing attitudes such as these are
important for there is a circular relationship between utility and
acceptability: 'low utility will diminish acceptability and low
acceptability will reduce utility by increasing political costs.'[7] Martin
adds this very important rider, which is too often overlooked, namely
that a sense of 'unacceptability sufficiently high to encourage an
attitude of appeasement in one power would increase the utility of
force for another.' Expressed differently, it is the old warning that
governments which favour 'peace' at almost any price abdicate, if not
encourage, the running of international politics in favour of those
willing to pay the costs of conflict.

The military instrument is therefore always costly, and it is often
likely to be a blunt tool for the purposes for which it is employed.
But are there any alternatives? For some purposes there are: non-
military instruments figure prominently in the promotion of some
national purposes. Furthermore, the importance of certain national
objectives for which armed forces were traditionally used (especially
territorial conquest) have declined in significance, while for some
societies the maintenance of armed forces is not acceptable, nor
are they as usable, as thirty or fifty years ago. Nevertheless, despite
these dents in the old picture, what is most impressive is the *traditional*
outlook adopted by many societies to both the acceptability and the
usability of their armed forces. The extreme view about the obsolescence
of military force is not supportable.[8] Military hesitation and scruple are
decidedly Western phenomena: even here, however, the utility of armed
forces has not been undermined to the extent that it has become
fashionable to suppose.

The utility of navies

The preceding section outlined the costs and values involved in
maintaining and using armed forces under modern conditions. In this
section the focus is on the utility of navies, but the organising framework remains the usage of armed forces in general, because the

maintenance and use of navies cannot be properly assessed apart from the general utility of military power and force.

The functions of armed forces can be classified, without too much distortion or overlap, as follows:

(1) *Projection of force functions*
    (i)   General war
    (ii)   Conventional wars
    (iii) Limited wars and interventions
    (iv) Guerrilla wars
(2) *Balance of power functions*
    (v)   Strategic nuclear deterrence
    (vi) Conventional deterrence and defence
    (vii) Extended deterrence and defence
    (viii) International order
(3) *Diplomatic functions*
    (ix) Negotiating from strength
    (x)   Manipulation
    (xi) International prestige
(4) *Domestic functions*
    (xii) Border/coastguard responsibilities
    (xiii) Nation-building

The subsequent discussion based on this classification is inevitably general; it can only provide a guide and perspective for the specific analyses which must be the ultimate aim when assessing such a subjective and contextual concept as utility.

(1) Projection of force functions

(i) *General war*

General war cannot be regarded as a rational instrument of policy. Wars in which the participants have every reason to expect annihilation cannot be regarded as a 'continuation of politics': the nub, in Kahn's brilliantly conceived question, is: 'Will the survivors envy the dead?' But such wars can occur: political pointlessness and catastrophic consequences do not rule out the possibility of accident, miscalculation or madness. Furthermore, the *threat* of general war is thought to have important utility in terms of deterrence, so that the ultimate futility has to be prepared for with all the effort, cost and seriousness as if it were politically 'thinkable'.

In the event of nuclear war breaking out, peacetime estimates of costs and values would change. Against such a new and horrible background naval forces would have utility in a number of critical operations. Naval strategy would be important, though not in traditional ways.

Sea-based forces might be involved in the first attack. If massive destruction is deemed the appropriate action by which to begin such a war, or by which to respond to a surprise attack, naval forces will be heavily involved: a significant portion of the nuclear potential of both superpowers is carried on or under the sea. In addition to its SLBMs, the strike carriers of the US Navy carry a residual nuclear capability: while their relative significance has declined since the advent of Polaris, their existence is an additional strategic and tactical threat, complicating problem, and potential cost for any enemy. As one of the three arrows in a strategic bombardment capability (the 'triad' in US jargon) sea-based forces have to be countered in any damage-limitation strategy, be it Soviet or American. The primary responsibility for the surveillance and destruction of strike-carriers and SSBNs will belong to naval forces, although land-based aircraft and missiles may have some role. The amount of success to be expected from a damage limitation strategy is not likely to be great, certainly as far as tracking and destroying the *Trident* and *Delta* class of submarines and their successors is concerned. But this does not mean that the task has been or will be left by default: so far at least, both superpowers work on a 'no free ride' rule-of-thumb. However, if SSBN technology continues to outrun its counters, then there will presumably come a time when economic constraints shout 'Enough'. To date, however, the utility of the damage limitation mission for the Soviet Union is proved by the effort invested in their shift to forward deployment.

It is conceivable that war might take place between the superpowers in which nuclear weapons are not used, or are used only selectively. In the nightmare world of graduated deterrence and controlled escalation sea-based forces will also have a special role. Nuclear-strike systems at sea can be 'withheld': SSBNs can disappear and strike carriers can head for the relative safety of the southern oceans. Such forces therefore derive some wartime utility from their ability to affect the post-exchange bargaining.

Naval forces have a further utility in nuclear war. While it is unlikely to commend itself as a justification for having a navy, the fact that some warships will survive and that their crews are likely to be as organised and as disciplined a body as will exist, means that they will be in some position to bring some hope of succour, rescue, relief or escape.

If in the nuclear scenario some naval forces have a central importance, the role of warships is not so clear in the more traditional aspects
of naval war. It was this problem which accounted for the creeping
doubts about the future of the major navies in the 1950s. During this
time, the members of NATO, with their memories of two world wars,
used a third battle of the Atlantic as the scenario which gave general
shape to their naval efforts; this involved the need to defend Allied
shipping against a prolonged war on communications. As time passed,
however, the idea of a 'broken-backed' war declined: the prevailing
view came to be that a major European war would be short rather than
long, at the most a matter of weeks rather than months. If general war is to
be short, there is no substantial requirement for warships to carry out the
historic tasks of blockade, convoy protection, and commerce destruction. Some capability is maintained for such purposes, because they just
might be used: most Soviet submarines have a role in the initial exchange,
but they nevertheless all carry an anti-shipping capability. While the short
nuclear war scenario rules out some of the most traditional functions of
maritime strategy, it does leave others intact. In Europe there would be
amphibious operations on both flanks, and involving both alliances. For
NATO this would be primarily for deterrence and reinforcement purposes: for the Soviet Union it would be to take control of the maritime
exits (northern Norway, the Danish and Turkish Straits) and to support
by amphibious hooks the fast-moving land battle for which they prepare.
In the long war scenario, sea control functions will have to be attempted
by the surviving NATO naval units, in order to reinforce and resupply
Western Europe. The Soviet Union would attempt to prevent the achievement of this aim by a mixture of land- and sea-based systems.

General war is not thinkable, but it remains a finite possibility. Within its changed environment of costs and values, the major powers will find
a variety of important if not historic roles for their warships. Whether
'victory', punishment or rescue is the objective, naval forces will have
considerable utility in this unlikely scenario.

(ii)   *Conventional wars*

The proponents of the thesis that the use of military power was becoming obsolete have almost entirely concentrated their attention on those
states locked in the balance of terror. They seem to have ignored the obvious fact that outside this confrontation military power has been useful
in many familiar ways. Indeed, in some important parts of the world, war
still retains the *natural* and legitimate connotations which it had in the

Western world until at least World War One: for many countries war is still Clausewitzian, being national, rational and instrumental.[9] From their experience in recent years, as winners or losers, Israelis and Egyptians, Indians, Bangladeshis and Pakistanis, and North and South Vietnamese all know that war is functional.

In the conventional wars which have taken place in the last thirty years, naval forces have not usually had an important role. This is largely because the wars have been between neighbours, and between countries which, with one exception, have not possessed sizeable naval forces. Furthermore, the wars which have occurred have usually been short; this has restricted the opportunities for the employment of such strategies as blockade and large-scale amphibious assault.

The only sizeable naval power to have been involved in conventional wars in recent years is India. Significantly, India used its naval forces to good effect in the wars of 1965 and 1971, against an enemy whose territory was physically separated by India itself. In the Indo-Pakistan war of 1965 the naval operations involved bombardment, but in 1971 they were on a larger scale: they included a blockade (which was not formally declared, but which involved visit-and-search on the high seas), air strikes on Chittagong from the Indian carrier *Vikrant* and a variety of actions (by both sides) against the other's ships. The 1971 war was the only clear example since 1945 of naval operations having been carried into the high seas. One neutral merchant ship, the *Venus Challenger*, was sunk with all hands by a *Styx* missile which probably strayed during an engagement between Indian and Pakistani warships.[10]

In the Middle Eastern wars of 1967 and 1973 small warships have had a variety of roles, including coastal defence, ASW, ship-to-ship attack, small-scale amphibious operations, and coastal bombardment. In the 1973 war the Israelis appear to have had few doubts about their investment in naval forces, relatively modest though they were. The Israeli Naval Force did not have a decisive influence on the final outcome, but then the basic Israeli strategic concept did not assume otherwise.[11] Of additional interest is the suggestion that this conflict represented a 'new era' in naval warfare: this was because of the battle of Latakia, the 'first naval missile battle in history', and because of the character of the overall naval side of the conflict. As the engagements were between the missile boats of small countries, and took place in closed seas, they could be regarded as a sign of things to come.[12]

One manifestation of the utility of naval forces for the small and not-so-small powers is the increasing sophistication of some of their weaponry. Despite the opportunity costs involved, a country such as

Iran has clearly been interested in maintaining as modern a navy as is within its capability. But as the decline of Indonesia's Soviet-built forces shows, it is one thing for a relatively non-industrialised country to want to exhibit impressive naval power, but it is another matter entirely to maintain a modern navy in proper order over a number of years. However, while the sensitivity of many countries on matters relating to maritime sovereignty grows, it would be logical to expect that they will give increasing attention to sea-based forces. With potential arms suppliers looking for longer production runs and a degree of influence, the situation suggests a further proliferation of modern naval vessels, if not embryonic medium-sized fleets.

Amongst other things, the proliferation of more sophisticated vessels represents an increased danger to third parties in the event of the outbreak of conventional wars, because of their spillage on to the sea. There is little doubt that such wars will occur, as a result of both maritime and territorial conflicts. In the years ahead the potential for conflict is considerable, and smaller powers have fewer inhibitions about the use of force. Third parties will have to suffer the disruption of trade resulting from blockade, or perhaps worse, because of the scope for the 'capricious behaviour of missiles'.[13] Such possibilities present important legal and operational problems for those states with a critical stake in maintaining the use of the sea for their own vessels.

While the conventional wars since 1945 have been decided mainly on the ground or in the air, warships have been given and have played a limited role. The operations have been small beer when compared with the traditions of the great maritime powers, but they have been significant within their own context. Within their limited capabilities naval forces have been fully employed in 'usable' situations, and so may be deemed to have had utility for the countries concerned.

(iii)   *Limited wars and interventions*

Fear of total war has directed the attention of strategists into the rag-bag concept which has been euphemistically called 'limited war'. These are wars in which at least one of the belligerents (implicitly a superpower) exercises some deliberate restraint: according to one's definition, this restraint might relate to the objective, the means, or the geographical scope of the conflict. Korea was the mould in which the concept of limited war was baked, or half-baked.

The attention given to the weapons and strategies of limited war confirms that some believe that military force can still be used profitably by the major powers for acquisitive or non-acquisitive purposes. However, few are likely to disagree with the view that under modern conditions the acquisitive use has declined markedly in utility. The age of imperialism as it was historically understood, involving great power intervention for territorial conquest, has passed. While the logic of the post-Suez and post-Vietnam world might suggest that one might confidently extrapolate this tendency, it is well to remember that the time-scale has been short: anything can happen in international politics, and often does. While crude imperialism might have passed, interventions of various types cannot be ruled out: Knorr's thesis of a decade ago has by no means been overthrown, but at least some doubts have been raised as a result of the world energy crisis, which served as a reminder of the closeness of the state of nature.[14]

On a number of occasions in the last twenty years great powers have injected force in various places in order to protect their interests. The US interventions in the Lebanon in 1958 and in the Dominican Republic in 1965, and the British interventions in Kuwait in 1961 and in the Malaysian-Indonesian confrontation of 1963-6 were sea-borne examples, while the Soviet interventions in Hungary in 1956 and in Czechoslovakia in 1968 involved the injection of ground forces into neighbouring territories. From the point of view of the superpowers concerned, few can doubt the utility of force for preserving a compatible world when, as in these episodes, it was achieved relatively clinically. Furthermore, in episodes where military force has not achieved its ends, as in Vietnam, it should not be automatically assumed that force has lost its utility; rather, one might question the appropriateness of the particular strategies and tactics adopted. As long as there is someone able to call himself a 'winner' there will be someone who can argue the case for the utility of military force. While 'Vietnam' is the symbol of the declining utility of war for many Americans, to the North Vietnamese and Vietcong the outcome represented a heroic triumph of national, revolutionary and military determination.

With the decline of imperialistic self-confidence amongst the traditional maritime powers, and with the rise and strength of nationalism in their former targets, the era of great power 'grab and hold' appears to have passed. This clearly has many implications for what was formerly one of the most adventurous and special uses of naval power. But interventions from the sea cannot be ruled out entirely. There remains at least the possibility of limited interventions to protect friendly régimes ashore. It remains to be seen whether, in a world of increased insecurity about the supply of primary resources, there will be any resurgence of more far-reaching interventionist practice: what is certain is that the character of many parts of the world will present many opportunities for intervention. These situations will arise not only because of the ambitions of the powerful, but also because of the inadequacies of the weak. In this respect Inis Claude has persuasively argued that we should turn our old way of looking at power and aggression on its head.[15] He has argued that our images are too dominated by the 1890s and 1930s, when war and intervention were the result of the aggressive decisions of the great powers: instead, we should concentrate our attention and anxieties upon the incapacity of the weak rather than upon the capacity of the strong. Many states today can hardly cope with their problems. They are overloaded with difficulties, and are short on capabilities. They cannot avoid trouble.

If this appreciation is valid, there is no guarantee that the more powerful will always deny themselves the opportunities presented for economic, political or military gain. Powers which have commitments of one type or another may be dragged into disputes and problems because they feel that they cannot afford to stand aside. In such circumstances, naval forces may still be the vehicle for large-scale military interventions; and if naval forces are in the vicinity of a troubled situation, this instrument might well shape an ostensibly sober will. Naval-based intervention will therefore remain a possibility: furthermore, it might not always be possible to keep an intervention under control. It has sometimes been said that 1914, when events 'slipped out of control', will be the model for World War Three rather than the aggressive ambitions of 1939. Latter-day Agadirs are not unimaginable in an era of multi-polar influence-building in troubled parts. Although it was inconceivable twenty years ago, it has since become a commonplace that one of the occasions for a major international crisis might be the result of a US-Soviet naval confrontation.[16] Getting there first with warships might be the imperative for haste, hostile thoughts and dangerous actions.

To the extent that limited wars and interventions might have utility for the superpowers, then naval forces have a considerable significance. Without its naval forces for transportation, sea control, and projection of force ashore, the United States would not have been able to support its policy in Korea and Indo-China and elsewhere, while Britain could not have maintained its position in a number of localities east of Suez. On the whole, in their technical and tactical aspects, the United States and Britain have used their navies effectively and impressively in the various operations in which they have taken part since Korea. From the relative sanctuary of the sea, a number of important missions were discharged off Korea, Suez, Kuwait, the Dominican Republic, Vietnam and elsewhere. From the varied use of aircraft carriers to the use of riverine operations on a new scale, navies have supported policy on shore in useful ways. Although maritime support by itself obviously cannot 'win' such engagements, it has been a vital ingredient for success: it has been a necessary but not sufficient factor. This is well illustrated by the impressive fact that despite all the advances in air transport, 93 per cent of US military traffic to Vietnam was sea-borne. While such logistic support does not always require warships (as opposed to merchant ships) it does require naval effort in an environment of potential threat. Prudent strategists believe it safer to assume that limited war 'sanctuaries' at sea have retained their character as a result of expediency and incapacity on the part of the enemy, rather than as a result of any addiction to American strategic theology.

The direct costs of maintaining a capability to project force from the sea at considerable distance from the homeland have become so great that they are now only within the reach of the superpowers. While Britain and France retain some intervention capacity (for unopposed landings), they have relinquished more ambitious options; they have quietly dropped out of the game. The Soviet Union remains an enigma in this respect. Whatever volitional constraints there have been on Soviet involvement in limited war, they have certainly been constrained by their relative weakness in naval forces; this incapacity has prevented them from embarking on distant military interventions, even had the intention been there. A sceptic would say that their lack of capability has enabled them to make a virtue of a necessity; the official Soviet line has obviously been that the intention has never been there. Mr Khrushchev, for example, has written in his memoirs that 'some people may have asked': — which presumably means that some people in the Soviet Union definitely *did* ask — 'what about personnel transport ships for landing operations and convoys?' His stock answer was that

we are a socialist country; in accordance with Lenin's principle of peaceful coexistence, we are against imperialist wars, and we do not aspire to occupy other countries. Therefore we have no need for those vessels that are used by countries like the United States to pursue aggressive and imperialist goals.[17]

With a few notable exceptions, word and deed seem to suggest that carrying revolution on Red bayonets has not been an operating principle of Soviet strategy since the early 1920s. This may have been a matter of expediency as much as principle.[18] Furthermore, Admiral Gorshkov is not the only Soviet spokesman who has recognised — with professional admiration if not ideological approval — the great utility of the US Navy in the fighting of limited wars. Restricted capability, lack of experience and balance of interests might suggest that Soviet leaders will not use their Navy as the vehicle for large-scale interventions; however, many observers have come to fear that now the Soviet Union has at least an embryonic intervention capability, it may be drawn in to support favourable *coups* and to protect pro-Soviet governments. After the experience of Vietnam nobody can be confident about controlling the extent of even small 'assistance' programmes. There are sometimes advantages to limited capabilities. So far, Soviet intervention capabilities from the sea remain limited, especially in terms of sea-borne air power and afloat support, but its leaders could cobble together a small interventionist force. Whether it will ever wish to is one of the most intriguing questions currently facing students of Soviet strategy.

A word must finally be said about one particular variant of limited war, the contingency planner's dream, or nightmare, of 'limited war at sea'. If the competition between the superpowers cannot be satisfied with the surrogate activity of crises, then some commentators have stressed the advantages of restricting ensuing violence to the sea: property would not be destroyed, apart from warships; casualties would be limited; and it is assumed that it would be relatively easy to control. In an extreme formulation it has been suggested that nuclear weapons might be used in such conflicts, while still limiting the fighting to the sea. Given the importance of maritime communications for the Western world, concern about the possibility of the Soviet Union applying pressure has been understandable; it is proper that the US Navy in particular has devoted some attention to this scenario. But there are considerations which make the 'wet war' unlikely. Not only has the Soviet Union presented the Western powers with growing numbers of potential hostages in terms of its own merchant vessels and warships, but the dangers of escalation will be intense if a campaign is prolonged, or if important losses are suffered. Could the Soviet leaders assume that its adversaries would not retaliate against Soviet ports? If ports were attacked, and there might be strong pressures to attack them, the image of the sea as a jousting arena will have been seriously impaired. Even the war at sea might be more difficult to restrict than is sometimes imagined, with the need to counter attacks by submarines and long-range missile-boats. The wet war scenario has also been suggested as a possible Western option in retaliation against Soviet moves on West Berlin. Again, coercive action at sea might provide some leverage in a crisis, but its extent would be limited by the fact that the Soviet Union is not ultimately dependent on using the sea; on the other hand, some hurt could be inflicted, and there may be circumstances in which the Western powers felt that they had no other less risky options. The idea of a total wet war is a feasible but not attractive option to either adversary: but between harassment at sea and a total wet war there lies a range of options which, if presently unlikely, might in some circumstances appear as the most usable type of coercion. At present, limited war at sea would appear to be more feasible and usable as an instrument of retaliation for the Western powers than as an instrument of compulsion for the Soviet Union. In general, however, discussion of such scenarios have a rather out-dated (but yet sometimes futuristic) ring about them.

As long as we live in a troubled world, with regular crises inviting the involvement of external powers, the possibility of great power military intervention will remain. If this is at any distance from the homeland of the intervening power, and is prolonged, then it is certain that the sea will play some part. After the experience of the last twenty years, it would appear that the utility of such interventions will be in inverse proportion to the extent and length of any ensuing war. Recent experience would confirm that naval power has an important utility for any interventionist state; but as far as the future is concerned, it is not the utility of navies as instruments for projecting force that is in question, but whether any of the potential interventionist states believe in the utility of large-scale military involvement in distant lands.

(iv)   *Guerrilla wars*

Intra-state violence in its manifold forms has been one of the characteristic features of the post-war period. The *next job* for many of the world's armed forces will be within their own borders, in an internal struggle, rather than in an international war. While the appropriateness of particular strategies and tactics can be questioned, there is little doubt about the utility of force for both revisionist groups wishing to overthrow the *status quo* and for those wishing to maintain it; in each case this usually involves a little help from their friends. Even those who have condemned the efforts of those seeking to maintain the relevance of the Clausewitzian philosophy of war in modern conditions have nevertheless acknowledged the utility of revolutionary violence and counter-insurgency.[19]

The various types of internal violence involve a 'grimmer'[20] type of strategy. For obvious geographical reasons naval forces will not be at the forefront of it: this will be the soldier's unenviable task. However, naval forces will have some utility, and recent experience would suggest that the sea is likely to be more useful to the counter-guerrillas than their opponents.

There have been some examples of 'waterborne guerrillas'. In 1970 subversive forces were intruded into Guinea from Portuguese Guinea. In the early 1970s waterborne guerrillas were reported operating off Chittagong and in the Mekong Delta. At the beginning of 1975 the Palestine Liberation Organisation landed a unit from the sea and attacked civilians in Tel Aviv. Government forces have organised naval counters to such efforts. The Soviet Navy's West African Patrol in support of the government at Conakry was one response. In March 1975 Israeli naval patrols were stepped up to counter PLO infiltrators, and there were expectations that the Israeli Navy's role in this regard would grow: given the length of Israel's sea frontiers, its Navy has obvious utility against this constant threat. Through the 1960s and early 1970s Portugal deployed naval forces off the coasts of Angola and Mozambique because of its fears of a similar threat of intrusion. 'Riverine operations' against guerrillas now take place in several countries, but particularly in south-east Asia. Earlier illustrations of this role were the counter-guerrilla patrols of US and Latin American navies during the fervour about Castroism, the patrols of the Seventh Fleet in support of the South Vietnamese Navy in the early 1960s, the patrols of the Dutch Navy against Indonesian infiltration into West New Guinea in the early 1960s, and Royal Navy patrols against Indonesian infiltrators into Malaysia in the first half of the 1960s. The most extensive use of naval forces against insurgents, however, were the operations of the US Navy during the Vietnam War. With carrier aircraft in the background striking against supply routes and providing a variety of support roles, the 'brown-water navy' operated in-shore, providing flexibility and mobility in patrol and support roles, and in carrying out landings on search and destroy missions.

In contrast with the large-scale guerrilla activities discussed above, the sea is also relevant in another of the characteristics of our time, namely associated 'terrorist' activity. Terrorist activity at sea has been a regular fear in some quarters in recent years, but as yet it has been virtually non-existent in practice. Understandably, the relative success and high publicity achieved by air hijackers bent on political or private gain has resulted in fears that this might encourage similar attempts against fixed installations at sea, or ships. Because of their inherent value, oil rigs have been thought to present a particularly attractive target for the terrorist. Given the growing significance (and symbolism) of the North Sea oil finds for Britain's immediate future, it is hardly surprising that the Royal Navy has had to pay attention to this matter in recent years, and has developed ships and tactics for the task, if not of the type and quantity some observers think is adequate. Such is the profusion of oil installations in the North Sea and elsewhere that actual 'point defence' is impossible. On the other hand, while their value and vulnerability make oil rigs an obvious cause for concern in violent times, their remoteness also presents potential attackers with some disadvantages. It is not yet clear that fixed installations at sea are a more 'attractive' target than a bus-load of schoolchildren, a foreign businessman, or the Post Office Tower: they are no more than one of a depressingly long list of potential targets. Turning from fixed installations, it is obvious that the terrorist-at-sea has an abundance of other potential hostages; and some of the world's shipping, notably super-tankers, are both valuable and vulnerable. However, airliners will remain more dramatic targets for hijackers, and will cruelly compress time for the target decision-makers.

The sea will not be a critical arena for guerrilla operations: these are pre-eminently land operations, and increasingly urban operations at that. Nevertheless, experience suggests that naval forces will have an important role in some counter-guerrilla operations in certain situations. The costs of providing such forces will not be high: compared with the addition of another nuclear submarine or aircraft carrier, few are likely to question the value of cost of providing for additional river gunboats or coastal patrol boats. To the extent that geography allows them, naval forces play a valuable role in this relatively new and certainly grim type of conflict.

(2) Balance of power functions

(v) *Strategic nuclear deterrence*

The basic framework of relations between the superpowers is controlled by their ability to inflict unacceptable damage upon each other. The cost of nuclear war has given the deterring of it a novel doctrinal and practical importance in modern strategy. For this reason it is not valid to argue that because these very expensive weapons are not used they are therefore useless. In fact, the opposite is true: their useless-ness will only be evident on the day when they are used. As long as nuclear weapons are believed to deter direct attacks on the homelands of their possessors, and are believed to contribute to maintaining a stable balance of terror, then (for better or worse) their utility is assured in the eyes of those who control them.

Within strategic nuclear deterrence the utility of sea-based forces is readily apparent. While US strike-carriers have declined in relative significance as platforms for strategic nuclear bombardment, the SSBN has come to have a prominence and role which is so familiar that it does not need labouring. The essential feature of the SSBN is the *invulnerability* which results from its long patrol times, its very wide operating radius, its concealment ability, its high mobility, and the dispersal effect which numbers make possible. There is presently no counter. These considerations enhance the utility of SSBNs as nuclear strike platforms, and this fact was encapsulated in the SALT I agreements of 1972. The same considerations make SSBNs an attractive option for the smaller nuclear powers: the British and French missile-firing submarines give their possessors a flexibility and significance in nuclear strategy which would not be the case with an equivalent number of land-based missiles.

There are periodic alarms about the increasing vulnerability of SSBNs. However, authoritative opinions continue to reaffirm that their invulnerability remains high.[21] It is certainly evident that both superpowers regard them as critical elements in their inventories, and intend to rely on them for a long time into the future. While the development of tracking systems proceeds, the constant perfecting of the SSBN gives them greater capacity for concealment, speed, destruc-tive potential and distance. It remains true, as Ian Smart has argued, that most claims about an ASW breakthrough are purely speculative, being

> apparently based upon the simple assumption that technology will inevitably, in time, produce a counter to any military weapon. Even if that assumption is generally justified, which is far from obvious, there is, however, no concrete indication in present technology of an efficient response to the SSBN.[22]

Because of the central importance of sea-based deterrence, it is frequently suggested that arms control efforts should focus upon ASW. This view has strategic logic: to the extent that ASW progress increases the chances for the successful tracking and destroying of SSBNs, to that extent it undermines whatever degree of 'delicacy' exists in the balance of terror. Despite the logic of this case, however, it will be extremely difficult to work out acceptable agreements aimed at limiting ASW efforts, 'destabilising' though they may be (though it should be added that the delicacy of deterrence is often exaggerated). For one thing, especially for the Western navies, ASW is important for the defence of shipping; and this is a problem completely apart from the nuclear deterrence game. Furthermore, the efforts of both superpowers are to some extent affected by damage limitation impulses: this involves the development of techniques to improve the detection of SSBNs. The problem of ASW control is one of the not unfamiliar dilemmas in nuclear strategy when the requirements of defence (damage limitation) pull against the strategically logical requirements of stable deterrence.

Sea-based forces will continue to contribute importantly to the general strategic context within which international politics take place. General war cannot be won in a politically meaningful sense, but it may be won in some sense, and the SSBN will be a factor in everyone's calculations about the outbreak and course of such a war, although these vessels cannot win control of the sea. Furthermore, in peacetime these vessels retain some shadow of the former glory of the battle fleet. Thirty years ago Lord Chatfield described the traditional role of the British battle fleet as being 'like the queen on the chess board; it may remain at the base but it still dominates the game'.[23] The SSBN performs a similar function in peacetime today.

The linkage between strategic weapons and local situations is usually uncertain. In many cases there will be a minimal relationship. On numerous occasions in the post-war period situations have developed in which the fact that one of the participants has possessed nuclear weaponry has been almost irrelevant, as with Britain during east of Suez operations, or as with the United States or Soviet Union in their relations with some smaller powers. Military power in the background is presumably only politically relevant if it is 'usable' (that is, appropriate for the situation, credible to potential targets, and seen as functional by the users). The patent fact is that in most situations short of a nuclear confrontation with a superpower, or a direct attack, the SSBN is not usable. Its impact on most local situations is therefore likely to be tenuous. There are exceptions, however,

and this is when *core* interests come into play in local situations.[24]
Berlin is an obvious focus of core interests, and therefore a situation in
which strategic weapons have a high salience. Furthermore, in at least
one case, that of Turkey, an SSBN has been used for demonstrative
purposes, in an attempt to establish the linkage between a local situation and the overall strategic balance. When the United States removed
its IRBMs from Turkey, the SSBN *Patrick Henry* was sent to Izmir,
in order to reaffirm in concrete terms to both Turks, Americans and
onlookers that Turkey remained within the perimeter of states protected by US strategic nuclear deterrence.[25]

The linkage between strategic and local matters is not one-way:
local forces play a part in strategic deterrence. Local naval forces can
provide a trip-wire, as ground forces do, in order to provide a flexible
escalation capability. Local naval forces may promise to meet threats
at their own level and also pose the risk of escalation: they are also
'power in evidence'. Furthermore, as Hill has rightly argued,[26]
when a nation's interests are in part protected by an alliance, it is
difficult to identify the point at which the alliance is bound to operate:
he goes on,

> In the sea affair, because the build-up of conflict may be slow and
> the threat to vital interests not immediately apparent, this operation
> is unlikely to occur at the first shot, or even at the first serious
> engagement. It is essential therefore for powers with vital maritime
> interests to ensure that they have force enough to hold the ring
> until their alliance is triggered by the obvious seriousness of the
> situation and their obvious determination not to let go.

For a variety of reasons, therefore, warships retain important
utilities when they are not being actively or directly employed. In this
context it is worth remembering that historically it was only when the
Grand Fleet was *at* Jutland that there was a real risk of the Royal Navy
losing the war: while at Scapa Flow it had all the latent potential of
the queen on the chess board. Though always costly, great powers in
the past could afford to have deterrence break down: war was thinkable. This is no longer the case. We live pre-eminently in an age of
deterrence. One recalls Michael Howard's interesting thought that
future battle honours will refer to battles deterred rather than battles
won, and one also recalls the traditional influence of the unseen warship
on conflicts in the past:

> [When Jellicoe] assumed the name of 'Viscount Scapa' there was
> a good deal of scoffing that an admiral should take the name of a
> desolate place where his fleet had remained at anchor almost
> continuously for four years. Yet by those four years, the British
> Fleet exerted the decisive pressure . . .[27]

In what passes for contemporary peace, the unseen SSBN, operating
in even more desolate places and for the foreseeable future, will
continue to exert a decisive pressure in strategic nuclear deterrence.

(vi)   *Conventional deterrence and defence*

The possession of any degree of military power threatens an intruder
with increased costs. Armed forces give a state some ability to operate
from a position of some strength: they show that the community
intends to defend its patch of territory. In so doing the beginning of
some sort of rough international order is established. Armed forces
are also a practical insurance policy against the uncertainties of the
future. The utility of military power for these purposes is evident from
both the words and actions of governments. As troubled as they have
been with economic and other problems, the newly independent countries of Africa and Asia have quickly provided themselves with
national armies. Internal factors have played a part in this, but at least
equally important has been the acquisition of military forces as a
concrete declaration of sovereignty.

   In contributing to conventional deterrence and defence, navies are
important because they minister to the three essential interests of
coastal states mentioned in Chapter One.[28] These interests are *sovereignty* (a coastal state will desire full sovereignty over some part of its
adjacent waters), *resource enjoyment* (a coastal state will expect to
enjoy the proceeds from the exploitation of resources adjacent to its
coast) and the *maintenance of good order* (a coastal state will desire
good order to be maintained in the seas off its coast, so that its own
well-being is not degraded). All countries with coasts will have these
interests in what happens offshore. The area over which these
interests are relevant will vary, as will the ability of different countries
to deploy naval power. Generally, the shape of a country's maritime
defence efforts will be determined by whether or not it perceives a
sea-based threat (and the character of that threat), the extent of the
sea area over which it has ambitions, whether it hopes to command that
sea area or merely deny its resources and space to others, whether it
has allies, the level of its technological capacity and its ability to secure

and use warships acquired from more advanced naval powers.

While security remains the basic value and obligation for all govern-ments, the potential external threat to most countries is not primarily or importantly sea-borne. For many countries, therefore, naval forces will form the least important arm of the national services by which adversaries will be deterred or fought. There are exceptions to this generalisation: for a number of countries the threat from the sea is a real one, and their naval forces play an important part in the overall defence system. But even for these countries, this was truer historically than it is today; formerly, navies were senior services for the (relatively few) maritime powers. Today they are rarely better than third amongst equals.

Naval forces continue to play prominent roles in the defence systems of the economically developed countries involved in the central balance. NATO and the Warsaw Pact both contain sizeable navies with modern warships. They carry out well-established tasks in contiguous sea areas, such as preparing to support land operations, and protecting and/or attacking maritime communications. In addition, for the superpowers, the requirements of defence in the nuclear age have demanded distantly deployed warships. The containment strategy of the United States and the damage limitation strategy of the Soviet Union have both entailed the permanent presence of their warships in forward positions.

Within each alliance, the very fact of the US and Soviet super-navies has affected the shipbuilding patterns of those sheltering under their wings. There has been some tendency towards a division of labour on naval matters in NATO, though this has not gone far. Logically, it might be expected to go further as rising costs increase the pressures for co-operation: but logic does not always determine such matters. Membership of a superpower-dominated alliance might either discour-age independent efforts (the superpowers are always liable to suspect free-riders) or encourage them (to give their possessors more of a voice within their alliance). Because of the temptation to smaller countries of sheltering under a superpower wing in a harsh economic climate, it is often misleading to judge the utility which some countries attach to naval power simply from their own national efforts: the utility which Norway and Japan attach to navies, for example, cannot be assessed merely nationally, but only in relation to the *pax Americana*.

Outside the NATO-Warsaw Pact confrontation a number of economically developed countries have deployed modern warships because of the possibility of maritime pressure. The costs of violating

Swedish neutrality, whose land approaches are difficult from the East, are pushed up by a small but advanced and hard-hitting navy. South Africa fears isolation and a possible international blockade mobilised against it. Not only does a strong South African navy help discourage such possibilities, but it also gives the South African government an opportunity to project itself as a valuable partner to the Western powers in a strategically sensitive region. Australia is another isolated country. Accessible on a large scale only by sea, and hopeful of bounteous resources off its coast, Australia has a requirement for some degree of modern maritime defence. Canada has a similar need. Although next-door to the United States, and therefore never likely to be decoupled from the latter's security, Canada has its own maritime interests, including a heightened concern for its independence, the enjoyment of its resources, and the maintenance of good order off its coasts; these values demand the protection of modern naval forces. The character of Canada's naval priorities probably represents a norm for medium-sized developed states.[29]

Developed states are certainly not the only ones with maritime defence requirements. As they have traditionally done, maritime forces play a part in establishing local military equilibria, as in Latin America. They may also be an element in moves to a preponderant regional position, as seems to be the case in the Gulf, with the Iranian acquisition of modern weapons of many types. In addition, maritime forces are of new significance because of the sensitivity which all recently independent states have on issues of sovereignty, including maritime sovereignty. These issues have been intensified in the 1970s because of the work and publicity attached to the UN Conference on the Law of the Sea, and the promise of great resources on continental shelves. Already there have been a number of clashes and disputes over the possession of potentially resource-rich areas. The anxiety to stake out claims has already resulted in naval and land battles between South Vietnam and China over the disputed sovereignty of the Paracels in 1974; the South Vietnamese were ousted from the islands. China, a country which had been traditionally poached, proved itself to be an effective poacher. The *Mayaguez* incident is relevant for different reasons, as a manifestation of a small country's sensitivity about sovereignty for its own sake. The *Pueblo* episode was similar. Whatever the precise location of the *Pueblo* when it was captured, the episode serves as a reminder to the traditional naval powers that their 'blue water' is somebody else's maritime backyard.

With regard to the protection of maritime sovereignty, technological and international political trends over the past twenty years have favoured the smaller powers. Missile-firing patrol boats have greatly intensified the stings which coastal Davids can inflict on maritime Goliaths. The doyens of these craft are the Soviet-produced *Osa* and *Komar* class of fast patrol boats (FPBs), which in 1975 were in service with sixteen navies, including the Soviet Union. In the late 1960s these units created a flurry amongst the traditional maritime powers because of the firepower packed in their missiles, their relative cheapness, and their ready availability to pro-Soviet régimes. They were a cost-effective method by which small powers could raise the dangers of maritime intrusion. While alert and modern forces can defend against the *Styx* missile, and while the range and sea-keeping capabilities of the fast patrol boats are much more limited than the major surface vessels they would face, they do represent a significant bee-sting capability, depriving potential intruders of a free ride, and challenging highly expensive warships relatively cheaply.

The publicity given to the gift-wrapped *Osa* FPBs from the Soviet Union has somewhat hypnotised the naval powers. It has helped to distract attention away from mining, a traditional weapon of the relatively weak. In some circumstances mining could be used with considerable effect in localities such as the Malacca Straits or the Gulf. Furthermore, the proliferation of advanced land-based aircraft poses potential naval intruders with great risks of tracking and attack. Together, all these developments push up the costs of intervention from the sea.

No country, however powerful, can afford to meet 'worst cases' as far as potential threats are concerned. At the most, 'fairly bad' cases are the standard. With maritime defence, however, many states do not attempt even to meet this standard; there is a tendency to let the matter go by default, relying on international stability and faith in allies. In many instances, naval services more than other branches of the armed forces are liable to be made to operate on the principle of what can be afforded, rather than on any clearly worked conception of threat. But this is not always the case, and the fact that the 'worst case' cannot be met does not mean that countries necessarily forgo maritime defence. In the 1950s, the fact that Chinese naval forces were not able to match the Seventh Fleet in combat did not stop their developing a coastal defence navy, at first with the help of the Soviet Union; this force could put up a fight if there was any intrusion by the Nationalists, and it showed that the new government intended to defend its stretch of water. Even if there is no clear sea-based threat, and even if they cannot match powerful navies, all coastal states operate on the rule-of-thumb that there should be no free ride for potential intruders. The sharper bee-sting and the no-free-ride idea are confirmations in the maritime context of the 'spirit of the age', which has determined the rising costs and declining benefits of territorial conquest.

The mini-navies possessed by many small countries are often a function of their inability to sustain larger forces rather than of any disinterest in exercising sovereignty over their stretch of water. Iceland is perhaps the best example of this, having extensive claims, significant challenges and minimal forces. Nevertheless, its 'Maritime Police Force', for all its lack of punch, pushes up the cost of intervention and gives the country a leverage in maritime matters which would be almost entirely absent if the country had no defence vessels. One cannot generalise far on the basis of the Anglo-Icelandic Cod Wars, because of the particular character of the relations existing between the two countries involved. Tradition, affinities and interests constrain the possibility of violence. But even where there are no such affinities and interests, naval force is not as usable as formerly. This was evident in the case of the US response to the seizure of the *Pueblo*. The United States had a surplus of capability for punishing North Korea, and had little or nothing to fear in retaliation from North Korea in a military sense. Nevertheless, the US administration abjured using an instrument which in former times would have been unexceptionable when a great power wished to punish — for an insult on the high seas — a country which was both small and hostile. The limits on the usability of maritime force by great powers, as a result of a mixture of expediency and principle, has been a notable feature of the post-colonial situation, though it is not one which potential targets can prudently extrapolate into the distant future.

Most countries, therefore, see maritime defence as part of maintaining their sovereignty and independence. Alliance membership and economic incapacity have both tended to limit naval efforts. However, as sensitivity about maritime sovereignty grows, so will the utility of protecting the country's seaward frontiers. Conventional deterrence and defence in the contiguous seas have always been — and will remain — the extent of the mission of most of the world's navies, and it has been an irreducible requirement for even the most ambitious. Naval forces can limit what other states can do to it in its own maritime backyard. Most navies are concerned solely with the independence and integrity of the state in a limited geographical sense, and have no capability or responsibility for advancing foreign policy beyond this: the navies of most countries do not act 'over there', in distant waters. While the seas are dominated by *status quo* navies, which the small powers cannot match and/or which they do not perceive as imminent threats, most navies can afford to remain relatively small. But whatever their size, they derive utility by confronting potential intruders with the need to have sufficient incentive and will to cross the important dividing line between shooting and not shooting.

(vii)   *Extended deterrence and defence*

Great powers have always established 'vital interests' beyond their homelands, which have required protection by military means. Alliance membership, colonial responsibility and strategic access have been the three chief reasons why some states have extended the radius of their military efforts.

Extended deterrence and defence require either a permanent physical presence or a capacity to project force when necessary. Navies have always had an important role in this respect: the great powers with far-flung interests have been the great naval powers. This generalisation has remained valid for those states which have wished to act in a military sense beyond their homeland or beyond immediately adjacent areas. In the post-war period, in large and small ways, naval power has proved to be of considerable utility for those states wishing to extend their defensive and deterrent capabilities.

The alliance policy of the United States is the primary example of the utility of naval power in this role. As one writer put it some years ago:

> None of the eight collective defence treaties that the United States and forty-three other countries have entered into since World War II would be credible without the promise of the continued use of the sea. Each of the pact signatories relies on the US Navy as the primary force to underwrite the alliances.[30]

This is such an obvious point that it is often overlooked by all but those professionally concerned with the movement of men and goods across the seas. Supply and reinforcement for any prolonged operation requires transport by sea. The promise of control of the sea was essential if the United States was to be able to offer its support credibly to countries such as Norway or Turkey, which would otherwise have been isolated and defenceless in the event of any Soviet pressure. The US Navy made the promise of countervailing power credible.

One aspect of the utility of navies in alliances is that they provide an opportunity for a variety of methods of symbolic co-operation. This will be discussed later, but for the moment it is worth noting that the adjective *Atlantic* in the phrase 'Atlantic Alliance' is not merely a geographical expression: it is also a reflection of the importance of the use of the sea both as a cementing and a permissive factor in the relations between the members.

Outside Europe there have been numerous examples of the use of naval forces to extend deterrence and defence in the recent past. The Seventh Fleet was sent to patrol the Taiwan Straits to deter Communist China from invading Taiwan (and in time it served to prevent the Nationalists from risking action against China proper). The Sixth Fleet was used in 1970 to extend assistance to Jordan during its crisis with Syria. Since the mid-1960s the Soviet Navy has been used on a number of occasions to extend deterrence and defence, notably the West African Patrol and the deployment to Egyptian harbours in 1967. The Royal Navy was used to extend British support to Malaysia during its confrontation with Indonesia; British naval forces patrolled against intruders, resupplied foot-patrols, instituted show-of-strength patrols to deter escalation, and provided general deterrence in the background. The end of colonialism has reduced one of the traditional utilities of navies, the protection of colonial interests from threats within and without. However, there has been a series of incidents in which colonial or post-colonial obligations have resulted in Western powers sending or using warships to support their policies, including the British cruisers sent to deter Guatemala from pressing its claim to British Honduras in 1947 (in the watered-down version of this problem in 1975 a frigate was sent), the Dutch Navy's action off West Guinea in the early 1960s to deter Indonesian pressure and to defend against intrusion, and the Royal Navy's general covering role during Britain's withdrawal from east of Suez in the late 1960s.

Extended deterrence and defence increase the responsibilities of naval intelligence. Over recent years this function has had unaccustomed publicity, with the sinking of the *Liberty*, the capture of the *Pueblo*, the shadowing and photographing of Western navies by Soviet ships, and by the ubiquitous Soviet intelligence-gathering fleet. Such activities are essential for the collecting of information about the tactics and standard operating procedures of adversary navies, as well as for gathering intelligence of a more general or political type. Because of the character of the work of intelligence ships, and their usually unescorted and unarmed character, these are vulnerable and tempting targets for those wanting hostages.

For reasons stated, one of the chief utilities of warships in the past has been their instrumentality for extending deterrent and defence capabilities beyond contiguous waters. This important role has been undermined by a number of developments in the last twenty years, notably by the declining perception of major war, by the ending of colonialism, by the decline of the long-war scenario in Europe, by the turning inwards of the traditional maritime powers, and by the growing belief through the 1960s (spurred on by Suez and Vietnam) that foreign military forces in an age of violent nationalism are likely to be counter-productive as protectors of distant interests (although in this last respect naval forces will rarely be as provocative as land-based forces).

But naval forces still have some important residual roles in extending deterrence and defence. This has been the implication of some of the small-scale Soviet activities in various parts of the world, including the close shadowing of US warships in a number of crises. Doctrinally, this mission is referred to as 'countering imperialist aggression'.[31] While the record suggests that the Soviet leaders are not prepared to run great risks in pursuit of this mission, it is one which has frequently been used as a justification for Soviet naval activies. As expressed by Gorshkov in 1970, the presence of Soviet ships in key areas 'binds the hands of the imperialists [and] deprives them of a possibility to interfere unhindered in the internal affairs of the peoples'.[32] Without having to sink or significantly harass US warships, the Soviet leaders hoped that the presence of their own vessels would constrain US naval behaviour. In the event, their effect has been marginal, though Soviet naval spokesmen and Western critics have sometimes claimed the opposite. Like all propagandists, Soviet naval spokesmen do not stop to discuss all the causal links in the process they are describing. However, in such matters the important considera-tion is what the hearers want to believe, and there have been some, including President Nasser, who have wanted to believe in the significance of the Soviet Navy in terms of changing power relation-ships.[33] On the other side, the Sixth Fleet has been of considerable importance to associates of the United States. Significantly, Mr Eshkol once claimed that the US Navy in the Mediterranean was Israel's strategic reserve.[34] While neither superpower navy can 'counter' the other in a physical sense without undertaking very risky and probably unacceptable behaviour, this does not mean that they lack diplomatic instrumentality. The perceptions of onlookers can ensure their utility in this respect: superpower navies can signify changing relationships and create uncertainty, and they can also help balance a sense of adversary pressure.

While the Soviet Navy has attracted increasing attention, the naval implications of the Nixon Doctrine have tended to be overlooked. This doctrine, while placing a bigger emphasis on countries helping themselves, has not been synonymous with isolationism: in fact, there has been a consciously 'big navy' element in the US policy of partial withdrawal. This was only logical for a prudent but not neo-isolationist superpower: if the United States was to continue to maintain a forward presence, but without the *front line commitment* implied in Cold War containment, then the building of modern warships, the allocation of large sums to the Navy, specific operational cruises in crises, and ensuring the general visibility of the Navy were rational responses. In the carrying out of a strategy of containment during a period of *détente* and in a foreign policy moving towards more carefully considered commitments, naval forces have inherent advantages over the other services.[35] The developing base at Diego Garcia is in line with such a policy. Although the fact that it is a fixed base might seem to contradict the trend of thinking represented by the Nixon doctrine, the sordid Anglo-American attempt to remove the local population indicates that Diego Garcia is the exception which proves the rule.

Major navies are therefore thought to retain an important peacetime role in supporting distant relationships. The ability of the United States to maintain its maritime credibility is important to allies and associates as well as adversaries. In this respect, once again, perceptions of 'balance' are important. If potential adversaries, by their own naval actions, can undermine that credibility, they can thereby affect the way the allies and associates of the United States look at and behave towards it. A decline in the credibility of US naval power might be one of the *effects* of Soviet naval activity, whatever the original motives for the latter's forward deployment. Furthermore US naval capability, much to the chagrin of the latter's naval establishment, depends on much more than the actual military balance of naval forces (as might be perceived by an omniscient observer): Soviet naval propaganda and domestic critics in the United States are amongst the factors affecting third-party perceptions. Something does not have to be tactically or strategically *true* to be politically *significant*.

(viii) *International order*

It is the capacity and willingness of states to defend themselves which
provides the basic framework within which the business of international
politics is carried on.[36] For practical purposes, governments regard
alternatives to the balance of power system as chimerical; to the extent
that the balance of power system provides local or world-wide order,
military power is still highly instrumental. Furthermore, for states
wishing to upset a particular *status quo*, armed force still retains its
place as the *ultima ratio*, although its usage is more circumscribed. At
sea, as on land, a stable balance of power system encourages the freedom
of the smaller powers. On land this means freedom to exist relatively
independently: at sea it means freedom for the safe passage of ships.

One important difference between balance of power systems on land
and at sea, however, is that whereas the former has usually been based
on an *equilibrium* of power, the latter has been based on a *preponde-
rance*. Over the last century-and-a-half, the high level of order and
freedom at sea was the result of the *pax Britannica* followed by the *pax
Americana*: since both the preponderant naval powers concerned
valued the concept of the freedom of the seas, and used their monopoly relatively benevolently, the liberty of the smaller maritime powers
to use the seas was assured. If it be objected that the *pax Americana* is
not what it was, because of the growth of the Soviet Navy, it is comforting to see that Soviet ideas about the high seas conform with those
of the Western maritime powers. Although the international law of the
sea is passing through a difficult period, the degree of order which
has existed over a longer perspective has been noteworthy. As with
international law in general, it is easy (but mistaken) to exaggerate its
fragility and the extent of non-compliance: in fact, for most of the
time governments are geared to maintaining the existing régime, upholding treaties, sustaining customary procedures, carrying out well-
established commercial practices, and so on. Because of the relatively
high degree of order at sea it has been possible for great asymmetries
to (safely) exist between the size of a country's merchant and fishing
fleets and the size of its navy.

To some extent all nations are interested in, and dependent upon,
the passage of goods across the sea. In some cases this dependence is
extreme, as with some highly industrialised countries for oil and
sometimes food; but non-industrialised countries also rely on
international trade for the sale of their raw materials. Even a

relatively self-sufficient country such as the Soviet Union requires maritime stability for the safety of its far-flung and important fishing fleets, and in order to secure the advantages which it derives from foreign trade. Almost all states therefore have an interest in order at sea. While the existing régime might not be the *preferred* system for some states, they can only pose a minimal challenge in a physical sense. On a day-to-day basis, they have to work with it, even if their ultimate hope is to change it.

In peacetime the sea is not a particularly dangerous place. Piracy still does occasionally take place in parts of south-east Asia, and there has been an occasional hijacking at sea ('ship-jacking') but such incidents are very rare when compared with similar incidents on land or in the air. The suppression of such incidents at sea has been directly attributable to the operations and pervasiveness of naval forces. There have been relatively few major incidents at sea. One *cause célèbre* was the Corfu Channel case in 1946, when British efforts to maintain the right of innocent passage through the Corfu Channel resulted in Albanian shelling and mining, and the loss of 44 British lives. A few years later, in 1951, British naval forces were sent to the Red Sea in order to prevent incidents against British ships as a result of the attempted Egyptian blockade against Israel. US destroyers were sent to perform a similar function in the Straits of Tiran and Gulf of Aqaba in 1957. Ten years later, for the same part of the world, the British Cabinet contemplated and then rejected the idea of forming an International Maritime Force to deal with this by-now familiar problem.[37] Such problems are not confined to the access routes to Israel, however. In 1961 a US force was called upon to reaffirm the right of innocent passage through the Lombok and Makassar Straits. In 1969 Iranian warships escorted a threatened merchant ship to the Gulf. Such trouble-spots are but the most dramatic of a regular pattern of disorderly incidents at sea. For the most part, however, they are not very serious. They usually involve the harassment or capture of fishing vessels, because they have allegedly infringed regulations: such incidents are usually small-scale, and are settled without violence. Neither these incidents, nor the collateral damage resulting from wars (notably the sinking of the *Liberty* or the *Venus Challenger*) can really support the case that the sea is presently a dangerous place. On the other hand, the potential for disorder is probably greater than at any other time in this century outside major war. The future degree of order at sea will depend upon a complex interaction of foreign policies, naval postures, economic interests and legal attitudes.

To the extent that there is order at sea, it is based upon naval power: as it was succinctly put in one study, 'no policeman, no law'.[38] But this does not mean that the policeman must be omnipresent. Just as enlightened self-interest on land ensures that good traffic control (the rule of the road and so on) continues in remote areas distant from the nearest policeman, the same is true at sea: short of wartime situations, enlightened self-interest determines that there is likely to be little straying from the accepted norms of the behaviour of the international maritime community.

This means that naval power has considerable utility for those with a stake in the *status quo*. Furthermore, while the smaller powers might vociferously assert what they call their 'rights' for the utilisation of the resources of the sea, they cannot match the naval or exploiting potential of the developed powers. These 'rights' are therefore in the gift of the developed states. As long as the latter have predominant naval power and are willing to use force, the smaller powers can only achieve their 'rights' through changes in international law; this in turn can only be brought about by the changed attitudes of the developed powers (though in this respect the smaller powers may be able to put a variety of non-military pressures on the developed powers, because of their control of important raw materials, and the wish of the developed powers to retain a harmonious relationship with them). Overall, therefore, the utility of navies for maintaining order at sea is both high and evident. Either in the way that navies represent the long arm of the law, or in the way that they provide the backdrop against which negotiations take place, naval forces have, and will continue to have, a critical role in the determination of what type of régime operates in what is increasingly a 'troubled common'.[39]

(3) Bargaining functions

(ix) *Negotiating from strength*

As has been apparent on a number of occasions in this book, armed forces have many roles apart from that of actually being used to kill and destroy. Not surprisingly, because of the growing costs of all types of war, much attention has been focused in the last twenty years on the exploitation of military power short of war. As Schelling has explained with considerable clarity, modern military power tends to be threatened in peace rather than used in war. For the superpowers at least, the instruments of war 'are more punitive than acquisitive': whether we like it or not, military strategy is not 'the science of military victory', but 'the diplomacy of violence'.[40]

In crises, the utility of armed forces for deterrent or compellent purposes is usually relatively clear. In 'normal' diplomatic intercourse the relationship between military strength and a country's bargaining strength is usually much less obvious, but not for that reason insignificant. Military considerations may be a negligible factor in the relationships between some pairs of states, but between many other pairs the possibility of violence, however remote, is one of the frameworks within which diplomacy takes place. In many circumstances, directly and indirectly, the demonstration of military power affects the structuring of the minds of policy-makers. Attitudes and policies towards particular countries are sometimes seriously affected by what such countries can do in a military sense. Even if in a particular episode military considerations might appear remote, military power retains some utility by enabling states to negotiate from a position of some strength.

Warships are no strangers to the explicit activities of the 'diplomacy of violence' or the more generalised task of contributing to negotiation from strength. Indeed, 'gunboat diplomacy' at the end of the nineteenth century was one of the phenomena which played a part in broadening the concept of strategy beyond that of the battlefield into explicit usages short of war. Naval reviews and other background demonstrations of fleet strength were used in attempts to structure the thinking of foreign governments. In view of the importance of naval forces in the days of imperialism, it was hardly surprising that practically any movement of even the smallest naval unit took on a political meaning.[41] Since that time, however, it can be argued that 'armed demonstrations' have not had the same efficiency: this is because of a declining credibility in many situations that 'the demonstrating Power was nearing the end of its patience and was contemplating serious measures'.[42] But it does not necessarily follow that such demonstrations lack utility, either internal or external. Externally they can contribute to what Schelling called 'manipulating the shared risk of war', from which they might hope to garner the fruits of exploitable danger. Internally, demonstrations prove to observers at home and allies abroad that the country's forces are attentive, 'and are moving with actual or symbolic strength into positions which may carry them from demonstration to what Germans call the *Ernstfall*, the case of extreme gravity, war'.[43]

While naval demonstrations might not be as universally effective as hitherto, warships nevertheless maintain some utility in crisis diplomacy. The primary example of naval forces being used to manage a crisis successfully was the Cuban missile crisis of October 1962. This crisis confirmed the value of superior local conventional force as a support to nuclear deterrence. However, one can exaggerate the degree of clinical control by which the naval units were manipulated in this episode.[44] Furthermore, the fact that the crisis occurred in such special and favourable circumstances for the United States means that it is probably not repeatable. It is therefore of limited value for generalisation. An entirely different type of naval demonstration was the display of massive but politically unusable US naval power after the *Pueblo* incident. Like the more successful action after the *Mayaguez* affair , this action at least performed a cathartic effect on US attitudes, by moving to the case of extreme gravity. The opportunities for the exercise of naval power in such ways are always likely to be few, although as stated earlier, naval forces do possess some specific characteristics which make them particularly well suited for crisis management roles.

Two specific techniques by which navies can engage in the diplomacy of violence are blockade and mining. Martin has written very clearly about those characteristics of blockade which make it a suitable technique for bringing naval power to bear, and as a crisis management technique for 'transferring the onus of escalation to the other side'.[45] While there might be some occasions when a naval blockade (outside war) will have utility, the peacetime and 'non-belligerent' record of this technique is not a good one. Judging from the Beira Patrol, it is not a promising instrument of international coercion, for it seems that as long as there are opportunities for evading international commitments and making a profit, so there will be people who will attempt to evade commitments and make a profit. On the other hand, the Rhodesian situation *has* developed since 1965, and the blockade may have had a contributory effect: it is probably too soon to say. In contrast to blockade, mining is a relatively cheap and perhaps underappreciated technique of the diplomacy of violence. Mining has typically been a weapon of the weak, but it can also be used effectively by the strong. This was the case with the US Navy's mining of North Vietnamese waters in 1972, the results of which were significant: 'The mines did not sink one important ship, but they had psychological and political effects quite out of proportion to the expenditure involved.'[46] This mining campaign demonstrated three things. Firstly, that mining is cheap (no aircraft were lost in any of the offshore mining operations) and effective (no major ships and very little cargo entered or left any of the mined ports). Secondly, that the political and psychological effects of hidden automatic weapons can be quite potent. And thirdly, that he who has the means to clear such weapons or who knows when they will render themselves ineffective, has a useful bargaining counter in negotiations. In sum, the episode 'demonstrates once again the value of simple weapons imaginatively used'.[47]

Just as mining can affect the course of negotiations, so can the display manifestations of warships. While the motives and effects of the passage of a Soviet cruiser and destroyer off Singapore during the Commonwealth Heads of Government Conference in January 1971 are open to various interpretations,[48] the fact is that the warships did intrude into the psychological environment of the conference participants, and did cause much speculation. A clearer case was the visits to ports in Cuba (a location of high sensitivity and symbolism for US opinion) by GII class SSB on the two occasions when the United States was preoccupied in reaching an agreement over SALT.[49] In more confrontational bargaining situations 'interposition' is a well-established naval technique. To be first on the scene, preferably with one or more superior warships, can constrain the actions of any adversary, can give him cause for concern, can put the adversary to greater effort, can raise questions in the minds of others about his ability to achieve goals, and can put the onus of escalation upon him. While interposition *can* have those effects, it obviously also entails a variety of risks.

The illustrations above involved rather specific naval actions. Naval forces might also contribute to 'negotiation from strength' in a rather more generalised manner. This can be seen in the way that the Soviet Union has tried to use its Navy to build up a claim to have natural rights as a Mediterranean state.[50] The corollary of the Soviet thesis is that navies of non-Mediterranean powers should be excluded from the area. A diplomatic campaign was built up in support of the naval deployment. This pattern has become a rather familiar one in Soviet naval diplomacy: if Soviet naval vessels can be used to bargain away the advantages which the US Navy has had, then they can secure important objectives relatively cheaply. Of note in this respect has been the possibility of 'strategic horse-trading' in the Caribbean: a Soviet naval presence in that sensitive area could be used to serve as a bargaining counter in its efforts to evict the Sixth Fleet from the Mediterranean.[51] Some observers have 'long suspected' that the ultimate objective of the Soviet naval deployment in the Indian Ocean was to establish a bargaining counter for mutual limits on naval deployments. The possibility of a mutual superpower naval withdrawal from that ocean in order to create a 'zone of peace' has been manipulated successfully enough to generate a degree of local support; it might have been expected that this would increase the pressures for withdrawal on the political masters of the US Navy.[52] Similar local support has also been generated by Soviet diplomatic initiatives in support of its naval efforts in the Mediterranean. A number of littoral countries have expressed concern about the naval situation; such countries as Albania, Yugoslavia, Algeria, Tunisia, Libya, Syria, and even Spain and France have publicly urged mutual withdrawal.[53] These episodes have been only the most prominent of various Soviet efforts in the post-war years to support naval objectives by political, diplomatic and legal initiatives. One must also consider their ideas regarding nuclear-free zones, zones of peace, and closed and regional seas.[54] While there have been instances when naval and diplomatic behaviour has been co-ordinated in pursuit of Soviet maritime and foreign policy objectives, it is sometimes easy to exaggerate the degree of calculation which may enter into Soviet efforts to exercise leverage by naval deployments. If leverage results, it may have been the result of the fears and predispositions of onlookers rather than the calculated outcome of Soviet manoeuvrings. Few, if any, Soviet naval spokesmen in the early 1960s could have predicted the political prominence of their warships only ten years later.

For some years there has been a persistent view amongst academic observers as well as naval establishments that the utility of navies short of war has been growing. One manifestation of this idea was General Moulton's suggestion that the old type of war was giving way to 'war as confrontation';[55] this was another variant of McNamara's comment that there is no strategy any more, only crisis management.[56] Moulton drew an analogy between the present situation and eighteenth-century confrontations, which were characterised by strategies of position and manoeuvre, rather than the strategies of annihilation which were characteristic of great power struggles in the first half of the twentieth century. The appropriateness of this analogy is suggested by the tactical positioning of superpower naval forces during many crises in the 1960s and early 1970s, notably off Cuba, in the Mediterranean Sea and the Indian Ocean. Although in such cases it was hoped to achieve one's objectives without shooting, the tenseness of the situations and the seriousness of the issues inevitably meant that the risk of violence was increased. These dangers place a premium on the players in naval confrontations understanding whatever passes for 'rules of engagement'. While the threat of escalation certainly imposes a marked degree of rationality on the decision-makers of the superpowers, the possibility of a latter-day Napoleon, who will break the rules and play for larger stakes, cannot be discounted. And his temptations might grow as a result of successes at the lowest level. Warships may have a role in such a scenario. They may one day be called upon to earn their keep by containing a violent crisis which one side is determined to *win*.

For this reason, although the use of force is more circumscribed for Western powers than in earlier periods, it will still have an important role, especially for the United States. Naval demonstrations, mobilisations and manouevres will be seen as 'an indispensable instrument of policy' by US Presidents 'lest potential adversaries stumble into a clash of arms by underestimating his will to use force'.[57] These are important words, and should be remembered by critics of alleged US 'over-reactions'. In such episodes as the Indo-Pakistani War or the *Mayaguez* affair, the US President not only has to deal with the local situation, but has also to keep ahead in a much wider and more important game.

But in this wider game it is not always easy — indeed it seems to be increasingly difficult — to determine which are the potentially most useful instruments of diplomatic effectiveness. The debate about the significance (or not) of precise *numbers* of weapons is but one manifestation of this problem. Is 'superiority' politically meaningless, as Dr Kissinger has suggested, or do numbers have psychological impact, as Dr Schlesinger has argued? The uncertainty is also reflected in arguments about the role of military power as 'tickets' to international negotiations. On the one hand, the superpowers alone engage in SALT, but on the other hand, the negotiations on the law of the sea have shown that the norms of the naval mighty can be challenged, rather successfully, even by those without significant naval power. Furthermore, in a less structured context, while it might be argued that the utility of naval presence is in decline because of various political and legal developments,[58] can it be asserted confidently that such warships do not have political effects, or that conditions will not change such that they will become more significant factors in future? Would the international politics of the Mediterranean region be the same were US warships to be withdrawn, leaving only the Soviet squadron and the littoral navies? Would the attitudes of local states to the Soviet Union remain static? Would Soviet expectations and behaviour change? It would be an imprudent observer of international life who would confidently answer in the negative. The way governments perceive their vulnerability to external pressure helps to determine how they behave in their relations with different states. To the extent that the numbers and visibility of weapons affect these perceptions, they affect confidence and hence are politically significant. While superpowers might face more inhibitions in the use of their naval forces than formerly, military potential can still have important effects. Those with doubts have to ask themselves what the international politics of particular regions would look like if the military power of one superpower were absent; in particular, they have to consider how its absence would affect the confidence and expectations of its allies, associates, third parties and adversaries.

The particular utility of warships as instruments in the diplomacy of violence is related to the growing costs of all types of war. However, for the exploitation of military power short of war to evoke politically significant effects, it is essential that at least some of the parties involved believe that there is some possibility that violence may be used. This means that if the tactics of naval confrontation are to have utility they cannot escape the requirement of having them performed by impressive and relevant fighting units, and of their being operated by political and naval leaders with the will to use them when necessary. If nobody concerned believes that violence is a possibility, the activity ceases to be a continuation of politics, and instead becomes a ritual military minuet.

Warships have a number of special assets as instruments in the diplomacy of violence. However, it must be conceded that there will be many situations in which they will not be appropriate. But as exceptional situations such as the Cuban missile crisis demonstrated, there will be some circumstances in which warships will be uniquely appropriate. This point (and the illustration) underlines the critically important consideration that the utility of warships must be judged not only from their use, but also *in terms of the potential costs of not having them as an option when they are needed.*[59] Warships are always costly: but there are always plenty of circumstances, small as well as large, in which the cost of not having them will be even greater.

(x)   *Manipulation*

Coercive instruments can be used to support policy in a variety of non-coercive ways. They can be used to gain international influence, to probe relationships, and to try and move others in desired directions without any targeting of military capabilities. Manipulation generally involves the granting or withholding of rewards.

Military aid has become especially important as a technique of manipulation. Despite the fact that military aid does not buy control over the recipients, major powers continue to use this technique to try to win or consolidate amicable relationships. Military aid has draw-backs and weaknesses as an instrument of diplomacy, but it retains a measure of utility in the eyes of the major powers because of its scarcity value: in some situations it will be the only promising instrument in an influence-building effort. In addition to military aid, bilateral relations can be manipulated by making (or withdrawing) shows of support, or by regular or specific visits (or non-visits). Smaller powers are sometimes able to manipulate their military relations with larger ones by granting or withholding facilities such as bases, training areas, or alliance commitment. The 'damned dots'[60] of Malta and Iceland, for example, have been able to manipulate their relations with the mighty because of their geographical and strategic scarcity value.

The current level of utility attached to warships for political mani-pulation is suggested by the widespread perception in many Western countries of the success, albeit on a small scale, of the 'political mis-sions' engaged in by the Soviet Navy. The occurrence of local problems and the forward deployment of Soviet naval vessels has given the Soviet leaders opportunities for using their ships in support of foreign policy. In terms of influence-building, the following episodes have attracted attention: in October 1967 they maintained a presence in Port Said to deter Israeli attack; between February and March 1969 they deployed ships into the Gulf of Guinea to effect the release of Soviet fishing vessels arrested by Ghana; after December 1970 they maintained the West African Patrol to deter insurgent intruders into Guinea from Port-uguese Guinea; from April 1972 they deployed minesweeping and salvage forces to Bangladesh for port-clearing operations; in April 1973 Admiral Gorshkov and a naval task group visited Iraq during its border conflict with Kuwait; and Moroccan troops were sea-lifted to Syria in April and July 1973.[61] Such episodes have given the Soviet Union the opportunity to try to consolidate its relations with various countries, though such low-level naval diplomacy is not able to divert basic contradictory trends in any relationship. Soviet support of the Arab cause against Israel in 1973 did not reverse the changed relationship with Egypt which followed July 1972, nor did the generally ineffi-ciently handled port-clearing in Bangladesh advance the cause of Soviet influence-building with that country. The significance of naval diplo-macy will diminish as a particular relationship grows in complexity.

At the outset of a relationship, however, warships can sometimes have a good deal of utility, especially if the countries concerned are widely separated and have had a low level of interaction; a port visit is a well-established technique by which one country seeks to develop a relationship with another.[62] In this regard, the Soviet Union has used warships, together with visits from fishing vessels (with the latter being supported by sales and trading agreements) to penetrate and to increase its interaction with some Indian Ocean countries such as Mauritius. As was stated in an earlier chapter, however, it is easy to exaggerate the influence potential of a goodwill visit. In addition, because of the possibility of tactlessness on the part of the naval power or antagonistic perceptions on the part of the host, visits can redound to the disadvantage of the naval power concerned. On the other hand, port visits can make an incremental contribution to influence-building. For at least a fleeting moment, they are a tangible expression of a commitment, and their symbolism might be quite out of proportion to their numbers or their military potential in a major war. Certainly the utility of port visits has been stressed by a number of Soviet spokesmen in recent years,[63] and to the extent that evidence exists (and unfortunately it is all rather impressionistic), the Soviet use of the tactic of port visits has been a useful by-product of their various naval presences. However, since this is a market which can be easily saturated, this tactic is likely to be a declining asset.

Once a bilateral relationship has developed beyond a minimal level, navies can be supportive in a variety of ways, either as channels of naval aid or as vehicles of alliance support. Naval aid can make some contribution to winning friends and influencing people, especially amongst states which are involved in conflicts. In the age of overt imperialism great powers held markets and resources by brute force; although this period has passed, major powers are still very interested in a 'compatible' world, and arms deliveries have been one important method by which they have supported associates, maintained advantageous local balances of power or improved disadvantageous ones. In some cases, the objective of military aid diplomacy might go beyond support to an attempt at creating a 'client' relationship, in which the recipient would be controlled rather than merely influenced. Military aid diplomacy has not proved to be an effective instrument of control, however, though it retains an important scarcity-value. Most recipients of military aid (who are often interested in it for internal as much as external purposes) have a greater need for equipment and training for ground and air forces than naval forces, and this obviously reduces the utility of naval aid in general. However, in particular cases (e.g. Indonesia, Bangladesh and Iran) naval aid in one form or another has been a highly relevant instrument.

Naval aid is certainly not a panacea, even when maritime factors have a high salience for the countries involved. An important example of this was the Soviet naval aid to Indonesia in the early 1960s. During these years a large number of Soviet warships and auxiliaries were transferred to Indonesia: there was a *Sverdlov*-class cruiser, a dozen W-class submarines, eight destroyers, eight escort ships, a dozen *Komar*-class missile boats, and 'numerous' torpedo boats, patrol craft and support ships.[64] Within a short time, however, President Sukarno had moved towards Communist China, and within a few years he fell from power. Soviet influence had quickly collapsed in Indonesia, regardless of its 'gift-wrapped navy'. Fifteen years later, a large proportion of the Indonesian Navy is not operational because of a shortage of spares.

If naval aid does buy a degree of influence it is usually cashable in terms of concrete benefits (such as naval facilities) or formal support on diplomatic issues. In most cases it is difficult to discern the effectiveness of the naval aid instrument as distinct from the other influence-building techniques which a country might be employing. Its effectiveness is not likely to be independent of those other techniques, nor is it likely to be other than incremental.

Observers should not expect too much from the instruments of diplomacy. Naval aid does not have to buy control or even positive influence in order to be politically worthwhile. The building up of a local navy might have a number of utilities short of control or influence: it might help buttress a country's non-alignment; it might help give it more independence in its general relationships with others; it might help reinforce anti-Western or anti-Soviet or anti-Chinese tendencies; and it might be actually useful in war. Assisting such tendencies might be valuable for suppliers of naval aid, even if there are no immediate direct benefits to be cashed. Indeed, the consolidation of anti-Western tendencies is always likely to have been a factor in the thinking behind the off-the-shelf navies provided by the Soviet Union to some Third World countries. Regardless of whether such aid gave the Soviet Union any leverage with the countries concerned, at least it helped to build up proxy threats to Western navies and so was indirectly supportive of Soviet objectives. Anti-Communist aid has similarly played an important part in general US military aid diplomacy, though until recent years there was no far-flung Soviet naval challenge against which to encourage proxy naval threats. In addition to these utilities, aid also buys or contributes to a superpower's presence in a country or region, and this may increase its diplomatic importance by establishing for it the right to be consulted on local matters. On the other hand, such presences can also be counter-productive: they might polarise relations within a region, thereby decreasing the superpower's overall influence potential and at the same time perhaps provoking counter-action by an adversary, and they might result in the superpower concerned being dragged into local disputes in a way which might be both dangerous and/ or unhelpful to its prestige.

The main recipients of naval aid have been countries on the shores of the Mediterranean Sea and Indian Ocean. Naval aid has also gone to some African countries, though with no appreciable effect. Soviet naval aid to Nigeria during its civil war (mainly consisting of patrol boats to blockade Biafra) attracted a good deal of attention, but it was not sufficiently impressive or significant to the Nigerians to encourage them to develop their relationship with the Soviet Union further. This must have been a disappointment for the Soviet Union, given Nigeria's regional importance. Occasionally naval weapons supplied by external powers have been used in war, as was witnessed in the sinking of some Pakistani naval and merchant vessels by India in 1971, by missile boats provided by the Soviet Union. One might expect that gratitude would be extended to the suppliers on such occasions, but one can never be sure, for it seems to be one of the truisms of all types of military aid diplomacy (as with babies) that the appetites of the recipients grow with feeding. The dividing line between gratitude for what has been given and disappointment (and perhaps resentment) that more is not forthcoming is usually very thin. The lavish military aid provided by the Soviet Union to Egypt is the recent classic case of this.[65]

Naval aid can encompass more than the provision of ships; it also includes the provision of advisers, and such activities as port-clearing. Once again, the provision of aid should not be mistaken for the achievement of influence. In this respect the Soviet port-clearing operation in Bangladesh has been illuminating. While the episode is commonly taken as evidence of Soviet 'influence' in the new state, this oversimplifies what happened. In fact the Prime Minister of Bangladesh, Mujibur Rahman, accepted the Soviet offer only with reluctance, after having failed to receive a promise of UN support.[66] Thus the Soviet Union stepped in to help an underdeveloped country – and not for the first time – after Western countries failed to mobilise the necessary wherewithal. The Soviet interest in this opportunity was almost certainly political influence-building, and the occasion for it was a particularly (exceptionally) appropriate one for naval aid. As Peterson has put it:

> Bangladesh depended upon her seaports for economic survival;
> were they to remain out of commission for much longer, she would
> starve. By restoring these ports the Soviets could make a crucial
> contribution to Bangladesh's economic recovery; a contribution for
> which, as they probably believed, they would be rewarded with
> political influence.[67]

However, despite the significance of naval aid, and the Soviet willingness to minister to a vital need, the Soviet leadership was not rewarded
as it would have liked. As Petersen concludes:

> There was no evidence . . . that the Bangladesh Government has
> returned the favour with more than minor political concessions.
> Though it never fails to stress the importance of 'friendly relations'
> with the Soviet Union, on major issues affecting the Subcontinent,
> Bangladesh follows the Indian rather than the Soviet lead.[68]

The lack of influence goes further: Rahman not only 'conspicuously
failed' to praise the Soviet work, but there were some negative results
for the Soviet Union. These included a retreat by the Soviet Union from
its original commitment, the UN's rapid clearing of Chalna (which the
Soviet team had given up as a bad job) and rumours about the establishment of a Soviet naval base in Bangladesh. These were all embarras-
sing to the Soviet Union in terms of influence-building in Bangladesh.
From the Soviet point of view the results of this experience 'cannot
have been entirely positive'. Thus Petersen concluded that Soviet
leaders may well be more cautious in future about commiting their
navy to such projects.[69] On the other hand, practical lessons were presumably learned, which might encourage them to believe that they will
do better next time.

In addition to influence-building with non-aligned countries, navies
also provide some scope for manipulating relationships within an
alliance. Countries can improve their alliance-worthiness, or their
relative decision-making power, by the relative size and quality of their
maritime commitment (as is the case with Britain and NATO) or by
maximising a limited potential by showing special competence in a
single area (as is the case with the Belgians and minesweeping). In
addition, some countries become important in a maritime sense simply
as a result of their location, and this contributes to their leverage

within an alliance: Turkey, Norway, Portugal and Denmark are such examples within NATO. Navies also provide an opportunity for demonstrating alliance solidarity in a concrete if not always militarily perfect fashion, as was the case with the aborted MLF idea, or as is the case with joint exercises between the NATO or Warsaw Pact allies, or between US and Latin American warships, or in such a NATO organisation as the Standing Naval Force Channel (STANAVFORCHAN) which was formed in 1973 and consists of mine countermeasures ships from Belgium, Germany, the Netherlands and the United Kingdom.

Just as warships can be supportive of alliance relationships, so the warships of adversaries can sometimes help to undermine alliance cohesion. If adversary naval behaviour can contribute to changing a country's thinking about the reliability, credibility and reinforcement and support capability of its major ally, this obviously promises to undermine alliance solidarity. Furthermore, if the smaller allies question the credibility of the maritime assurances of the larger allies, then even the latter might start losing confidence in their ability. But the implication of this is two-fold: the result might either be a further weakening of alliance ties, or alternatively a strenuous effort to stay in the same place. From a purely strategic point of view, an adversary might find either of these outcomes satisfactory.

While there are many limits on warships as instruments of manipulation, there are some circumstances in which they will have utility, either because of the particularly maritime nature of a problem (as in the Bangladesh port-clearing) or because of the lack of other influence-building instruments (as with the establishment of relations with distant states). By acquiring a degree of influence states may improve the pay-offs from the relationship in terms of concrete facilities for strategic purposes, diplomatic support, economic benefits, and the denial of options to adversaries. But the acquisition of a marked degree of influence is never likely to be the independent result of naval efforts. The utility of warships in this respect will always be difficult to separate from the utility of the diplomatic, economic and other military instruments with which they may be concerted. It has been stressed that however skilfully naval diplomacy is practised, its effects are dependent upon the perceptions of others: it must also be stressed that the influence potential of superpowers in Third World countries at the present time faces a number of major constraints, mainly arising out of the latter's newly minted sense of national identity. Invariably, therefore, the success of naval diplomacy is likely

to be small-scale and incremental. Of course, it will be no less welcome
for that: the superpowers have had to adjust in the last twenty years
to the realisation that in contrast to the era of military intervention,
great economic and military resources do not necessarily buy political
influence with weaker countries. Smaller countries rightly suspect that
neither military, political nor economic support (or offers of support)
are given entirely or mainly altruistically. In the present international
climate superpower 'carrots' are rarely impressive enough to overcome
incompatibilities in political goals, except sometimes for the most
weak or needy. States recognise that there may be more penalties
than rewards from superpower support. These continuing suspicions
by the potential targets of superpower naval diplomacy — in many
cases the old actual targets of great power naval coercion — will mean
that the relationship between the possession of a physically impressive
navy and the exercise of political influence will remain an uncertain
one.

(xi)   *International prestige*

The historically high correlation between military power and international status has passed. Most would argue that there still was some
relationship, looking at the fact that the five Permanent Members of
the UN Security Council were also the five nuclear powers. On the
other hand, none would argue that the relationship is as direct as this
illustration suggests.[70]

   Navies, which in some periods of history have been in the front rank
of status-endowing attributes, are not as prestige-worthy as formerly.
Nevertheless, in some circumstances there is a prestige bonus to be
had from the possession and wise use of naval power, and there are
still plenty of people (especially those with a vested interest) who
would argue that a considerable navy was a badge of great power
status, and that it would help to give its possessor the political influence which the attribution of prestige bestowed. The writing of
Admiral Gorshkov has been most prominent in this respect. Even small
countries can derive some respect from the possession of a navy: indeed,
they can derive respect without suggesting any of the overbearing
connotations which a major navy might have. In the context of a
regional situation, the search for naval prestige might be more pressing
than the jaded military appetites of some Western observers feel able
to accept. This has long been the case in Latin America; it was the
case with Ghana under Nkrumah; and it seems likely to be the case in
Iran's build-up in the Gulf. In the latter example, whatever the military

rationale for Iranian warships, it is evident that the Shah has also a particular conception of his personal status and of his country's role which demand commensurate military hardware.[71] But even for less ambitious countries, the possession of some naval force will be part of the country's badge of sovereignty, together with a national army and flag, and a seat at the United Nations. Naval forces bring respect because, as Martin has put it,

> In addition to whatever prestige may be derived from extremely modest naval forces, any capacity to undertake combat at sea, however hopeless in purely military terms, is very significant politically in a world so interconnected and with such inhibitions about the overt use of force as the present one. Even the smallest naval force affords the ability to cross the all-important line between shooting and not-shooting, and may deprive much larger naval powers of the opportunity to present some enforcement action as pacific.[72]

In a period when the expectation is that the politics of the sea will be more rather than less troubled, one might expect that the status-endowing quality of warships will increase rather than decrease.

In addition to the prestige which warships may derive from their primary foreign policy functions, it is worth remembering that the image of navies, with both home and foreign communities, is sometimes augmented in important ways by what are really fringe activities, such as search and rescue. Nevertheless, although these are fringe activities, they can have worth-while effects. Prestige at home is important because it will affect the quality and quantity of recruitment, especially in democracies, and this in turn will affect operational performance.

In the modern world small allies have a greater degree of freedom than hitherto in their relations with their main ally. Because major war is not likely, they do not have to fear abandonment:[73] the opposite, excessive superpower interest, is usually the case. Consequently it is important for the superpowers to maintain their prestige amongst their allies. Naval forces are used occasionally for this purpose, albeit in small ways. Thus the United States in the summer of 1975 sent an all-nuclear task group, including the *Nimitz* to Europe; and the Soviet Union has used the *Leningrad* to entertain 'vacationing' Communist Party leaders from Bulgaria, East Germany, Mongolia, Poland and Czechoslovakia.[74] On the whole the superpowers know where they stand with their adversaries: on the other hand they have to spend a good deal of their daily time worrying about how they themselves stand with their friends.

Great warships are nowhere as prestigious in themselves as in former times, but as was argued in an earlier chapter, they sometimes contribute in important ways to the enhancement of their state's status in the eyes of relevant observers. But it is more difficult than formerly to separate their effect from the effect of other instruments of policy. Nevertheless, they are believed to contribute to the military and political capital of a number of countries. If people believe that warships give international prestige, then they do, for the believers at least. But it is probably true that fewer people are likely to think in this way than previously. For many leaders economic status has a greater salience than military status. In this respect it is worth recalling that it was often said that when he was Britain's Prime Minister, Harold Wilson regarded the pound as a more important symbol of Britain's international virility than the H-bomb.[75]

(4) Domestic functions

(xii) *Border/coastguard responsibilities*

Policing the immediate coastal zone has always been an important, if usually undramatic role for naval forces. Order is maintained in a constabulary rather than a military sense, in furtherance of the interests of sovereignty, good order and resource enjoyment. For a large number of the world's navies, the coastal policing role is the overriding task. And because of the increasing economic importance of coastal zones (not to mention the expanding definition of this concept) there is a widely held view that offshore maritime policing will become a more prominent task for many navies. Because of the economic importance of resources in contiguous seas, a number of the more modern navies (such as Britain and Canada) have somewhat reoriented their sights in this direction. The task of promoting resources has resulted in calls for relevant planning and training for low-level confrontation.[76] This view has been strengthened in Britain because the vulnerability of oil rigs to terrorists created a political mood in which at least some gesture had to be made to protect the country's maritime resources.

The value of warships for coastal policing is self-evident. While strategists debate the utility of major warships acting 'over there' and taxpayers bemoan their cost, few are likely to question either the

value or cost of the lesser amounts of money spent in the attempt to
prevent unwanted egress or ingress, to control shipping in coastal
areas, to maintain access and surveillance over fixed installations,
to prevent smuggling, discourage pollution, and so on. In this sense
navies (sometimes organised as a separate coastguard) are simply a
seaward extension of national police forces, and the utility of the
latter is not questioned: indeed, in many countries the requirement
is likely to be for more rather than less law-enforcers. The utility of
these activities is evident for all states, from the oldest maritime
powers to the newest of countries: the latter, if they are coastal, are
especially sensitive about their sovereignty, and they will provide themselves with at least a few patrol boats (albeit an armed dhow or two).
No-free-ride is a trusted rule of thumb whether it is the criminally
or militarily aggressive (or criminally negligent) which are being
deterred. The future of many navies will lie in the carrying out of a
variety of coastguard functions in those areas of water over which
a degree of national jurisdiction is claimed.

(xiii) *Nation-building*

It is a cliché that 'security begins at home.' The task of internal security
involves armed forces in patrolling the country's borders, be they on
land or sea, in contributing to the maintenance of civil order, and
generally in providing 'aid to the civil power'. The armed forces of all
states have important contributions to make in these roles: sometimes
it is a regular low-level commitment; on other occasions it involves a
commitment to intervene to help resolve a crisis. In many types of
states in recent years, be they underdeveloped or industrialised, difficult
problems of governability have arisen. One result of the disorder or
threatened disorder which has resulted from this has been a fairly
widespread perception that armed forces have been and will be drawn
into domestic life more than we have been accustomed to regard (in
the Western world at least) as proper and normal. While radical
critics might regard such military intervention as a retrogressive step,
those who value 'order' (perhaps the vast majority in all states) regard
legitimately used military power in such roles as proper and valuable
and confirming the utility of military forces. This is so, if unwelcome,
even in countries where the military have traditionally had a minimal
role in internal security operations.

Because of the obvious geographical reason that internal security
problems occur on land, and that navies are equipped to operate (on
the whole) only as far as the shore-line, warships in most circumstances

have only a restricted role in such operations. However, in times of serious internal conflict they can support government forces acting on land in a number of ways: examples include riverine patrols searching for guerrillas, or the blockading of a coast during local crises or civil war (as was the case with the blockade of Biafra during the Nigerian civil war). Occasionally, warships are used even more directly for controlling or suppressing internal troubles. It is salutary for the British to be reminded that within living memory its government used naval forces for a variety of tasks during the General Strike of 1926.[77] Equally salutary for Chinese Communist propagandists is the fact that the present government of China was the last government to send gunboats up the Yangtze. This ironic turn-about occurred during the troubles associated with the Cultural Revolution.[78] As well as being used on the government side to suppress troubles, it is also well to remember that in at least one classic case, that of the *Aurora* in 1917, a warship played a part in fomenting revolutionary disorder.

In addition to their contributions to internal order, navies, like the other branches of a country's armed services, can also contribute to nation-building through ceremonial and socialising roles, and through internal development of various sorts. In their ceremonial role they are a badge of sovereignty, and can symbolise national identity and independence: they can provide some psychological reassurance to the home community, perhaps symbolising past glories or present hopes. In their socialising roles armed forces can provide a degree of political indoctrination, youth control, general socialisation and education, and can foster national rather than regional or sub-national consciousness. Furthermore, in many developing countries the armed forces have been important channels for 'modernisation'. Taken as a whole, this means that armed forces have had a high utility for nation-building in many new states. They also have some utility in this respect for those industrialised countries which are not homogeneous and in which the leadership is not very confident.

Inevitably the nation-building role of navies is quite restricted when compared with that of armies. In all countries armies are larger and more pervasive: even in the ceremonial role navies usually have to take third place behind those services which can parade through or fly over the national capital. Nevertheless, in some countries navies do make a contribution to nation-building: in parts of Latin America and South-East Asia the inaccessibility of some communities and the advantages of waterborne transport provide a series of opportunities for local naval forces to exercise this role.

Some naval forces today operate in ways which are far removed from issues of strategy and clashes of force: they contribute to civic action programmes of various types in coastal regions or along big rivers in some of the developing countries. They help in the development of communities and communications, by providing power plants, maintaining navigation, providing charts, giving medical assistance, helping with traffic control, and assisting the development of waterfronting regions by building piers and harbours and providing navigational aids. They can also assist in local education programmes. The type of work which can be done along these lines is well exemplified in the Philippines, where the Navy is contributing to the development of the country in several ways, including the use of a Naval Construction Force for building stretches of roads, bridges, schools and buildings. More prominently, in developed as well as underdeveloped countries, navies assist when necessary by providing assistance in natural disasters.

Naval officers as nation-builders obviously require different skills from those of captains of ships, and certainly captains of war.[79] They need the political and developmental skills necessary for the building up of the infrastructure which their countries can utilise. Naval organisations can and do make some contribution to the development of coastal and riverine regions in a few developing countries: in this sense they contribute to the significant internal utility of armed forces in the developing world.

The utility of navies: concluding remarks

In a world which has changed markedly over the past twenty-five years, and certainly over the last fifty, it is only proper that strategists in every country keep asking the question: why do we need a navy? For naval establishments to ask such a question might create an impression of a lack of self-confidence in the eyes of others, and may produce a degree of uncertainty in the naval service itself, especially if familiar and well-established answers become discredited. On the other hand, such reassessments are a necessary part of adjusting military means to political interests. For some years this business of reassessment has been a particularly disturbing activity for the major naval powers, because technological and political changes affecting the maritime environment have left traditional answers about the roles, missions and utility of navies in a state of flux.

But the breast-beating uncertainty about the utility of naval forces is almost exclusively a concern of the Western maritime powers.

Uncertainties may exist in the Soviet Union, but they are not overt. The problem for the former monopolist maritime powers is that some of the foreign policy goals for which navies always had essential supportive roles have either changed or disappeared: this has obviously brought into question the character of their naval needs. Most dramatically, the benefits to be gained by major war or intervention are almost universally thought to have vanished. In other respects, however, naval forces maintain much utility: this is so in the case of basic deterrence and defence, and in terms of preserving order at sea. As with armed forces in general, naval *strategy* in the modern world is less concerned with contributing to victory in war than with furthering national interests short of war.

In these changed circumstances, it is not surprising that the old problem of how much to spend on naval forces has become more frustrating. This is partly the result of the fact that the old yardstick, the test of major war, is increasingly perceived to be a distant possibility (though all admit that it is a possibility). The requirements of major war still provide some yardstick, because of the need to deter that very eventuality: but in a deterrent situation, where war is not admissible, it is obviously much more difficult to answer the question 'how much is enough?' These problems are intensified because of the soaring costs of all types of warships, because all these ships have to be justified within domestic political contexts in which armed forces are often not as acceptable, and because the international context is such that there will be fewer circumstances in which they might be used. It must be added, of course, that these are not peculiarly naval problems.

The problems involved in assessing the marginal utility of extra military insurance are always difficult. Answers are likely to be particularly difficult, and parsimonious, in a period when both industrialised and developing countries are largely turned in on themselves; in each case the opportunity costs represented by defence spending are particularly visible and sensitive. Furthermore, as the belief grows in some countries that war is an increasingly remote risk, so the desire for high insurance slackens. When governments assess their military insurance needs, national cultural factors will affect their appreciation. Some countries will tend to overinsure, as with the Soviet Union, while others tend to succumb to the temptations of peace. When considering the insurance quality of warships, and questions of marginal utility, it is always important to remember that the appropriate analogy is not with life assurance, in which an individual's family receives benefits after his death, or fire insurance, in which a family or business receives some recompense after a calamity: instead the valid analogy is with the kind of insurance provided by locks on houses, safety-belts on cars, and police forces against criminals. In such cases, unlike life assurance, there is some relationship between the amount spent (assuming it is spent on good equipment which is properly used) and the likelihood of the threat materialising, and the degree of calamity experienced.

The utility of navies, and for that matter the use of force in general, should not be based on generalisations from a few familiar cases. Naturally, the outlooks of the traditional maritime powers concern us most, but theirs is only one view. An important distinction must therefore be made between those few states wishing to use their navies in support of foreign policy in distant seas, and the majority interested in exercising naval power only within their own coastal waters. However, as more states have become attached to what some regard as the 'common heritage of mankind', interest in the use of the sea has grown amongst all coastal states. However, the development and maintenance of a militarily effective navy for distant operations (even policing a 200-mile exclusive economic zone) will be beyond the capability of many countries. But despite such constraints, there can be little doubt about the utility which many smaller countries attach to their sea forces. Maritime sovereignty remains a high value, and some naval capability is within the reach of all, especially because of the interest of major powers in proliferating arms for a mixture of economic, political and strategic reasons. The utility of naval forces for furthering policy in contiguous seas is attested to by the fact that most of the world's navies are of this type. It is no coincidence. While jet-setters and drop-outs might deride suburban housing and bourgeois habits, the latter have conspicuously high utility for the bulk of Western industrialised society: they represent a satisfactory balance of aggregate values over aggregate costs. Similarly, coastal navies suit the limited pockets and unassuming intentions of most of international society.

Small countries will rarely have the doubts about their navies that the larger naval powers have demonstrated. Furthermore, it is worth considering that an additional coastal patrol craft for, say, oil-rich Abu Dhabi might be regarded by the local rulers as having greater utility for them than a US government might regard the acquisition of an extra aircraft-carrier. In general, small countries do not have the doubts which face the great naval powers. They are usually clearer about the purposes for which they require their ships. In contrast, those countries which want to act effectively on a global scale have manifold problems, and never know what might come in handy. Furthermore, the smaller navies do not have such intense problems of marginal utility, because the units in which they are interested are less conspicuously costly. It is only when a country becomes involved in acquiring major surface and submarine forces, especially aircraft carriers and nuclear submarines, that the public sacrifice in terms of hospitals, roads, social services and so on becomes politically important. There is little or no evidence that the many small-navy countries are dissatisfied with the return which they receive from the money invested in ships. Their warships continue to be used in ways and for jobs for which no other means is as suitable. In addition, while warships are always a burden in a direct and indirect economic sense, naval organisations as such are not prominent in the other aggregate costs of armed forces. Admirals do not often figure in *coups* and naval establishments rarely threaten legitimate authority. Navies are not usually prominent in the minds of the liberal critics of military values. Furthermore, the external political costs of using navies are usually limited when compared with the all-or-nothing actions which so often characterise the use of troops or aircraft.

Despite the growing problems, the great naval powers — the 'producers' rather than the 'consumers' of international order at sea — cannot opt out of their responsibilities without facing significant risks. This means that there will be a pressure to modernise as long as they think that war or lesser disorders at sea are possible, and so need deterring, and as long as they wish to support foreign policy in distant regions. This last activity is of some interest to all. While many states may seem to be interested in an active sense only in what happens immediately off their shores (perhaps up to twelve miles), many of them will also be interested more generally in what happens beyond, at least to two hundred miles. Whatever a particular state's attitude to the ongoing order at sea — whether it wants to challenge it, suffer it, defer to it, or enjoy it — its ability to employ the use of force at sea will have some bearing on the success or not of its diplomacy in specific instances. If states (or their protectors) make no effort in a naval sense, they must be willing to face the possibility that important sea areas may be dominated by adversaries or potential adversaries. If there is no benevolent naval power available, shipping will be at the mercy of those willing to use violence. For those interested in order at sea the 'no policeman, no law' relationship remains valid. For those interested in disorder, the rule is 'no force, no leverage'. In both equations the common factor is the utility of naval power.

The direct costs of using military force in the international arena have changed. Although the theoretical range of functions which navies can serve is unaltered, the values guiding the choice of those functions have changed. Most states are now more inward- than outward-looking; they are more concerned with the fruits of domestic economic development than with the now bitter fruits of territorial conquest. To the extent that the utility of force has declined, it has done so because of rising costs and because the traditional great military actors no longer place a high priority on doing those things for which their navies were so useful in the past. Furthermore, governments are aware of a wider range of alternative instruments for the support of foreign policy. If the arrows in the foreign policy quiver are not as sharp as in the recent past, at least there are more in the quiver. As economic levels and dependencies have spread and risen, governments have come to possess other means of inducement and punishment. There are more substitutes for force.

But military power is not without utility. For one thing the rising cost of war enhances the use of military power for deterrence. Consequently, the non-acquisitive utility of force has been maintained or even increased. Its acquisitive utility would seem to have declined, however, though it should be added that between smaller countries there are fewer of the military inhibitions which have come to characterise relations between the great powers. In addition, for all types of state, armed forces have increased their utility because of their domestic usage, though navies can invariably play only a marginal role in this respect.

Navies therefore have decreasing military utility for the great naval powers in an acquisitive sense, but they have an increased utility for all states in enhancing the non-acquisitive functions of military power. Naval forces have increasing utility for policing functions for all types of states. They have a residual diplomatic utility for the great naval powers, and have increased diplomatic utility for the newer naval powers which are challenging existing perceptions about naval balances either globally (as is the case with the Soviet Union) or regionally (as is the case with Iran). Since most coastal states in the world are satisfied with using their navies for policing and non-acquisitive military functions, this suggests that their naval forces have no need to fear for their future employment. This limited outlook is well suited to the international climate outside the central balance. But in some parts of the world force is used and conceived in traditional and sometimes acquisitive ways. During the late 1960s and early 1970s, when it was commonplace to hear Western commentators decrying the utility of military force, Iran was spending vast amounts of money on modern military equipment to make itself policeman of the Gulf, Israeli commanders were conquering territory to improve their state's security, Indian forces were detaching East Pakistan and helping carve out the new state of Bangladesh, and the North Vietnamese and Vietcong were successfully rounding off a prolonged war. The leaders of these groups do not need asking whether force has utility. Furthermore, some would argue that, apart from nuclear war, the Western attitudes to the use of armed force which characterised the Vietnam period might be more transient than we yet think. In this respect the oil crisis at the turn of 1973-4 drew attention to possible tensions in a world of scarcer resources. Especially with the Vietnam memory still strong, Kissinger's raising of the possibility of US military intervention in the Middle East took on additional significance. While some Western commentators might have regarded the announcement with some scepticism, potential targets certainly had to take it seriously.

The contrast between the different perceptions of the historic maritime powers and some smaller powers has an important implication. There has been a natural tendency when armed forces fail to achieve a particular objective for critics to argue that the utility of the instrument is declining. This has been so in the naval case: such an argument was heard, for example, following the demonstration of force by US warships after the seizure of the *Pueblo*. However, one must never automatically equate failure with disutility without first asking: were the tactics right? were there enough (or too many) warships present? were warships the most useful response? Even if one still decides that one's warships are or were irrelevant for a certain policy objective, one nevertheless has to recognise that one of the reasons for this may have been related to the increasing usefulness of the adversary's warships. One of the reasons for the declining utility of intervention by great powers is directly related to the increasing utility of the defensive military power of smaller countries.

It has been the objective of this chapter to provide a comprehensive framework in which a more coherent discussion of the utility of naval forces can take place. With this in mind it must always be the objective of students of the subject to move from the general to the particular. They must ask, in relation to a particular country: what are its interests in the use of the sea, as seen by decision-makers and opinion-formers?

what naval capabilities are thought to be needed for what purposes? do such military, political and economic purposes justify whatever has to be spent on the necessary capabilities? what are the opportunity costs involved? are there alternative means by which the purposes can be pursued more efficiently, more cheaply, or more effectively? how acceptable is the maintenance and use of naval forces to the interested public in that country?

Clearly, there will be many national purposes to which naval forces cannot minister. In military terms their slowness and vulnerability have increased. It is no longer possible to exercise 'command' or 'control' in the old style against a determined and major enemy. If technological trends can be extrapolated, it will become relatively easier to deny rather than to secure the use of the sea. Furthermore, in less drastic situations than all-out war, changes in international circumstances have restricted the usability of naval force. Nevertheless, most of their inherent assets remain, as do most of the functions which they have always performed. Warships are still usable in many situations, and even their non-use has a variety of important (mainly deterrent) utilities. What has changed for the major naval powers is not so much the instrumentality of warships as the purposes for which they have been considered useful: there has been much uncertainty about some of the purposes to which warships have traditionally ministered. Some objectives have simply been given up in the face of national and international developments: other roles, worthwhile in themselves, have been ended because the cost to the electorate could not be justified. The historic naval powers have had to adjust and are in the process of adjusting their thinking to the new circumstances, although they still sometimes have ships which were built for purposes which have become increasingly uncertain, and for wars which are increasingly remote. The smaller naval powers have not had to face such problems of adjustment. But for both groups of countries one thing seems certain: given the propensity for international conflict and given the growing significance of the sea in international politics, there is little reason to suppose that the utility of navies is in doubt, though their size, character and purposes may be somewhat removed from the traditional Anglo-American image.

The troubled common

The 'wide common', as Mahan called the sea,[80] has not yet degenerated into the 'jungle' that some have claimed.[81] On the other hand, the common is certainly not the relatively stable, relatively empty,

relatively unused, relatively unpolluted, and economically marginal
two-thirds of the earth's surface that it was through the many decades
of *pax Britannica* and *pax Americana*, when the British and US
navies exercised a benevolent hegemonic order. For a mixture of
military, economic, technological and political reasons, the common is
now much troubled. Well-established 'rights' are thought to be vulnerable, and the sea is thought to be a more dangerous place. Fear has been
expressed that maritime affairs may degenerate into a degree of disorder which has not been evident outside wartime for centuries.

It is the intention of this final section to look at the sources of
order and disorder at sea: the balance of these pressures will help shape
the environment within which existing warships will operate, new
warships will be conceived, naval organisations will develop and adapt,
and new strategies and tactics will evolve. Already the problems of the
troubled common have resulted in limited clashes of violence: but on
the whole conflicting interests have focused on questions of international law and its future. After a slow evolution, the international
legal regime at sea has suddenly been buffeted by rival interests and
undermined by new problems. The old law is now in process of rapid
development, as seen most obviously in the growth of claims regarding
the breadth of the territorial sea and in the general challenge to well-
established norms. There is a widespread belief that a comprehensive
and generally agreed new system will have to emerge if maritime affairs
in future are to proceed on some other basis than 'first come first
served', supported by national military power.

The current salience of law of the sea problems is the result of the
coincidence of three pressures. Firstly, the arrival of new technologies
which have made the exploitation of the sea easier. This has been an
accelerating development, impelled by such factors as the doubling of
marine scientists every four years.[82] Secondly, perceptions about
declining resources on land have increased the significance of resources
at sea. And thirdly, the whole issue has been galvanised by the powerful
nationalism of the developing countries. On some issues in the mid-
1970s this group showed a new consciousness of strength, and a new
degree of unity and assertiveness. These three pressures have together
encouraged two temptations: the temptation for the developed and
technologically capable to grab what they can, and to exploit it before
conditions change; and secondly, for ambitious countries of all types,
the more general temptation to make extensive maritime claims, and
to hope to make these ambitions concrete by securing a change in the
law. For all these reasons the sea will become increasingly used and will

be of novel international political importance. For most states the sea has formerly been a marginal issue-area in international politics: today it has a centrality which as a by-product is threatening the old stability.

The potential sources of conflict are many, and are by now familiar. (1) There are problems resulting from the depletion of non-renewable resources on land, especially oil. This has resulted in exploration for oil and many other minerals on or under the sea-bed. Problems in this area have been intensified by the accelerating demand for these re-sources. It is hardly surprising that the oil problem has caused disputes about jurisdiction over the continental shelf between, amongst others, Greece and Turkey, Indonesia and Vietnam, Japan and Taiwan. (2) There are problems arising as a result of the increasing importance of the sea as a source of foodstocks, as world population increases. Not only is the demand increasing, but intensified exploitation threatens both traditional patterns of fishing and present catches. This in turn stimulates efforts to protect stocks and livelihood; such a situation almost inevitably results in disputes such as the 'cod wars' between Britain and Iceland. Disputes about fishing rights have been a regular feature of maritime affairs in many parts of the world, and there is reason to suppose that they will increase rather than decrease. (3) There are problems resulting from the new technologies; these are making new exploitation possible and old tasks easier. New fixed systems are frequently a cause and a result of this exploitation. In turn, oil and gas rigs, pipelines and cables can cause legal and military problems. Other installations, such as power stations and airports, may be moved to the sea and cause different problems. (4) There are problems resulting from the military uses of the seas, including the use of fixed systems for submarine surveillance, the tensions associated with the cat-and-mouse activity of ASW, and the dangers involved in the operation of fleets in close proximity. While some controls and agreements have been reached on this subject – the Seabed Treaty, the agreement on the prevention of naval incidents between the United States and USSR, and the SALT I restriction on SSBNs – such agreements do not preclude tension at sea arising out of the deterrent game in all its manifestations. (5) There are problems arising from the claims which have been growing about the territorial sea and exclusive economic zones; these affect the rights of ships, especially warships, passing through a number of the major shipping straits. Troubles may arise if coastal states extend their powers of regulation, and especially if they close off important areas of what was hitherto regarded as high sea. A principal example in this respect is the Indonesian archipelagic concept of internal waters. States making such claims will obviously improve their bargaining strength if they can support their legal claims with naval power, be it only a minimal force such as Iceland's gunboats. Closed seas will interfere with the traditional legal immunity of warships on the high seas; the growing claims will therefore affect those wishing to deploy warships in distant waters, for deterrence or other purposes, or even those with a more limited stake in naval mobility.[83] They will also affect overflying rights. Whether or not such claims are backed by naval forces, those with an interest in naval mobility will feel obliged to effect patrols to maintain rights. (6) There will be problems arising from challenges to the existing character of international law, and from the problems which may result from differing interpretations, ambiguities and claims concerning whatever agreements materialise. (7) There are problems because of the fears (variably perceived) about pollution, especially where it involves threats to cash and livelihood. (8) In addition to these newer problems, there are also many of the traditional ones, such as the need to protect neutrality in crises and war. In recent times these problems have been witnessed as a result of the US action during the Cuban missile crisis, the Indian blockade of Pakistan, the Middle Eastern crises, and the US mining of North Vietnam. (9) Finally, it is not only the 'common' that is troubled, but also the lands around it. The propensity for disorder in the years ahead is very high, because of economic, political, social and military strains in many parts of the world. Some of the conflicts which result can be expected to spill over on to the sea.

In sum, there are numerous pressures on the traditional régime at sea. The sea will be used more rather than less. Its resources, which were previously marginal, now have an importance whose potential is considerable, if ultimately uncertain. That national jurisdiction in various forms and for various purposes will extend over new sea areas seems to be one of the very few safe predictions in current international politics. In one form or another the foreign ministries of the world are likely to be concerned with maritime boundary problems to a greater extent than ever before. The old régime is changing, and there is an expectation of being on the brink of another. The implications of these trends for the future of navies remain to be seen, but implications there will be, wherever the equilibrium comes to rest between the extremes of a free-for-all or an internationally agreed treaty system.

The old order is changing, but it is not inevitable that disorder will be the outcome. There are some important sources of stability. Many states are conscious of their interdependence with others in terms of the movement of goods, security, pollution and international trade. There is always a tendency to exaggerate the limitations of international law in international politics, but as one standard work in the field has pointed out, foreign ministries are generally geared to maintaining agreements rather than to breaking them.[84] In addition, there are many non-governmental international economic actors (much more important than the diplomat in the minds of many) who are actively engaged in carrying out business in one form or another, and who have a strong commitment to stability. Clearly shippers and bankers and their ancillary activities, and all the companies who rely upon them for profit and employment belong to this group. On each and every day there are thousands of merchant vessels going about their business, keeping to the rules, and with no thought or requirement for the protection of their country's warships. While there are occasional exceptions to this picture of busy inter-dependence, the extent of daily stability is an important corrective to the too-easily drawn picture of the sea as a dangerous place.

There are other reasons for not taking too pessimistic a view. Although the developing countries would not appear to have the same vested interest in maintaining the old order as the 'have' countries, they nevertheless do have some stake in orderly international behaviour: that would appear to be the most likely way for them to secure trade and aid. Furthermore, whatever verbal and moral pressure they can bring to bear on the larger powers, they are mostly unable to present any military challenge. It is significant that despite all the warning signs of the early 1970s about the 'Third World' acting together as a unified force, the UN meetings on the Law of the Sea have not (so far) been as acrimonious as many had feared. Other hopeful signs have been the orderliness with which some areas of the sea have been distributed amongst the littoral states, and the fact that despite the fears of terror-ism against ships and fixed installations, actual incidents have been negligible. Another sign of the times is the extent to which international law currently affects naval planning, and the expectation that inter-national legal policy will increasingly become a factor in naval doctrine.[85] Furthermore, all these trends are developing against a back-ground in which the major naval powers share roughly the same interests in law of the sea questions: if there is any trouble between the super-powers on maritime matters it is likely to be the spill-over of conflicts elsewhere, rather than being the original cause of trouble.

The future, as ever, appears balanced between the forces of order and disorder. Order at sea is not fragile, but *The Times* was expressing a widely held view when it forecast that if an acceptable international régime was not established, the competition for the resources of the sea could hardly do other than breed conflict.[86] Both 'haves' and 'have-nots' recognise the need for change: both groups of states have strengths and vulnerabilities and share a preferred commitment to 'jaw-jaw' as a solution (a situation of 'no law', as well as the *status quo* favours the traditional naval powers, so that the challengers have to take care in the way they present their demands). But even with the 'best will' in the world on both sides (and how often is *that* present in international relations?) nobody is expecting that the process will be easy or that the outcome is destined to be successful. It is no part of this chapter to suggest outcomes, merely to point out that since the late 1960s the forum for these contending interests has been the UN conference on the Law of the Sea. While the results of these meetings have not been as successful as many hoped, neither have they been as troubled as some feared. The sessions showed the importance attached to the issues, the national sensitivities about maritime sovereignty, the complexity of the subject, and the difficulties facing the reaching of an agreement between such a large and variegated group of states. They also showed the changeability of some aspects of international politics, especially in the way that well-established norms about the maritime régime could be challenged even in the face of the vested interests of the developed maritime powers. In view of these factors, any new system which is hammered out will be the result of hard bargaining over a long period rather than any grandiose diplomatic *coup*. The new system is likely to be a rather messy (but not necessarily unsatisfactory) bundle of regional and bilateral agreements, possibly with some universal agreements, some *ad hoc* agreements over certain issues, and various *modi vivendi* in those areas which expediency or chance leaves uncovered by agreement. However coherent or however cobbled the eventual outcome, few states will achieve all their objectives, and there will be ambiguities, omissions and problems which will give rise to the possibility of further disputes. Furthermore, partly because of the speed of change and the uncertainty of evaluations, the degree of international commitment to whatever norms are 'legitimised' will not be evident for some time.

In such changing circumstances, in which maritime affairs are increasingly important as international political issues, the major international actors will continue to need some capability for exercising force at sea. If there is minimal or no international regulation, naval forces will be needed to support national claims: if there is agreed international regulation, naval forces will be needed to maintain and enforce it. In either case warships will be necessary to deter conflicts, or to keep them within manageable bounds if they do break out. Inevitably, while the character of the new role is still inchoate, there is a feeling among some observers that few navies are well-equipped for carrying out 'the new offshore constabulary tasks'.[87] Others, however, are confident that navies can rise to the new challenge.[88] In either case, can there be much doubt about the verdict that maritime forces 'are likely to be more rather than less in demand both at home and away' in the context of the changing law of the sea, while the other requirements of deterrence at all levels seem unlikely to diminish?[89]

The warships of the future may not always act merely nationally. Enforcement might be carried out on an international basis. Such an idea — 'an international peace-keeping naval force' — was contemplated by the British Cabinet immediately preceding the June War in 1967. The idea was that a body of maritime powers would co-operate and if necessary assemble an international naval force to escort convoys through the Straits of Tiran, an international waterway which was being closed to Israeli ships by Egypt. Opposition within the Cabinet and the outbreak of war ruled out the idea.[90] In a sense, this idea was a naval example of what some writers have seen as a necessary response by governments if the international system is to develop in an orderly fashion: that is, national security will have to be seen by each state to have both a national and a community aspect, which means having international forces in readiness either for collective security or for peace-keeping.[91] Extensive claims on the sea, rigidly supported by individual countries, are likely to present the international community with opportunities for such employment.

It is clear, therefore, that law, in one form or another, by its presence or by its absence, will have a novel impact on naval policy. Legal considerations will affect the shape of naval planning, and they will affect the character of policy by unloading on governments a variety of maritime troubles. Also, as Hill has put it, 'Every state, in one way or another, will be trying to use the law to lick reality, whether of geography, poverty or power.[92] This, of course, has always been the case to some extent, and the naval powers have manipulated the law well or badly in support of their policies. One of the continuing regrets of many writers on British naval history was the government's adherence to the Declaration of Paris of 1856, which blunted the advantages of

British naval power.[93] In a different way, the German naval establishment failed before the war to think through the international legal problems of submarine war against commerce, and suffered as a result.[94] In contrast, the operations of the US Navy during the Cuban missile crisis were carried out with a sophisticated legal eye, with the legal instrument being well used in support of policy.[95] In the present international community the realisation of the desirability of having the law on one's side is now more prevalent than ever before; there would appear to be no good reason to disagree with Professor O'Connell's verdict that naval planning will be determined more than ever before by international legal considerations.[96] This means that legal issues will increasingly be the occasion for naval operations, and that naval planning will be framed increasingly with an eye to the law. On the whole these law-based situations will be such that force is usable: they will be of a different character to East-West confrontations. In future it may make more sense to talk about lawships rather than warships.

The international context within which naval policy is made is changing in many ways. A variety of new actors, technological possibilities, economic interests, military developments and political issues have made Mahan's 'wide common' a troubled one. The resulting tension between the forces of order and disorder, international collaboration or national scrambling will be the environment within which naval policy will be framed in the immediate future. But two familiar things will be certain on the troubled common. Law, as ever, will be a continuation of politics by other means. And warships, of one type or another, will continue to be built as insurances against unknown contingencies, in order that nations can try to exert a degree of control over an unfriendly environment.

Notes

1. Above, Chapter Six.
2. The following paragraph is indebted to Klaus Knorr's most useful essay on the subject: *On the Uses of Military Power in the Nuclear Age* (Princeton: Princeton University Press, 1966), pp. 5-16.
3. Ibid., pp. 8-9.
4. Space forbids an extended discussion of these assumptions, but they are well covered in strategic literature. In particular, see: Stanley Hoffmann, 'The Acceptability of Force', and Laurence Martin, 'The Utility fo Force', in *Adelphi Papers* (London: IISS, 1973), No. 102; John Garnett, 'The Role of Military Power', Chapter 3 in John Baylis *et al.*, *Contemporary*

Strategy. Theories and Policies (London: Croom Helm, 1975); Klaus Knorr, op. cit.; Robert E. Osgood and Robert W. Tucker, *Force, Order and Justice* (Baltimore: The Johns Hopkins Press, 1967).

5.   Knorr, op. cit., pp. 9-10.

6.   See Hoffmann, op. cit.

7.   Martin, 'The Utility of Force', p. 14.

8.   See, for example, Walter Millis, 'The Uselessness of Military Power', in R. A. Goldwin (ed.), *America Armed* (Chicago: Rand McNally, 1961).

9.   This formulation is by Anatol Rapoport. See the Introduction to his edited *Clausewitz On War* (Harmondsworth: Pelican Books, 1968).

10.   D. P. O'Connell, 'Naval Policy and International Law and International Relations', in *Britain and the Sea* (The Collected Papers and Records of the Conference held at the Royal Naval College Greenwich, 12-14 September 1973), pp. 30-1. Extracts were reprinted in the *New Scientist*, 25 October 1973.

11.   Chaim Herzog, *The War of Atonement* (London: Weidenfeld and Nicolson, 1975), Chapter 17.

12.   Ibid., pp. 264, 269.

13.   On the missile threat, see D. P. O'Connell, *The Influence of Law on Sea Power* (Manchester: Manchester University Press, 1975), pp. 86-90.

14.   This possibility was raised by Mr Schlesinger in January 1974 and by Dr Kissinger a year later with regard to the Middle East. See the analysis in *Strategic Survey 1974* (London: IISS, 1975), pp. 30-2.

15.   Inis L. Claude, Jr., 'The Enlarged Community in a Changing International Environment', Chapter I in Ieuan G. John (ed.), *EEC Policy Towards Eastern Europe* (Westmead, Farnborough, Hants.: Saxon House, 1975).

16.   E.g. Z. Brzezinski, 'Peace and Power', reprinted in *Survival*, Vol. X, No. 12, December 1968.

17.   Strobe Talbott (trans. and ed.), *Khrushchev Remembers. The Last Testament* (London: Andre Deutsch, 1974), p. 31. It is well to remember that a Soviet intervention *by definition* would not be an 'imperialist war'.

18.   Ken Booth, *The Military Instrument in Soviet Foreign Policy, 1917-1972* (London: RUSI, 1974), esp. pp. 31-56.

19.   Rapoport, op. cit., pp. 411-14.

20.   Michael Howard, 'The Transformation of Strategy', *Brassey's Annual 1972* (London: William Clowes and Sons Ltd., 1972), p. 9.

21.   E.g. Kosta Tsipsis, Anne H. Cahn, Bernard T. Feld (eds.), *The Future of the Sea-Based Deterrent* (Cambridge, Mass.: The MIT Press, 1973). See also Ian Smart's panegyric on the SSBN: 'From Polaris to the Future', Chapter 9 in A. M. J. Hyatt (ed.), *Dreadnought to Polaris: Maritime Strategy Since Mahan* (Toronto: Copp Clark, 1973).

22.   Smart, op. cit., p. 107.

23.   Admiral of the Fleet Lord Chatfield, *It Might Happen Again* (London: Heinemann, 1947), p. 100.

24.   Edward N. Luttwak, *The Political Uses of Sea Power* (Baltimore: The Johns Hopkins University Press, 1974), p. 28.

25.   Ibid., p. 2.

26.   Hill, 'Maritime Forces in Confrontation', op. cit., p. 36.

27.   Quoted by Geoffrey Bennett, *The Battle of Jutland* (London: Batsford, 1964), p. 155. In similar vein, Mahan's immortal words about the influence of the Royal Navy on the Napoleonic Wars were as follows: 'amid all the tramping to and fro over Europe of the French armies . . . there went on unceasingly that noiseless pressure upon the vitals of France, that compulsion whose silence . . . becomes to the observer the most striking and awful

mark of the working of Sea Power.'

28. See Captain J. R. Hill, 'The Rule of Law at Sea' (unpublished thesis, Department of Laws, University of London, King's College, 1972), pp. 172-3.

29. For a brief account of the principles on which Canadian naval policy is based, and how they are translated into capabilities, see: G. R. Lindsay, 'Canadian Maritime Strategy in the Seventies', in Hyatt, op. cit., pp. 64-76.

30. Daniel J. Carrison, *The United States Navy* (New York: Praeger, 1968), p. 37.

31. For a sensible discussion of this, see MccGwire's arguments in Michael MccGwire, Ken Booth and John McDonnell, *Soviet Naval Policy. Objectives and Constraints* (New York: Praeger, 1975), pp. 529-30.

32. Barry Blechman, *The Changing Soviet Navy* (Washington: The Brookings Institution, 1973), p. 22.

33. Mohamed Heikal, *The Road to Ramadan* (London: Collins, 1975), pp. 47-8.

34. Ibid.

35. See Chapter Two.

36. This argument is well expressed by Michael Howard, 'Military Power and International Order', *International Affairs*, Vol. XL, July 1964, pp. 397-408.

37. George Brown, *In My Way* (Harmondsworth: Penguin Books, 1972), pp. 128-9.

38. James M. McConnell and Anne M. Kelly, 'Superpower Naval Diplomacy in the Indo-Pakistani Crisis', Chapter 31 in MccGwire, *Soviet Naval Developments*, p. 451.

39. This is discussed below, pp. 274-81.

40. Thomas C. Schelling, *Arms and Influence* (New Haven: York University Press, 1966), Chapter I.

41. Alfred Vagts, *Defence and Diplomacy: The Soldier and the Conduct of Foreign Relations* (New York: King's Crown Press, 1956), p. 248.

42. Ibid., pp. 256-9.

43. Ibid., p. 259.

44. See above, Chapter Six.

45. L. W. Martin, *The Sea in Modern Strategy* (London: Chatto and Windus for the ISS, 1967), pp. 81-3, 150-65.

46. *The Economist*, 21 July 1973.

47. Ibid.

48. Geoffrey Jukes, 'The Indian Ocean in Soviet Naval Policy', *Adelphi Papers*, No. 87, May 1972 (London: IISS, 1972), pp. 13-15.

49. Michael MccGwire, 'The Evolution of Soviet Naval Policy: 1960-74', Chapter 28 in MccGwire, Booth and McDonnell, op. cit., p. 527.

50. Ibid., p. 524.

51. Michael MccGwire, 'Soviet Naval Interests and Intentions in the Caribbean', Chapter 33 in MccGwire, *Soviet Naval Developments*, pp. 482-3.

52. James M. McConnell, 'The Soviet Navy in the Indian Ocean', Chapter 28, ibid., pp. 401-2. It seems to have had the opposite effect to the one desired.

53. Ibid. Oles M. Smolansky and Carey B. Joynt, 'The Political Background to Soviet Naval Policy·in the Mediterranean', Chapter 28, ibid., pp. 378-9; Barry M. Blechman, 'Soviet Interests in Naval Arms Control: Prospects for Disengagement in the Mediterranean', Chapter 35, ibid.

54. William E. Butler has shown the continuity of Russian thinking about

'closed' and 'regional' seas, noting that this doctrine has been favoured by both Tsarist and Soviet leaders at times of naval weakness. William E. Butler, *The Soviet Union and the Law of the Sea* (Baltimore: The Johns Hopkins University Press, 1971).

55. Major General J. L. Mouton, 'Convulsive War and Prolonged Confrontation', *Brassey's Annual 1970* (London: William Clowes and Sons Ltd., 1970), pp. 130-41.

56. Quoted by Michael Howard, 'The Transformation of Strategy', *Brassey's Annual 1972* (London: William Clowes and Sons Ltd., 1972), p. 8.

57. Ann L. Hollick and Robert E. Osgood, *New Era of Ocean Politics* (Baltimore: The Johns Hopkins University Press, 1974), pp. 85-6.

58. Elizabeth Young, 'New Laws for Old Navies: Military Implications of the Law of the Sea', *Survival*, Vol. XVI, No. 6, November/December 1974, p. 267.

59. As the Foreign Office put it at the beginning of the century, there were important 'British interests in distant seas where the opportune presence of a British ship of war may avert a disaster which can only be remedied later at much inconvenience and considerable sacrifice'. Quoted by A. J. Marder, *From the Dreadnought to Scapa Flow*, Vol. 1 (London: Oxford University Press, 1961), p. 53.

60. *The Economist*'s phrase, 31 July 1971.

61. See Robert G. Weinland, 'Soviet Naval Operations – Ten Years of Change', op. cit.

62. A list of Soviet port visits is provided by Michael MccGwire, 'Foreign-Port Visits by Soviet Naval Units', Chapter 21 in MccGwire, Booth and McDonnell, op. cit.

63. McConnell, in MccGwire, *Soviet Naval Developments*, pp. 395-7.

64. Norman Polmar, *Soviet Naval Power: Challenge for the 1970s* (National Strategy Information Centre, Inc., 1975), pp. 67-8.

65. For the Egyptian view, see Heikal, op. cit., *passim*.

66. These comments are based on Charles C. Petersen, *The Soviet Port-Clearing Operations in Bangladesh* (CNA Professional Paper No. 123, June 1974, reprinted as Chapter 17 in MccGwire, Booth and McDonnell, op. cit.).

67. Ibid., p. 27.

68. Ibid.

69. Ibid., p. 29.

70. See Chapter Three.

71. A sense of the Shah's role-consciousness is evident in the report in *Time*, 6 August 1973.

72. Martin, *The Sea in Modern Strategy*, pp. 127-8.

73. See, for example, Herbert Dinerstein, 'The Transformation of Alliance Systems', *APSR*, Vol. LIX, No. 3, September 1965, pp. 589-601.

74. *The Times*, 14 August 1975; Norman Polmar, 'The Soviet Aircraft Carrier', *USNIPs* (Naval Review 1974), May 1974, Vol. 100, No. 855, pp. 157-8.

75. Joseph Frankel, *British Foreign Policy 1945-1973* (London: OUP for RIIA, 1975), p. 271.

76. E.g. Hill, 'Maritime Forces in Confrontation', pp. 34-5.

77. Julian Symonds, *The General Strike* (London: The Cresset Press, 1957), p. 53; *The Times*, 5, 10, 11 May 1926.

78. *Keesings Contemporary Archives 1966-1967*, 22185B, 22186A.

79. However, Admiral Sir Ian McGeoch has reminded me that civic action, in aid of the underprivileged, in showing concern with the environment, and in upholding the law in peacetime without fear or favour was very 'Nelsonic'. Nelson was not only an incomparable captain of war: he was

also a fine example of a naval officer acting as a concerned citizen.

80. Alfred Thayer Mahan, *The Influence of Sea Power upon History, 1660-1783* (London: Methuen, 1965. First published in Boston by Little, Brown and Co., 1890), p. 25.
81. *The Economist*, 13 October 1973.
82. Ibid.
83. A thorough analysis of the possible effect of changing ocean law on US security interests can be found in Hollick and Osgood, op. cit., pp. 75-131.
84. Louis Henkin, *How Nations Behave: Law and Foreign Policy* (London: Pall Mall, 1968).
85. See O'Connell, *The Influence of Law on Sea Power*. Compare this with the days when naval planners did not give a damn. See Marder, *From the Dreadnought to Scapa Flow*, Vol. 2, p. 32.
86. *The Times*, 24 September 1973.
87. Elisabeth Young, 'Military Implications of the Law of the Sea', *Survival*, November/December 1974, p. 264.
88. E.g. the reply by J. R. Hill, 'Maritime Power and the Law of the Sea', *Survival*, Vol. XVII, No. 2, March/April 1975, pp. 69-72.
89. Ibid., p. 72.
90. George Brown, op. cit., pp. 128-9.
91. E.g. Hoffmann, op. cit., p. 13.
92. Hill, 'Maritime Power and the Law of the Sea', p. 72.
93. E.g. Roskill, *The Strategy of Sea Power*, op. cit., pp. 91, 94, 145: Richmond, op. cit., pp. 266, 279.
94. Marder, *From the Dreadnought to Scapa Flow*, Vol. II, Chapter XIV.
95. Roger Fisher, *Basic Negotiating Strategy* (London: Allen Lane, The Penguin Press, 1971), pp. 138-48.
96. O'Connell, *The Influence of Law on Sea Power*.

INDEX